COMMITMENT
ON CAMPUS

DEAN R. HOGE is Assistant Professor of Christianity and Society, Princeton Theological Seminary, where he is currently engaged in various research projects to explore changes in Protestantism in America today. He received his Ph.D. in Sociology from the Harvard Graduate School.

Jacket design by James Stewart

COMMITMENT ON CAMPUS

CHANGES IN RELIGION AND VALUES OVER FIVE DECADES

by Dean R. Hoge

THE WESTMINSTER PRESS
PHILADELPHIA

Support for the publication
of this study was provided by
The Barra Foundation, Inc., of Philadelphia.

PUBLISHED BY THE WESTMINSTER PRESS®
PHILADELPHIA, PENNSYLVANIA

PRINTED IN THE UNITED STATES OF AMERICA

Library of Congress Cataloging in Publication Data

Hoge, Dean R., 1937–
    Commitment on campus; changes in religion and values
over five decades.

    Bibliography: p.
    1. College students—Religious life—History.
I. Title.
BV639.C6H6   301.5′8   74-7236
ISBN 0-664-20706-5

CONTENTS

PREFACE

       As Dean Hoge writes, most religious histories tell us what theologians have thought and how religious organizations have changed. They do not tell us much about the beliefs and commitments of ordinary people and even less why such beliefs and commitments change in quality and intensity. This unpretentious study makes a major contribution to filling that gap for twentieth-century America.

Hoge's is not the first effort to consummate the marriage of survey research and history, but it is the most serious attempt yet to do so in the field of the sociology of religion. Working out of an area where survey research has been most continuous for a period of fifty to seventy years, undergraduate college students in Eastern and Midwestern universities, he combines this core of reliable information with a great many other measures to reconstruct important aspects of the history of belief in twentieth-century America. Supplementing his college studies with national samples wherever possible, he moves in Chapter 5 beyond questionnaire data to include the impressions of youth religiosity to be gleaned from newspapers and magazines over the last half century and to interviews with campus ministers as to their impressions of changes in recent decades. As a result of all this evidence, carefully marshaled and interpreted, we get a new and more sharply defined picture of the history of religious orthodoxy among ordinary believers. In brief, religious orthodoxy among young people, who seem only to exaggerate tendencies general in the society, declined from the early 1920's to the mid-1930's, rose from the late '30s to the early '50s and declined again from the middle '50s. But in the richness of implications he finds in those changes Hoge contributes both to our theoretical understanding of religion in modern society and to our knowledge of processes of change.

Unlike much "empirical" sociology this study is well grounded theoretically. Relying mainly on the Durkheimian tradition, Hoge both utilizes its insights and contributes to it. Religious orthodoxy is closely related, as Durkheim would have expected, to the degree of solidarity in established social groups such as nation, community, and family. As solidarity in such groups becomes emphasized, religious orthodoxy increases; as such solidarity is undermined, orthodoxy declines. From this we must conclude that religious orthodoxy as the sociologists of religion have defined it is the "totemic religion" of traditional American society. Hoge contrasts in good Durkheimian fashion the strength of traditional groups and their associated orthodoxy with the strength of individualism and its associated religious liberalism. The two tend to vary inversely. Other variables that might be expected to influence the degree of religious orthodoxy do not seem to do so directly though they may indirectly through their effect on social solidarity. Strikingly, economic fluctuations measured in a variety of ways seem quite unrelated to changes in orthodoxy. Even more interestingly, modern natural science seems to have no direct influence on religious belief, or at least that is what we can conclude from the fact that natural science majors consistently are higher on religious orthodoxy than social science and humanities majors. In his last pages Hoge is tempted to conclude, again on good Durkheimian grounds, that the long-term trend is the decline of religious orthodoxy and that the rise of orthodoxy in the 1940's and '50s was a temporary vacillation. This is because it is the long-term trend in modern society to move from highly solidary groups to ever more individualistic modes of social organization. Of course this long-term trend may indeed continue, but there are reasons even in the theoretical and empirical resources of this study for raising some doubts.

As Durkheim so carefully indicated, modern individualism, where it is not sheer social pathology, is based not on the absence of social control but on a certain kind of social control; it correlates not with the absence of religion but with a certain kind of religion: the religion of humanity. The categories of empirical social science seem much more oriented to traditional social forms and beliefs whose decline they accurately describe than to the newer social forms, commitments, and beliefs that may be taking their place. We may be seeing in twentieth-century America simply a long-term erosion of social solidarity and traditional belief. If that is so, I would think that a sociologically sensitive observer would hesitate to predict an indefinite continuation of that trend, for at some point the coherence of the society itself will be threatened. On the other hand, new modes of social organization and belief may be emerging that our traditional concepts and indices are not picking up, modes that may reverse long-term apparent trends by initiating entirely new tendencies. A new communalism, such as has recently been tentatively experimented with, may turn out to be essential for survival in late twentieth-century America, and may reverse many long-established trends. In such a situation the autonomy of the symbolic dimension of religion, not much in evidence in Hoge's data, may reassert itself. Symbolic innovations or reinterpretations may set the direction for new social forms rather than religious symbols largely passively responding to changes in social solidarity as has often been the case in twentieth-century America. I am not predicting that such a shift will occur, but I do not see how on the basis of Hoge's analysis such a shift can be ruled out. One interesting fact that Hoge has presented suggests at least the possibility of such a shift. Interest in religion among young people, as measured by class enrollment in religion courses, has not declined in the last twenty years and may have increased, even though orthodoxy has declined sharply. Does this not indicate a reservoir of support for new religious crystallizations?

I have allowed myself to indulge in speculation far beyond the confines of the present study. It is one of its virtues that, while providing us a well-crafted platform from which to observe twentieth-century American religion, it does not prevent us from raising the largest possible questions about what it discloses.

ROBERT N. BELLAH

ACKNOWLEDGMENTS

This study began in a reading course with Professor Gordon W. Allport in 1966. We started a process of theoretical reflection and data collection on religious change among college students. In the spring of 1967, Dr. Allport began to withdraw from the project because of worsening health, but he continued to support it however he could. It was a great loss to all of behavioral science when he died on October 9, 1967.

I continued the research, and in the succeeding months a great many persons cooperated in the data collection. Their help was indispensable: Dr. Roger Brown, Dr. George Miller, and Dr. Richard W. Shomer at Harvard University; Dr. Philip K. Hastings at Williams College; Dr. Ben K. Gold and Dr. Max Sheanin at Los Angeles City College; Dr. Thomas K. Drabek at the University of Denver; Dr. Douglas H. Heath at Haverford College; Dr. Robert Sokol, Dr. Irving E. Bender, and Allan Johnson at Dartmouth College; Dr. Vernon Jones at Clark University; Dr. Carl P. Duncan at Northwestern University; Dr. Leonard Vaughan and Dean David L. Harris at Ripon College; Dr. Gene P. Sackett, Dr. Ronald Faich, and Dr. Leonard Berkowitz at the University of Wisconsin; Dr. Maurice Troyer and George Dolch at Syracuse University; Dr. Judith Porter and Herbert Kritzer at Bryn Mawr College; and Dr. Gerald Gurin and Ed Krupat at the University of Michigan.

I would also like to thank my thesis advisory committee, Dr. Talcott Parsons, Dr. Erik H. Erikson, Dr. Samuel F. Sampson, and Fr. Joseph H. Fichter, for their help and criticism. Several persons reviewed and helpfully criticized the preliminary analyses of the data, including Dr. David J. Armor, Dr. Sampson, Fr. Fichter, Dr. David Riesman, Dr. Robert Bellah, Dr. S. M. Lipset, James Rule, Dr. Douglas H. Heath, Dr. Vernon Jones, and Dr. Robert Sokol. I would also like to thank the assistants who worked on various aspects of the research, especially Donald Luidens. Finally, my wife, Josephine, deserves special thanks for her assistance, her encouragement, and her forbearance throughout the project.

Financial support came mostly from the Laboratory of Social Relations, Harvard University, as research allowances under National Institute of Health predoctoral fellowships numbers 2-F1-MH-30,523-01, 02, and 03. The Milton Fund of Harvard University and the National Science Foundation also provided financial assistance. Dr. William H. Sheldon contributed financially to the Wisconsin replication study. Help in many forms came from Princeton Theological Seminary, especially from Dr. Samuel W. Blizzard and President James I. McCord. This support and assistance is much appreciated.

INTRODUCTION

So far as religion is concerned, our students are groveling in darkness. Christianity, as a system of belief, has utterly broken down, and nothing definite, adequate, and convincing has taken its place. Their beliefs, when they have any, are superficial and amateurish in the extreme. There is no generally acknowledged authority; each one believes as he can, and few seem disturbed at being unable to hold the tenets of the churches.

So concluded James H. Leuba, America's first reliable researcher of the religious beliefs of college students, after his first study in 1906 (1916:213). In the half century since then similar doubts, alarms, and longings for the glorious past have filled books and journals. Some of the alarms may be understood as the centuries-old criticism of youth by their elders. Some may reflect actual changes. Whether or not students had fallen dangerously away from our religious traditions in 1906 or have done so in the late 1960's is not clear from present evidence.

Efforts of sociologists to measure and understand religious change in modern society run up against two limitations. First is a paucity of trustworthy information on changes over time in religious beliefs and commitment. Whereas ecclesiastical and theological developments are rather well known, changes in religious beliefs and commitments are not. The problem is one of measurement, and the hindrances have been both technical and financial. Second is a disagreement on the models best depicting the situation of modern American religion in historical and social context. Theoretical approaches to "religion and society" are being developed, but so far they have been either very general or very rudimentary. Thomas S. Kuhn has noted that the social sciences are "pre-paradigmatic," and in the analysis of religion in modern society this is emphatically true. Our most promising starting points such as the social evolution model and the differentiation model need further specification for short-run change. This study hopes to contribute on both fronts. It reports an attempt to gather pertinent and trustworthy data on changing religious attitudes and behavior in certain groups within American society, and it puts forth some theoretical suggestions based on the data.

Although the backdrop of the study is the problem of understanding modernization and "secularization," we shall not enter into the current debates on that level. The study is more specific and limited. This is both because the subject demands specificity and because we believe that use of such variously defined and value-laden terms as "secularization" impedes rather than serves clarification. Our conceptualization will remain closer to the operational level. And we shall refrain from value judgments about the changes.

This study can say little about change within theological systems. Detailed analysis of such changes cannot be done with questionnaire or interview research. Our measurements are limited to a series of overall indicators of commitment to traditional Judeo-Christian religious conceptions, forms, and institutions. They are more like a pulse-taking or temperature-reading than a thorough physical examination. Yet this type of research offers some insights not available elsewhere—it can provide an overview of changes in beliefs and commitments in broad social groups and it can suggest new insights for explaining the changes.

Accurate descriptions and interpretations of religious change in modern society are especially important to ecclesiastical leaders and theologians. The questions of "secularization," "modern technological man," "post-Christian" thought, and so on, are central to theological discussion today. Seminary training convinced the writer that articulate description and interpretation of the present situation would serve theologians and ecclesiastical leaders as much as any offering from social science. Not only in religion but in all areas of society sociologists are paying new attention to indicators of change (cf. U.S. Dept. of H.E.W., 1969; Sheldon and Moore, 1968).

Our main focus is American college students, partially because finite time and money are available for research and also because college students have been the white rats of behavioral science. They have been studied longer and more intensively than any other group in society. Almost every innovation in social psychology is first tested and refined on college students. By now the literature on college students is very extensive. A recent review listed over one thousand studies of the effect of college experience on students. Therefore college students provide a fruitful point of entry for the close study of religious attitudes and behavior. Finally, college students, unlike white rats, are of momentous importance in themselves. In recent years their political action and protests have filled newspaper headlines and books. College students have gained new self-consciousness and confidence as a political force capable of altering government policies. In addition they participated in forming, during the 1960's, a distinct counterculture making a lasting imprint on American life.

The backbone of this study is a series of thirteen replication studies carefully repeating earlier surveys in various American colleges and universities. These thirteen were selected from the available reports of past research. Persons knowing the literature will recognize many of them. We excluded any studies in the Southern states and any in denominational colleges in order to limit the variations in the data. Most of the past research was done in prominent Eastern colleges and Midwestern universities. Chapters 2, 3, and 4 describe the findings in our thirteen studies and in the existing literature. The data are presented in somewhat detailed form, and a reader preferring to skim over the statistical details may refer directly to the summaries at the end of each of these chapters.

The method of referencing may be unfamiliar to some. The numbers refer to publication date and page. Thus the reference (Jacob, 1957:120) refers to page 120 of the 1957 work by Jacob. All works are listed in the Bibliography.

CHAPTER 1

Theoretical Approaches
to Religious Change

What religious changes have occurred in recent decades in America? How might they be interpreted and explained? Answers to these questions today are at best hesitant and speculative. This study addresses itself to both questions, and it is guided by theoretical approaches proposed by past researchers. These include not only conceptual schemes for studying religious change but also explanations for particular trends in America. In this first chapter we shall outline nine approaches and the hypotheses they produce.

1. *Dynamic Density of Groups.* Emile Durkheim's theory of religion focuses on human groups, and his theory of religious change is based on the dynamic density of groups. Dynamic density is a measure of the frequency, range, and stability of communications among group members. It is a measure of a group's vitality, and as it increases, group sentiments and loyalties will increase. Individuals' commitments and beliefs are products of the groups they belong to, and any change in them will be directly traceable to changes in the dynamic densities of those groups.

Durkheim holds a rather rigorous social determinism of ideas:

> Among peoples as well as individuals, mental representations function above all as an expression of a reality not of their own making; they rather spring from it and, if they subsequently modify it, do so only to a limited extent. Religious conceptions are the products of the social environment, rather than its producers, and if they react, once formed, upon their original causes, the reaction cannot be very profound. (Durkheim, 1951:226–227; cf. 1933:341,344)

Religious change is a product of changes in human groups. It is seldom consciously planned and seldom desired. Neither religious debate nor the confrontation between traditional religion and modern science is important in causing religious change (Durkheim, 1951:169–170).

What is "religious" about religious groups is not of foremost importance to Durkheim. He studies religious congregations and sects alongside political and familial groups in the analysis of group life and its effect on individuals (Durkheim, 1951:209). Religious commitments are not theoretically distinguishable from other group commitments.

Under what conditions will a group's dynamic density intensify or weaken so as to bring about religious change? Durkheim puts forth several suggestions. Social change occurs, of course, amid political revolution, economic upheaval, or military conquest. During such times religious change is inevitable. Also, he speaks of periods of "collective effervescence" (Durkheim, 1961:475). They are associated with revolution, disruption, military action, or a type of revivalism, and they produce a restructuring of groups and an intensification of new centers of community life. Durkheim discusses national wars which unite the people in new patriotic fervor; in such situations social interaction intensifies, dynamic density in the society increases, and new religious symbols and commitments are born (Durkheim, 1951:208). The particular sentiments strengthened will depend on the character of the group. In situations of perceived national threat, national commitments will strengthen. In times of family crisis or celebration, family commitments will strengthen. Traditional religious commitments will also intensify in times of national threat or celebration insofar as they are integrated with nationalistic commitments; the same is true about the relation between traditional religious commitments and family commitments. Durkheim would thus hypothesize that traditional religious commitments in America, insofar as they are associated with national commitments, will intensify during times of war or perceived threat to the nation. Similarly they will intensify during times of threat to the family or ethnic group insofar as they are associated with ethnic or family commitments.

A corollary of this Durkheimian theory concerns relations between groups. They too depend on the intensity of communication and the factors facilitating or inhibiting communication. Any migration of people, new trade practice, new technology, or the like which produces more frequent, more stable, and broader communication between two groups will increase positive sentiments in each group toward the other (Durkheim, 1933:284 ff.). It will produce increased tolerance in each group for the other's group sentiments (including religion) and will in turn erode sentiments of exclusivism within each group. The crucial mechanism in producing this tolerance and openness between groups is not an increase in physical proximity but an increase in density of communications.

In summary, Durkheim would expect religious change in any group or any society to be traceable to changes in group dynamic density, due to national excitement or perceived threat, due to ethnic group excitement or perceived threat, or due to changed communication densities across boundaries of traditional groups.

2. *Impact of Individualism.* Durkheim also discusses the long-term social evolution toward greater individualism and its impact on traditional religion. Societies undergoing modernization have a progressive de-emphasis on local groupings and loyalties in favor of more universal, national, and humanistic loyalties. Geographic and social mobility of people tends to reduce the strong religious sentiments of traditional groups. This mobility, especially when combined with "liberal" education, works to weaken customary religious beliefs and commitments (Durkheim, 1951:165). As individualism grows, traditional religious commitments everywhere weaken in favor of new sacredness of the individual and of personality. The end result will be a "religion of humanity" or a "cult of man" (Durkheim, 1933:169 ff.). Increasing individualism will bring with it an increase in tolerance and more individual free thought in religious matters. This trend is visible in human history. "[T]he history of the human mind is the very history of the progress of free thought" (Durkheim, 1951:375). But in the short run this trend may be reversed in specific situations by the intensification of small-group loyalties and commitments.

In summary, Durkheim sees a kind of irreversible trend toward individualism and tolerance in religion, due to social changes in mobility and education patterns. He would predict that the more individualistic religious groups would have less intense patterns of traditional commitments and that persons in the liberal branches of education would tend to be more individualistic.

3. *Social Mobility.* Hypotheses predicting the effects of social mobility on religion have been put forth by Max Weber (1963) and H. Richard Niebuhr (1957). They begin with a study of religion in various social classes and status groups and then proceed to a study of

religious change produced by changes in wealth, status, and power of these classes and groups. Weber points out that privileged strata tend to have religious beliefs stressing individual and inner needs:

> The salvation sought by the intellectual is always based on inner need, and hence it is at once remote from life, more theoretical and more systematic than salvation from external distress, the quest for which is characteristic of nonprivileged classes. (Weber, 1963:125)

In the modern world, intellectualism tends toward a nontheistic world view and tends to weaken the authority of any priestly group (Weber, 1946:351). Any social groups that move toward greater intellectualism will experience corresponding religious change. Also, attention to politics in any group tends to preclude development of salvation religion:

> [S]alvation religions usually emerge when the ruling classes, noble or middle class, have lost their political power to a bureaucratic, militaristic imperial state. The withdrawal of the ruling classes from politics, for whatever reason, also favors the development of salvation religion. (Weber, 1963:122)

Also in times of rapid social change men's thoughts turn from politics to more ultimate religious questions.

The theory of social mobility and religious change is most explicitly stated by Niebuhr. He shows that in seventeenth- and eighteenth-century England and America a series of new fervid sectarian movements arose among the urban proletariat and small landowners, groups that were neglected by the established churches. Each new movement fashioned a strict ethic of diligence and responsibility and was able in time to raise its economic position. With this economic rise, the religion inevitably changed.

> [T]he history of denominationalism reveals itself as the story of the religiously neglected poor, who fashion a new type of Christianity which corresponds to their distinctive needs, who rise in the economic scale under the influence of religious discipline, and who, in the midst of a freshly acquired cultural respectability, neglect the new poor succeeding them on the lower plane. This pattern recurs with remarkable regularity in the history of Christianity. (Niebuhr, 1957:28)[1]

As the members of the sectarian groups become upwardly mobile there is a "relaxation of ethical demands" and a decreased commitment to the religious institution (Niebuhr, 1957:31). With increases in wealth comes increased emphasis on individualism and the psychological needs of the individual person. At any one time in American society there is a spectrum of Protestant groups, with upper-class churches stressing intellectualism and individualism and lower-class churches stressing eschatology, personal righteousness, rigorous daily ethics, and a simple salvation theology. The history of no one group or type of denomination may serve as an indicator of American religious history, and the "secularization" of any one group should not be seen as "secularization" in the entire society.[2]

4. *The Third Immigrant Generation.* Will Herberg in *Protestant— Catholic—Jew* has put forth a "third-generation hypothesis" for explaining the upswing in organized religion during the 1950's. He stresses that American history is largely the history of immigrants and that immigrant history provides the key to understanding American social history. The largest wave of immigration was in the years 1880 to 1914. Many of them tarried in the Eastern industrial cities and settled in ghettos populated by very mixed groups. Often the new conditions of life precipitated a crisis of identity, and the pressures for assimilation into the dominant English culture produced for their children a profound ambivalence about the heritage. The parents were content to live in ethnic communities, but the children often felt restricted by the old-world language, names, customs, and attitudes. The third generation, in contrast to the second, was not troubled by foreignness. It was clearly American. But it was faced with a different problem—the problem of identity in the mobile American society. The problem of "Who am I?" arose. The third generation did not want to cling to old-world origins or ethnic groups, but it did tend to stress religious heritage in its quest for identity.

> The connection with the family religion had never been completely broken, and to religion, therefore, the men and women of the third generation now began to turn to define their place in American society in a way that would sustain their Americanness and yet confirm the tie that bound them to their forebears, whom they now no longer had any reason to reject, whom indeed, for the sake of a "heritage," they now wanted to "remember." (Herberg, 1960:31)

The tendency of the third generation to have religious affiliations as a means of self-identification is thus a main explanation for the upswing of religion in the 1950's. This theory should describe recently immigrated Catholics and Jews more than Protestants. Gerhard Lenski tested the hypothesis in Detroit and found that religious commitment increased from the first to the second *and* from the second to the third generation (Lenski, 1963:45). Thus the aptness of the third-generation hypothesis is open to question.

5. *Other-direction.* Another explanation proposed for the religious upswing in the 1950's was by David Riesman (1950). He depicted a broad and long-term change in American character which he labeled the shift from inner-direction to other-direction. This shift was seen as a result of several demographic and social changes. Both Riesman and Herberg suggested that it accounted for the increased religious participation in the 1950's. They suggested that college students in the 1940's and 1950's were changing from inner-direction to other-direction and that the other-directed students are more traditionally religious than others, especially in public religious participation.

6. *Structural Differentiation.* A third explanation for the rising religious participation during the 1950's was proposed by Talcott Parsons based on the theory of structural differentiation. The theory describes a process by which a social structure or institution having a single, relatively well defined place in a society divides into two or more structures or institutions having more specialized functions and different from the original (cf. Parsons, 1966b: Ch. 2). A familiar example is the movement away from household-based manufacturing, as in cottage industry, to the establishment of specialized factories and workshops manned by people unrelated to one another. With differentiation, the values of the society must be reformulated in more flexible and general terms so as to be applicable in the new diverse specialized institutions. The total value system of society must be reexamined and possibly readjusted to integrate the new institutions with all their social implications (Parsons, 1960:301).

From this theoretical starting point, Parsons suggested that the increased religious participation and interest in the 1950's was a result of rapid social change in the years after World War II. In those years American society had experienced not only tremendous economic growth but also some major structural differentiation and reorganization such as suburbanization and new forms of industry. Many persons were under pressure to perform new and different roles, and American values were coming under considerable pressure for respecification and readjustment. The effects on personalities were the sources of a new concern about values and a subsequent new emphasis on religion, for Americans looked to their religion for guidance amid the rapid social change and the respecification of American values. The intensely personal character of the new religious interest in the 1950's seemed to support the theory. Also the intensity of the McCarthy phenomenon in the early 1950's seemed to suggest that Americans were feeling new concerns about central societal values and roles.

The explanation for the religious upswing of the 1950's in terms of structural differentiation and attendant value changes was plausible in the situation, but after the 1960's it loses its force. For the 1960's experienced *decreasing* religious participation, and no one could argue that social change had decreased in its tempo or its societal effects in the 1960's. Unless the structural differentiation explanation could be adapted to fit the 1960's as well as the 1950's, it appears invalid for explaining religious change in America.

7. *Urbanization.* The Chicago school of sociology asserted that cities tend to "secularize" persons and to weaken their ties to religious traditions. The most forceful statement of this position was by Louis Wirth (1938), following the work of Georg Simmel (1950). Lenski provides a convenient summary of the theory:

> To begin with, urban conditions bring people of diverse backgrounds into constant and close association with one another. More than that, they find that they are obliged to co-operate in the production of goods and services, the maintenance of law and order, and a variety of other tasks essential to the well-being of the total community. As a consequence they find it necessary to ignore the differences which divide them. . . . Eventually, what began as a mere *modus vivendi,* or temporary arrangement for specific situations only, becomes generalized into a basic value applicable to all kinds of situations. In short, norms of *tolerance* and *secularism* inevitably arise in urban centers. Norms peculiar to one religious group or another are de-emphasized, leaving a common core of moral norms which are shared by all the various faiths represented in the community. (Lenski, 1963:9)

The theory is derived from Durkheim's analysis of group boundaries.

Since Wirth's article in 1938, the Chicago theory of urbanism has been scrutinized and tested by many persons. Herbert J. Gans (1968) reviewed the research and the criticisms that have been made. In his view, existing research indicated that a large number of urban dwellers in America remained isolated from the hypothesized consequences of urban social and cultural patterns. Hence the tolerance and secularism did not in fact arise to any significant degree. Rather, most of the American urban population consists of relatively homogeneous cultural groups which are shielded fairly effectively from other groups. This was especially true of residents living outside the center city areas (Gans, 1968:66). The "melting pot" effect of the city and suburb is not very strong. Lenski concluded that in Detroit communalism and primary groups survived and even thrived, contrary to Wirth's prediction. In Detroit the differences between the religious subcommunities "are at the very least as sharply drawn as ever, and there are numerous indications that they may become more pronounced in the future" (Lenski, 1963:322). Whether the Wirth theory of urbanization explains a significant portion of religious change in America is doubtful.

Harvey Cox's *The Secular City* (1965) proposed the Wirth theory as a principal explanation of apparent secularizing trends in the 1960's, in spite of the paucity of evidence supporting it. In a critique of Cox, Andrew Greeley pointed this out, saying that urban sociologists find as much *Gemeinschaft* and ethnic communalism in modern American cities today as earlier, and also as much in cities as in rural districts today (Callahan, 1966:104 f.). This critique seems to the point. Greeley summarizes:

> I am simply contending that the secular city does not exist, and given the human's tendency to preserve the traditional, and the primordial, the suprarational elements of his life, the secular city may never exist. (Callahan, 1966:107)

In our research this theory can be indirectly studied by comparing college students reared in urban centers with those reared in suburbs or in rural areas.

8. *The Influence of Political Events.* An explanation of recent religious trends in America has been proposed by S. M. Lipset, suggesting changing political sentiments as an important factor. His depiction of political sentiments in the 1930's, 1940's, and 1950's is central to the argument:

> The period 1930 to 1945 saw the predominance of liberal sentiment in American politics. This was largely the result of two factors, the depression and the threat of Fascism. The depression emphasized the need for socio-economic reforms and helped to undermine the legitimacy of conservative and business institutions. It was followed immediately by a war which was defined as a struggle against Fascism.

> The post-war period, on the other hand, has seen a resurgence of conservative and rightist forces. This has resulted from two factors, a prolonged period of prosperity and full employment, and second, the change in foreign policy. Where once we warred against Fascism, which is identified with the "right," we now war against Communism, which is identified with the "left." . . . Thus, the period from 1947–48 to 1954

presents a very different picture from the previous decade and a half. The conservatives and the extreme right are now on the offensive. The "free enterprise" system which provides full employment is once more legitimate. Liberal groups feel in a weak position politically, and now wage a defensive battle, seeking to preserve their conquests of the thirties, rather than to extend them. (Lipset, 1966:327–328)

Lipset stresses that McCarthyism in the 1950's, like the Ku Klux Klan in the 1920's, arose out of the status anxieties of certain groups feeling threatened in the changing social and political situation. The source of both McCarthyism and the Klan is only indirectly economic, for both rose and fell amid prosperity. Both movements included attacks by small-town and provincial city lower-middle-class and working-class groups against the "cosmopolitans" of the Eastern upper class. Lipset notes that the McCarthyism years were also years of a religious upswing, and he suggests that the same was true of the years of the Klan. Political sentiments in both cases produced new religious activity of a certain kind. Political events and attitudes are much more important in this regard than economic conditions and attitudes. Lipset cites national surveys showing associations between intolerance of minority groups, fear of Communism, and evangelical religious beliefs. Significant inputs affecting one set of attitudes also affected the other set (Lipset, 1963b:344). At any time an individual's religious attitudes will be similar to his political attitudes in certain respects such as openness to change, optimism, individualism, defensiveness, tolerance of diversity, and stress on adherence to tradition.

Lipset suggests that weakening religious participation after the middle 1950's was a parallel phenomenon to the weakening of cold war fears. Events in the world, such as the Khrushchev coexistence doctrine and the Sino-Soviet split, weakened both the strong fears of totalitarianism and the intense traditional religious commitments of the earlier postwar period.

Herberg also suggests that the cold war was an element in the rising religious interest in the 1950's. He calls the cold war "the contemporary crisis of Western civilization." In this situation organized religion is seen by many as a source of peace of mind and security and also as a weapon in the struggle with Communism. "Religion has suddenly emerged as a major power in the 'hundred years of cold war' that appears to confront mankind" (Herberg, 1960:61).

9. *Religious Revival and the Birthrate.* Herberg commented on the similarity of religious participation trends and the birthrate since World War II and suggested that both are responses to an intensified need for security.

The demographical fact would seem to confirm the impression many observers have had in recent years that, amid the mounting insecurities of our time, increasing numbers of younger people are turning to the security to be found in the enduring, elemental ways and institutions of mankind; in the family, they feel, they can find the permanence and stability, the meaning and value they crave amid a world falling into chaos. Religion, like the family, is one of the enduring, elemental institutions of mankind; indeed, the two have been closely linked from the very earliest times. (Herberg, 1960:61)

Herberg's suggestions were tested by Lenski in Detroit. Lenski found that "in all three of the larger socio-religious groups, those who attend church regularly tend to have larger families than those who do not" (Lenski, 1963:254). Also both devotionalism and doctrinal orthodoxy were positively associated with fertility on all social class levels. These findings support Herberg's discussion about the association between the religious revival and the baby boom. They point to underlying social sentiments as the explanation for religious changes.[3]

ANALYSES OF RECENT
RELIGIOUS CHANGE IN AMERICA

What changes have occurred in American religion in the twentieth century? We shall summarize the conclusions of several persons who have tried to collect and analyze available evidence.

Michael Argyle's *Religious Behaviour* (1958) reviews information on trends in Great Britain and the United States in the twentieth century. He summarizes for the United States:

The figures for adult church members, Sunday School members and voluntary contributions all show a slow decline from 1900 to about 1940, followed by a rather more rapid increase since then. Surveys of beliefs and analyses of periodical articles show an increasing liberalism of belief. Protestants and Catholics have maintained about the same proportions, but the small Protestant sects have increased rapidly, and also changed in character, during this period. (Argyle, 1958:34)

In 1958 Louis Schneider and Sanford Dornbusch published *Popular Religion*, an analysis of forty-six best-selling devotional books published between 1875 and 1955. Several trends were visible in the concerns of these books, and the years 1935–1940 appeared to be the main period for new and changing themes. The idea that religion will make a better world (as distinct from purely personal salvation) increases greatly in importance around 1940, and after 1936 there is an increase in the notion that religion will link one to one's fellowmen and make one a member of a solidary community. The view that religion will bring "our nation" leadership or victory over our enemies comes to the fore during World War II and in the period of the "postwar anti-Communist crusade" (Schneider and Dornbusch, 1958:13). Also after 1940 the books seem to assume a less optimistic world.

Both Parsons (1960) and Herberg (1960) argue that interest and participation in religion have risen during the 1950's, and they cite various evidence such as polls, membership data, book sales, and church-building to support the argument. S. M. Lipset collected and interpreted all available indicators of religious change in an attempt to check on claims of a religious revival in the 1950's. He also compared accounts of European travelers in the United States in the nineteenth century with conditions in the 1950's. He concluded that indeed a religious revival had occurred during the 1950's but that the long-term history of religion in America was one of no noteworthy change for over a century:

> [A]lthough there have been ebbs and flows in enthusiasm, basic long-term changes in formal religious affiliation and practice have not occurred, and the current high level of religious belief and observance existed in the past as well. (Lipset, 1963a:150)

American religion has always been tolerant of denominational differences, activistic in orientation, this worldly, and focused on morality rather than transcendental belief, liturgy, or experience.

Charles Glock surveyed the indicators of religious change and the divergent conclusions drawn by Herberg, Lipset, and others. He agrees with Lipset in seeing little long-term "secularization."

> Actually, there is nothing in the literature that would constitute a serious and systematic defense of the secularization hypothesis. Its advocates are likely to be clergymen, church administrators, theologians, or journalists, and where they have been social scientists they have tended to be oriented to qualitative rather than quantitative observation. The evidence which they cite tends to be neither systematic nor thoroughly documented. (Glock and Stark, 1965:83)

Glock suggests that Niebuhr's model of rising membership of conservative churches and a gradual transformation of such churches with social mobility is the most apt in view of the data (Glock and Stark, 1965:84; cf. Stark and Glock, 1968: Ch. 10). Similar skepticism about the "secularization hypothesis" has been voiced by Andrew Greeley, based on existing research (Greeley, 1969).

The most recent review of all available indicators of religious change in America is that by N. J. Demerath III (1968). He analyzes the figures on church membership, attendance, and the like, concluding that conservative groups grew the most in the first half of the twentieth century while liberal groups grew the least. He concludes that the religious revival of the late 1940's and 1950's was confined mostly to the conservative and smaller Protestant groups (Demerath, 1968:359). Sunday school enrollment grew in the years 1940–1955, then leveled off. Beliefs of ministers and seminary students in the major Protestant denominations have become demonstrably more liberal since the 1920's. Ecclesiastical organizations have become much more elaborate and bureaucratized, and ecumenical structures have multiplied at all levels. But Demerath is cautious in his conclusions about any overall trends in commitment or participation.[4]

The main conclusion of these researchers is that most indicators show an upswing in traditional religious commitment and participation in the 1940's, with a leveling off or a downturn in the late 1950's or early 1960's. And probably the middle and late 1930's were a period of relatively great changes.

STUDIES OF RELIGIOUS TRENDS
AMONG COLLEGE STUDENTS

The data on religious trends over the decades among college students are meager. Two major reviews of research on values of college students provide a wealth of information on *individual freshman-to-senior changes,* and they include several studies investigating trends over the decades. The first was done by Philip E. Jacob in 1957, entitled *Changing Values in College.* The second was done in 1969 by Kenneth A. Feldman and Theodore M. Newcomb, entitled *The Impact of College on Students.* Both are impressive in their breadth and comprehensiveness.[5]

Between 1966 and 1969 the writer cooperated with various persons in carrying out thirteen new replication studies. Each study except that done at Haverford College was a questionnaire survey exactly repeating an earlier study. In all twelve we matched sample groups as closely as possible and used identical questionnaire items. All questionnaires were pretested on Harvard and Radcliffe students or on the target groups. Obsolete or ambiguous items were deleted from the replication questionnaires, and in most cases new items were added to enrich the analysis. All studies except the Syracuse University study were done at the same time of year as the original, insofar as it was known.

Our interest was not only in actual attitude changes in the colleges studied but also in the changes not traceable to shifts in the admission practices of these particular colleges. We calculated "adjusted responses" statistically holding constant the most relevant background variables from the original to the replication sample. We weighted the data from each replication sample so that it resembled the original sample in the most important background variables. For example, if 10 percent more Jews and 10 percent fewer Protestants were in the replication sample than in the original sample, we weighted the responses of the Jewish and Protestant students in the replication study data to decrease the effect of the Jews and increase that of the Protestants. Most studies required multiple weightings. Usually they included religious background, father's occupation, and major course. In several studies they also included rural/urban background, veteran/nonveteran status, strength of religious influence in upbringing, and scholastic aptitude. Appendix A describes the adjustment procedure. In all except the Syracuse, Denver, Clark, and Michigan studies the differences between actual and adjusted responses were small.

The thirteen new studies will be described briefly here. More details are found in Appendix A. Of the thirteen, three were replications of 1946 and 1948 surveys employing a questionnaire written by Allport and his associates; in 1966 we replicated their 1946 study at Harvard-Radcliffe, and in 1967 we replicated very similar studies done in 1948 at Williams College and Los Angeles City College. At Clark University in 1967 we replicated a series of older studies done between 1930 and 1956. Also in 1967 we replicated a series of studies done at Northwestern University between 1933 and 1949. In 1968 we replicated a 1948 study at the University of Denver, 1929 and 1949 studies at Ripon College, a 1930 study at the University of Wisconsin, a 1926 study at Syracuse University, and 1914 and 1933 studies at Bryn Mawr College. At Haverford College we gathered extensive data from freshmen entrance tests done between 1944 and 1966. In 1968 we replicated a 1952 study done at Dartmouth, and in 1969 we replicated the same study done at the University of Michigan. Also at Michigan we replicated parts of earlier surveys, and we gathered the results of periodic religious censuses between 1896 and 1969.[6]

These studies represent no "sample" of American colleges and universities in the late 1960's. Under the circumstances no attempt could be made to gather data representative of all college students. However, the thirteen colleges provide a certain amount of generalizing power. Six are private prestigious Eastern colleges, and three are large Midwestern universities and members of the Big Ten. The findings of this research are probably generalizable at least to Eastern colleges and Midwestern universities.

DEFINITIONS AND CONCEPTS

Several concepts should be clarified at the outset to minimize confusion. First is the concept religion. We shall avoid it as a technical term because of its ambiguity. It often implies exclusion of beliefs and practices outside the main historical world religions, thus prodding some writers to invent concepts such as pseudo religion, quasi religion, and secular religion. Such concepts are theoretically sterile. Our approach begins with the concepts meaning-commitment system and traditional Judeo-Christian religion. The term "meaning-commitment system" will refer to the total system of values, attitudes, commitments, and behavior of any individual person. It is somewhat similar to Tillich's concept of ultimate concern in that it refers to the central elements of one's personal religion. The term "traditional Judeo-Christian religion" or, for short, "traditional religion," will refer to beliefs, practices, forms, and institutions of the historic Jewish and Christian faiths. Another possible term might be "organized religion," but it seems to exclude personal behavior and commitments.

Paul Tillich gives an example of a meaning-commitment system:

> If a national group makes the life and growth of the nation its ultimate concern, it demands that all other concerns, economic well-being, health and life, family, aesthetic and cognitive truth, justice and humanity, be sacrificed. The extreme nationalisms of our century are laboratories for the study of what ultimate concern means in all aspects of human existence, including the smallest concern of one's daily life. (Tillich, 1958:1–2)

In this example nationalism is the supreme commitment and principle of organization for all else. Tillich mentions other commitments that may compete with it (economic well-being, health, family, and so on) and says that these must be "sacrificed." More accurately, they must be either sacrificed or coordinated in the service of the supreme commitment. In the meaning-commitment systems of individual citizens nationalism may or may not be found in its socially promulgated form. Most often it will not be, because most individuals in modern society have plural commitments, and no one completely dominates. The researcher must analyze the individual's meaning-commitment system to determine how and where nationalism, or traditional religion, fits into it.

The meaning-commitment system is composed of attitudes, defined as responses (or the readiness to respond on cue) to objects in the physical or social environment. Attitudes are commonly seen by social psychologists as having cognitive, affective, evaluative, and behavioral levels in some relation to each other. No general statements can be made about the causal interrelations of the four levels, but most social psychologists would tend to agree with Durkheim that the affective is more important than the cognitive.[7] We should not see the meaning-commitment system as totally unified.

> Only rarely will an individual exhibit such a high degree of unity of attitudes that we are justified in saying he has a single ideology or life philosophy. More commonly, an individual's political, religious, artistic, and scientific ideologies are somewhat separable. (Krech *et al.*, 1962:145)

These findings suggest that a term such as "ultimate concern" is seldom apt for describing individuals in modern society. Rather, the meaning-commitment system of most middle-class persons is a loosely organized coalition of clusters of attitudes and commitments. It should be visualized as a network of "subsets" of value commitments, related both to general values and to specific institutions and groups. The ego must organize the network into a viable identity system having tolerable levels of internal conflict. It will change in structure during the life cycle and with important changes in occupational status, wealth, citizenship, and so on. Many of the general conceptions and symbols included in its cognitive level must have considerable flexibility in interpretation if they are to coordinate the diverse attitudes and commitments. Insofar as any model is helpful for visualizing the total structure, probably the hierarchy is best (Katz, 1967:460). A widely known hierarchical model has been put forth by Abraham Maslow (1943).

Since time, money, energy, and attention are limited commodities, commitments of any individual are limited, and the whole will approximate a fixed-sum system. As one commitment strengthens, another must weaken. Methods for assessing total systems of commitments should include a fixed-sum conception. However, it constitutes only an imperfect fit, for the amount of conflict within the system affects the total resources available to it. For example, for some persons family commitments and traditional religious commitments may be mutually reinforcing, while for others they may conflict. Increased conflict within the system reduces the total resources available to it, and the resolution of internal conflicts has the effect of freeing increased amounts of energy within the personality system. Analyses of conversion commonly point this out. Although a pluralistic system of meanings and commitments has the constant problem of internal conflict, in one respect the pluralism may enhance the adaptive capacity and stability of the system. Diversified investments tend to be more secure, since no single loss is total loss; likewise pluralistic meanings and commitments serve for personal survival.

Traditional Judeo-Christian religion refers to those systems of beliefs, behavior, and institutions based self-consciously on the Jewish and Christian historical tradition. The relation of traditional religion to individual meaning-commitment systems is roughly the same as that of political parties to individual political ideology and commitments. An individual may be a member or he may be an "independent."

In taking measurements of traditional religion, a principal dimension in this study is *orthodox-unorthodox*. It measures distance from an orthodox "ideal type" somewhat resembling evangelical churches in the nineteenth century. The unorthodox dimension of the dimension is less defined, but empirically the departures from orthodoxy tend to be in one direction, including naturalism, biological evolution, a rather individualistic humanism, individual responsibility for formulation of beliefs, contextual ethics, and sensitivity to cultural relativity. The proper realm of human action is seen in improving the lot of the human race, especially its individual freedom, level of living standard and well-being, expression, and escape from suffering.

In attitude studies such as this an attempt to be theologically precise is hampered by several obstacles. First is the low level of theological and religious knowledge of many Americans and to a lesser extent of many college students. A 1950 Gallup poll asked, "Will you tell me the names of any of the first four books of the New Testament of the Bible—that is, the first four Gospels?" Thirty-five percent of the respondents named all four correctly, and 47 percent named at least one correctly; 53 percent could not name any (Rosten, 1963:327).

A second obstacle is the variety of theological systems current among religious leaders even within the same denomination. Attempts by researchers of attitudes to be explicit soon run into varying theological formulations behind the general affirmations and "slogans." Many laymen prefer to report assent to the socially accepted affirmations while at the same time reinterpreting them substantially to make them privately acceptable. Our approach is to avoid slogans and traditional rhetoric as much as possible in search for "effective" commitments and beliefs.

With these comments on conceptualization let us turn to the research findings.

CHAPTER 2

Changes in
Traditional Religious
Attitudes and Behavior

What have been the measurable changes in college students' religion over the past half century? Are changes in beliefs the same as changes in religious practices and church commitments? Have students from Protestant, Catholic, or Jewish homes changed more than others in their loyalty to their home traditions or in their religious attitudes? And is it true, as Durkheim has proposed, that the more individualistic religious groups have less intense patterns of traditional commitments? This chapter reviews all available data on religious changes, both from the literature and from the thirteen replication studies. It begins with the question of the interrelation of various measures of religiosity.

INTERRELATION OF ATTITUDES,
BEHAVIOR, AND INTEREST

The study of dimensions of traditional religious commitment is important in recent American sociology of religion (cf. Faulkner and DeJong, 1966; King and Hunt, 1969; Stark and Glock, 1968). Some of our studies included enough suitable items to construct and interrelate several indices. The results can be summarized in four parts.[8] First, in all studies an Orthodoxy or Conservative Religious Belief dimension is the most dominant in terms of strong correlations with other dimensions. Whenever we created a Religious Experience dimension it correlated strongly with the Orthodoxy dimension. Second, the strength of correlations among indices in our studies resembles that between indices in studies of adult populations. Third, in every study of students the correlations among indices were stronger for the Catholics than for the Protestants and stronger for the Protestants than for those without religious preference. Thus, the more orthodox the religious group, in our terms, the more strongly do the indices intercorrelate. Fourth, the rather strong correlations between indices weaken the arguments of some observers who attribute commitment to present-day churches to "nonreligious" motives such as the desire to find friends or to meet the right kind of people. Our data provide little support for this "country club church" theory. Orthodoxy of beliefs and strength of religious sentiments are our strongest predictors of churchmanship. Such a conclusion raises the question of the viability of liberal churches over the long run, for liberal persons tend to have weak commitment to organized churches.[9]

CHANGES IN RELIGIOUS ATTITUDES,
COMMITMENT, AND INTEREST

In this section our attention is limited to traditional religious *attitudes;* religious behavior is discussed later. We first review studies of changes over the last two decades, then studies showing longer-term changes.

Change Over Two Decades

Three of the studies of the period 1946–1967 used the same questionnaire items; Tables 2.1 and 2.2 show the changes on two items. These items show a decline in orthodoxy. The more orthodox responses have declined about 18 to 22 percentage points at Harvard, Radcliffe, and Williams, and about 9 at Los Angeles City College. The change on the various items is quite uniform. We noted the rise in choices of "None of these alternatives" and inquired about it in our pretesting sessions. Most subjects said that choice of this response indicated absence of a thought-out view on the item. It meant that the respondent had no definite view, probably because the topic was not crucial to his own identity system. It did *not* mean that our questionnaire was constructed on too low a conceptual level to fit the articulated viewpoints of respondents.

Why the change is smaller at Los Angeles City College than elsewhere is not clear. Los Angeles City College is quite different from the other colleges. It has minimal entrance requirements; it is a municipal junior college with students largely commuting from home;

TABLE 2.1

"Check the one statement that most nearly expresses your belief."
(In percentages)

| | HARVARD | | | RADCLIFFE | | | WILLIAMS | | | LOS ANGELES CITY COLLEGE | | | | | |
| | | | | | | | | | | Men | | | Women | | |
	1946	1966	Adj.*	1946	1966	Adj.	1948	1967	Adj.	1948	1967	Adj.	1948	1967	Adj.
N =	123	350		86	83		92	202		100	245		100	217	
Infinitely wise, omnipotent Creator; personal God**	25	16	} 29	40	13	} 34	29	11	} 38	34	25	} 45	37	39	} 64
Intelligent and friendly Being	27	19		19	18		27	24		15	22		30	27	
Vast, impersonal spiritual source or principle	10	7	} 70	7	14	} 65	13	13	} 60	6	6	} 56	5	5	} 38
I neither believe nor disbelieve in God	17	18		12	14		18	13		21	16		13	8	
The only power is natural law	7	15		9	14		1	8		10	9		3	3	
The universe is merely a machine	2	5		2	8		1	1		3	4		1	2	
None of these alternatives	12	20		11	17		11	28		11	19		11	17	
	100	100	99	100	98	99	100	98	98	100	101	101	100	101	102

* Adjusted scores. In these studies the adjustments remove the effect of changes in religious backgrounds and religious influence in upbringing.

** The responses here are abbreviations; on this and all following tables when the responses are abbreviations the full responses are in Hoge (1969, Appendixes A–M).

TABLE 2.2

"The church. (Check the view that best corresponds to your own attitude.)"

(*In percentages*)

	HARVARD			RADCLIFFE			WILLIAMS			LOS ANGELES CITY COLLEGE Men*			Women		
N =	1946 170	1966 349	Adj.	1946 63	1966 86	Adj.	1948 92	1967 199	Adj.	1948 306	1967 248	Adj.	1948 131	1967 218	Adj.
The one infallible foundation of civilized life**	6	1	} 24	6	0		8	1	} 43	17	6		22	14	} 66
On the whole it stands for the best in human life.	36	28		40	26		56	41		46	48		49	53	
There is certain doubt; it possibly may do harm.	18	25		13	20	(same)	12	19		12	12	(same)	12	9	
The total influence may be on the whole harmful.	6	10	} 76	2	9		3	11	} 58	7	7		3	6	} 35
Stronghold of much that is wholesome and dangerous	10	5		6	9		2	4		7	9		3	4	
Insufficient familiarity	4	5		8	5		5	7		6	6		4	4	
A different attitude	20	26		25	31		14	18		5	12		2	11	
	100	100	100	100	101		100	101	101	100	100		95***	101	101

* All men in 1948.

** The responses here are abbreviations.

*** These figures reported in 1948 are in error, but we lack the correct figures.

it is the only Pacific state college in our studies. Also it has not upgraded its entrance requirements over the last two decades, unlike all the other colleges studied. Which of these factors is most important we cannot know.

Two other items in these studies should be noted. One item asked about belief in immortality. Those believing in personal immortality declined 13 percentage points at Harvard, 16 points at Radcliffe, 19 points at Williams, and 8 points at Los Angeles City College (all scores adjusted).

TABLE 2.3

Six Items from the Conservative Religious Scale, Denver
(*Percentage of Protestant background students responding
"Strongly Agree" or "Agree"; both sexes*)*

	1948	1968
N =	622	319
I believe the Bible is the inspired Word of God.	51	33
The idea of God is unnecessary in our enlightened age.	6	17
The Bible is full of errors, misconceptions, and contradictions.	33	55
The Gospel of Christ is the only way for mankind to be saved.	34	16
I think a person can be happy and enjoy life without believing in God.	46	77
In many ways the Bible has held back and retarded human progress.	33	38

* Individual items were not adjusted; on most items adjusted change from 1948 to 1968 is somewhat greater than actual change.

A second item asked for agreement or disagreement with the proposition, "Denominational distinctions, at least within Protestant Christianity, are out of date and may as well be eliminated as rapidly as possible." At Harvard and Radcliffe, agreement declined 13 percentage points; at Williams it declined 9 points; and at Los Angeles City College it declined about 12 points (all scores adjusted). Sentiments favoring ecumenism diminished from the late 1940's to the late 1960's. Correlation analysis showed that those in 1966–67 disagreeing with this proposition tended to be Protestant and tended to be orthodox.

The Denver replication study covered the same period of time, 1948 to 1968. A Conservative Religious Scale was its main measure of orthodoxy. Among all students of Protestant background, there was an average decline of about 22 percentage points. Among students of Catholic background the decline was about 23 points (all scores adjusted). Several of the changes for Protestants are shown in Table 2.3. The items with greatest change were those having a particularistic emphasis, saying that Christianity or the gospel is the only truth, the only salvation, etc. These data suggest that a new sense of relativity is the most important single change over two decades. In general the changes at Denver resemble those at Harvard, Radcliffe, and Williams.

The study at Haverford College covers the period 1944 to 1968. It has two measures of traditional religious attitudes, a Conservative Belief Scale and the Allport-Vernon religious scores. The Conservative Belief Scale is composed of six items from the Minnesota Multiphasic Personality Inventory (MMPI) test:

98 I believe in the Second Coming of Christ.
#115 I believe in a life hereafter.
#249 I believe there is a devil and a hell in afterlife.
#258 I believe there is a God.
#373 I feel sure that there is only one true religion.
#483 Christ performed miracles such as changing water into wine.

On Item 98 the computer ignored all responses of Jewish students. Figure 2.1 shows the trends in scale scores from 1944 to 1968.

The scale scores peak in about 1950, then decline 23 percentage points to 1968. The adjusted decline is about 14 to 17 points. In a separate analysis of the data, Douglas H. Heath (1969b) deleted item 373 from the scale and found that the remaining items peaked in 1952–56. Item 373, expressing religious exclusivism, began losing support somewhat earlier than the other items in the scale. Also Heath constructed a Traditional Value Index from the Allport-Vernon Study of Values, and it was highest in 1952 and 1956. The Allport-Vernon Religious Scores at Haverford increased consistently from 1944 to 1952, then slowly declined until 1966, our last information.

FIGURE 2.1

Trends in Conservative Attitude Scale, Haverford Freshmen Nonveterans*

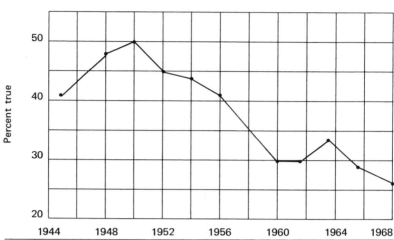

*To reduce short-run fluctuations, data from 1961-62, 1963-64, and 1965-66 are combined.

The Haverford study has our only direct comparison of religious attitudes in the late 1940's with those in the early 1950's. Paul F. Lazarsfeld and Wagner Thielens, Jr., in their 1955 survey of social scientists, found a trend toward conservatism in many attitude areas including religion during the late 1940's and early 1950's. They hypothesized that the conservatism and caution on campuses in the early 1950's resulted from the intense concern about national security. They included in the interviews a series of questions comparing the situation in 1955 with "6 or 7 years ago." "This referred approximately to the time when the concern with national security had begun to be acute" (Lazarsfeld and Thielens, 1958:38). Over half the social science teachers detected a decline in intellectual and academic freedom during those years.

> Actually, at the time of our field work, the difficulties had passed their peak in some respects. The elections of 1954 and the censure of Senator McCarthy had brought a change in the tone in which legislative investigations were conducted. With the end of the Korean War, the feeling of the country at large calling for intense vigilance had somewhat slackened. Perhaps as a reflection of this calmer atmosphere, the sense of apprehension of the professoriate at the time of our study might be said to

have reached a kind of uneasy equilibrium, with the pressures arising during the difficult years and the responding forces of moral resistance almost balancing each other. (Lazarsfeld and Thielens, 1958:98)

Many social science teachers mentioned that controversial topics such as race, political criticism, or religion were dropped from discussion on their campuses during the early 1950's (Lazarsfeld and Thielens, 1958:198). Students were judged by the respondents to be less willing to express unpopular political views than six or seven years earlier, also less ready to voice unpopular views in private talks or to join organizations with unpopular views.

We conclude that expressions of religious orthodoxy on many college campuses were stronger in the early 1950's than in the late 1940's and that the peak was probably in the years 1952 to 1955. Religious orthodoxy during the early 1950's was probably a part of a broader tendency toward conservatism and caution.

At Dartmouth and Michigan we replicated three items on traditional religion from 1952 to 1968–69. One item asked, "Do you personally feel that you *need* to believe in some sort of religious faith or personal philosophy?" Those responding "yes" declined 7 percent at Dartmouth and 9 percent at Michigan. A second item asked, "Do you feel that you *now* have an adequate religious faith or personal philosophy as a guide to your conduct?" At both Dartmouth and Michigan the responses changed little. A third item asked about conceptions of the deity. The two most orthodox response choices declined 14 percentage points at Dartmouth and 20 points at Michigan (adjusted).

In addition, at Dartmouth four items on religion from studies done in 1958 and 1961 were replicated in 1968. The results confirmed the declining orthodoxy and traditional commitment and suggested that the declines were sharper in the years prior to 1961 than during 1961–1968. In general, the changes at Dartmouth are in the same direction as those at Harvard, Williams, and Haverford, but slightly smaller. The changes at Michigan are similar to those at Harvard, Williams, and Haverford.

At the University of Texas, Robert K. Young, David S. Dustin, and Wayne H. Holtzman (1966) surveyed undergraduates in 1955, 1958, 1964. Included in the questionnaire was a twenty-three-item scale on acceptance of orthodox religious beliefs. They found very little change from 1955 to 1958, but from 1958 to 1964 the attitudes became less orthodox. Scale scores ranged from 0 to 92, and the mean score dropped about 7 points in those six years. This finding seems to match those at Haverford and Dartmouth.

In summary, all studies agree that orthodoxy declined from the late 1940's to 1966–68, and the best indications are that the high point came in the period 1952–55. The decline from 1946–48 to 1966–68 was about 13 to 23 points on orthodox responses to attitude items in all colleges except Los Angeles City College, where the decline was about 9 points.

Change Over Three or More Decades

We turn now to studies showing changes from the 1920's or 1930's to the late 1960's. One of the most eloquent studies was done at

FIGURE 2.2

Mean Scores on Thurstone Scales, Northwestern University

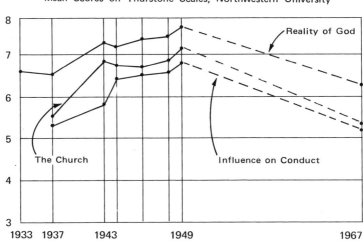

Northwestern University, where three Thurstone scales were administered to introductory psychology classes from 1933 to 1949 and then in 1967. The three were the Reality of God scale (No. 22A), the Influence on Conduct scale (No. 22C), and the Attitude Toward the Church scale. All three were scored so that favorable attitudes had high scores. See Figure 2.2 and Table 2.4.

The broken lines between 1949 and 1967 indicate the lack of information on trends during that time. Veterans and nonveterans were not distinguished in 1948 and 1949, resulting probably in slightly lowered scores; the sharp rise from 1948 to 1949 may reflect the reduced numbers of veterans in introductory classes from 1948 to 1949. The three scales vary quite uniformly over the years, suggesting that they measure very similar dimensions. The 1967 adjusted scores resemble those in 1933 and 1937.

TABLE 2.4

Mean Scores on Thurstone Scales, Northwestern University*

	1933	1937	1943	1944	1946	1948	1949	1967
N =	449	349	113	156**	180	156	284	179
Reality of God	6.6	6.52	7.23	7.07	7.28	7.41	7.77	6.26
Influence on Conduct		5.31	5.89	6.25	6.38	6.38	6.72	5.12
The Church		5.49	6.86	6.60	6.61	6.77	7.06	5.24

* The adjusted scores for 1949 were 7.60, 6.53, and 6.80, in that order. In 1967 they were 6.39, 5.38, and 5.39, in that order.
** In 1944 the N for the Influence on Conduct scale is 120.

In several respects the study at Clark University resembles that at Northwestern. At Clark the same three Thurstone scales were given to all entering freshmen in 1931 and 1967. In 1947, 1948, 1949, 1954, 1955, and 1956 selected items from the scales were administered to entering freshmen, sometimes one sex only. Since Clark had only men students in 1931, the thirty-six-year trends are only for men. See Table 2.5. The replication shows a slight decline in orthodoxy and commitment. The large difference between actual and adjusted scores in 1967 was caused by an influx of Jewish students in recent years.

In order to specify the changes from the early 1930's to the 1940's and 1950's we studied the individual Thurstone items administered by Jones during those years. From each scale two indices were constructed, one composed of very favorable ("positive") items and one composed of very unfavorable ("negative") items. The index scores were the percentage of respondents checking the index items. However, since the *total* number of checks in 1967 was somewhat lower than before, we computed "relative scores" showing the proportion checking the index items minus the overall tendency to check any single item. Thus a score of zero means that the percentage of index items checked equaled the overall percentage of items checked. Figure 2.3 shows trends on one of the scales. The other two are very similar. There was a slight rise in orthodoxy among the men from 1931 to the late 1940's, little change from the late 1940's to the middle 1950's, and a considerable fall to 1967. The adjusted scores slightly reduce the change from 1956 to 1967. The trends at Clark resemble those at Northwestern.

TABLE 2.5

Freshman Men's Mean Scores, Thurstone Scales, Clark University

	Freshmen 1930–33	Freshmen May, 1931	1967	1967 Adj.
N =	286	57	190	
Reality of God	7.23	7.17	6.28	6.84
Influence on Conduct	7.10	7.11	5.83	6.51
The Church	7.47	7.43	5.97	6.88

At Dartmouth the Allport-Vernon Study of Values was administered to samples of seniors in 1940, 1956, and 1968. The mean religious scores rose from 25.0 in 1940 to 33.9 in 1956 and then fell to 27.6 in 1968. For Allport-Vernon scores these are large changes. They show the same rise-and-fall pattern in traditional religious commitment seen at Northwestern and Clark Universities.

At Ripon College a short questionnaire on religious beliefs was administered to entering freshmen in 1929, 1949, and 1968. It had a series of short sentences or phrases to which the freshmen were asked to report one of five degrees of belief. Several of the items were: "Ten Commandments should be obeyed," "Existence of God," "Reality of sin," "Man is saved by faith, not by works," "Resurrection of the body," "Existence of the devil," and "Virgin birth of Christ." From 1929 to 1949 the average change on twenty-three of the items in those who "absolutely believe" or "are inclined to believe, but doubt" was a decline of about 2 percentage points (when adjusted, it was a rise of 3.7 points).[10] From 1949 to 1968 the average change was a decline of 17.6 percentage points (when adjusted, a decline of 14.3 points). No clear pattern was discernible in the amount of change in individual items.

At the University of Wisconsin the same questionnaire was filled out by psychology and sociology classes in 1930 and 1968. Five of the twenty items dealt with traditional religion. See Appendix B, Table B.1, items P–T, for a summary. The 1930–1968 trends showed a sizable gain in commitment to the church and small gains in belief in divine inspiration, the importance of belief in God for human life, and individual immortality. Also the emphasis shifted markedly from

FIGURE 2.3

Reality of God Indices, Clark University

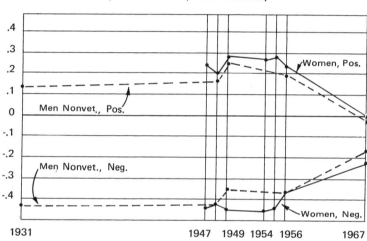

pure supernaturalism to greater attention to this-worldly concerns in religion. The shift toward orthodoxy at Wisconsin from 1930 to 1968 was not found in any other colleges in our research. The University of Wisconsin was known as a liberal college in the 1920's and 1930's, and these data confirm that reputation. Also the data serve as a warning against the often-heard statements that student radicalism in the 1960's was something new and unprecedented.

An item concerning the church (Item P in Appendix B) is the same as the item in the Harvard-Radcliffe, Williams, and Los Angeles City College questionnaires. The 1946–48 Harvard-Radcliffe and Williams students were considerably more favorable to the church than the 1930 Wisconsin students.

At Syracuse University liberal arts college undergraduates re-

TABLE 2.6

"(If you checked *3* above:) Check the *three* statements
in the following list which are your most important objections
to the present situation in religious worship." Syracuse
(*In percentages*)

	1926	1968	1968 Adj.
N =	780	231	
Churches are always asking for money, and we see no results.*	7	9	
Ministers have less capacity than they should have.	27	6	
One hears only platitudes, and the service is boring.	26	24	
People who stress church are often hypocrites and "Sunday Christians."	52	57	57**
Church membership would entail accepting doctrines I cannot honestly believe.	36	44	44
Although some clergymen have acceptable interpretation of dogmas, the old literal phraseology dominates the church.	17	29	
Church services make me gloomy and depressed.	3	3	
Church services appeal too much to emotions and are sentimental.	17	8	
Church offers no program for bettering humanity.	14	21	
Clergy and church members have narrow attitudes toward able and modern religious thinkers.	49	38	31
For some reason not mentioned.	30	45	

* The responses here are abbreviations.
** In 1968 only the three largest categories were adjusted.

sponded to identical items in 1926, 1932, and 1968. One item asked
about beliefs in God, and the adjusted responses showed a decline of
14 percentage points in the two most orthodox response categories,
saying that God was an infinitely wise and powerful personal Being
who answers prayer and that God was an infinitely intelligent Being

working under natural laws. Less orthodox or agnostic responses increased 14 points. From 1926 to 1932 the decline on the two most orthodox response categories was 10 points. A second item asked for beliefs about the miracles of the Bible. The changes in adjusted responses from 1926 to 1968 were minimal.

Another item asked if the respondent felt the need for religion and

TABLE 2.7

"Check the statement most resembling your belief about personal immortality, i.e., the belief in continuation of the person in another world. (Check one)." Bryn Mawr
(In percentages)

	1914	1933	1933 Adj.*	1968	1968 Adj.*
N =				228	
I believe in personal immortality for all men.	} 72	} 39	} 45	21	29
I believe in conditional immortality, i.e., immortality for those who have reached a certain state of development.				3	4
I believe neither in conditional nor in unconditional immortality of the person in another world.	22	37	32	31	24
I have no definite belief regarding this question.	6	24	23	45	43
	100	100	100	100	100

* Adjusted scores remove the effect of changes in religious background and major course of study. We found no discernible change in socioeconomic status of Bryn Mawr students over fifty-four years.

if the present church was satisfactory to him. In 1926, 38 percent said they felt the need and found the church satisfactory; in 1968 the figure was 22 percent (adjusted). In 1926, 50 percent said they felt a need for religion but found the church unacceptable; in 1968 the figure was 64 percent (adjusted). Commitment to the institutional church fell off from 1926 to 1968. Table 2.6 shows the second half of the same item.

The main objections to the church are rather similar in 1926 and in 1968. At both times the greatest objection was the hypocrisy of

TABLE 2.8

"Check the one statement most nearly expressing
your belief." Bryn Mawr
(*In percentages*)

	1933	1968	1968 Adj.
N =		227	
I believe in a God to whom one may pray in the expectation of receiving an answer. By "answer" I mean more than the natural, subjective, psychological effect of prayer.	31	19	19
I do not believe in a God as defined above.	60	63	59
I have no definite belief regarding this question.	10	17	21
	101	99	99

professed Christians. Objections to the clergy declined 21 points, and intolerance of laymen to modern thinkers declined 11 points (18 points when adjusted). Criticism of the clergy has largely disappeared, probably the result of much innovation among the clergy and especially the campus clergy. Yet objections to the institutional church as a whole are even stronger in 1968 than in 1926. There are more complaints of unacceptable doctrines, of old literal phraseology in worship, and of the lack of any positive program for humanity. The main objections are thrusts at the basis of church doctrine and practice, not just superficial jabs at particular forms and actions.

The overall pattern at Syracuse is a decline in orthodox beliefs over forty-two years. This decline in orthodoxy and commitment appears similar to that found at Harvard, Williams, and Haverford over a twenty-year period. Rose K. Goldsen *et al.* (1960:161) replicated the Syracuse item on the importance of religious belief and participation in their survey of Cornell students in 1950, and they found great similarity in the responses. This strengthens our conclusion that students' tendencies to orthodoxy were about the same in the middle 1920's as in the early 1950's.

Bryn Mawr undergraduates responded to two identical items in 1914, 1933, and 1968. See Tables 2.7 and 2.8. We lack the figures for the second item in 1914, but James H. Leuba tells us that "the proportion of believers in an interventionist God was considerably larger (at Bryn Mawr College) in 1914 than in 1933" (Leuba, 1934:298).

Some light on trends is shed by Leuba's survey of American scientists alongside his 1914 and 1933 surveys of Bryn Mawr students. Using the same items as at Bryn Mawr, he found 42 percent of the scientists expressing belief in God and about 51 percent expressing belief in immortality in 1914. In 1933 the figures were 30 percent and 33 percent respectively (Leuba, 1934:296 f.).

Table 2.7 shows that the Bryn Mawr students expressed considerably more belief in immortality in 1914 than in 1933 and more in 1933 than in 1968. The shift, however, was not to an expressed nonbelief but to the response saying "I have no definite belief regarding this question." The percentage expressing nonbelief *declined* 6 percentage points from 1933 to 1968. Apparently the long-range trend is not only a decline in orthodox belief but also a greater acceptance of having no opinion, of being noninvolved and unconcerned with traditional religious issues. The 1914 students felt a much greater need to have *some* opinion.

Judging from the adjusted percentages and also the ratios of believers to nonbelievers in both tables, we conclude that the change from 1914 to 1933 exceeded that from 1933 to 1968. The latter appears to be a decrease in orthodoxy of 6 to 12 percentage points. This seems larger than the change from the early 1930's to 1968 at Clark and at Wisconsin.

Leuba also carried out a 1906 study of nine colleges and one teachers college, using two open-ended items. We never learned the identity of the colleges, but we replicated the study at Harvard-Radcliffe, Williams, Northwestern, Clark, and Bryn Mawr. On the first item asking about conceptions of God, the clearest 1906–1968 trend was a decline of about 15 to 30 percentage points in those holding to any conception of God at all. On the second item asking what difference it would make if God were nonexistent, the responses show little 1906–1968 change among the men but an increase of about 12 to 24 percentage points among the women responding "no difference at all" or "doubtful or uncertain."

The Bryn Mawr replication seems to depict. more change in religious beliefs from 1914 to 1968 than does the nine-college replication from 1906 to 1968. The former is also more trustworthy as a measurement. Our best conclusion, from the Bryn Mawr study, is that reported levels of orthodoxy were probably higher in 1906–1914 than in the late 1920's.

The last of our studies producing information on long-range trends in religious commitments was at the University of Michigan. One item on religious attitudes from 1924 could be replicated in 1969. It asked, "Do you think an individual can formulate his own religious beliefs alone without the assistance of the church?" In 1924, 62 percent of both sexes said "yes," and in 1969, 83 percent of the nonveteran men said "yes." Although the samples are not comparable, there is probably an actual increase in agreement on this issue from 1924 to 1969. It suggests a rise in individual autonomy, a trend we shall comment on below.[11]

Also at the University of Michigan there have been periodic religious censuses of all enrolled students. The first reliable census was done in 1896, and since the 1930's they have been done annually as part of registration procedures. Most of the early reports are lost. The censuses provide information on the percentage of students giving a "religious preference." Because it is commonly known that campus ministers make use of the religious registration data for contacting students, the act of registering a religious preference implies some openness to religious gatherings and activities. The percentage of students expressing a religious preference seems a rough indicator of commitment to and interest in organized Judeo-Christian religion. The percentage of the total student enrollment reporting a religious preference or reporting church membership is shown in Figure 2.4. Several complications in using this figure as an indicator of religious trends are discussed in the notes. The percentage reporting church membership is shown through 1934. Sometime in the 1930's or 1940's this question ceased to be asked. No breakdowns by sex are possible because of fragmentary data in the early years. However, it can be concluded that the differences between men and women changed little over the seventy years studied. Women consistently reported more religious preferences than men.

The overall picture is a gradual decline until the middle 1920's, then little change until after World War II. In the early 1950's there appears to be a slight increase, but in about 1955 or 1956 there begins a sharp drop which continued throughout the 1960's. A portion of the overall downward slant over all seven decades may be traceable to the increasing individual freedom of action for students. The universities today ask less compliance with regulations and mechanical procedures (such as censuses). Any researcher wishing to replicate older studies becomes quickly aware of the change. The increased student freedom probably affects the reporting of religious preferences over the entire time span, for students in recent years may feel less obligated to make public statements about religion.

FIGURE 2.4

Religious Census Data, University of Michigan

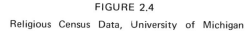

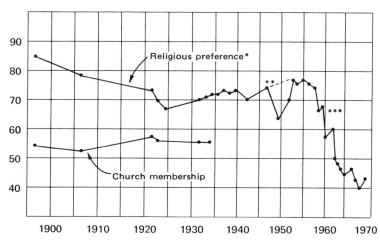

1900   1910   1920   1930   1940   1950   1960   1970

* The percentages are computed over the total enrollment at the Ann Arbor campus, including graduate students. Two important trends affect the data. First, the percentage of graduate students rose over the years. In 1924 it was 20 percent of the total enrollment, and in 1969 it was 38 percent. This shift alone would produce a decline in the curve since graduate students are less open to religious participation than undergraduates. Second, the proportion of women rose from about 16 percent in 1906 to 38 percent in 1969. The greatest increase in women occurred before 1940. Increasing numbers of women would tend to raise the curve slightly because of the greater tendency of women to register a religious preference. Probably the increases in graduate students and increases in women nullified each other in the years prior to 1940, but the increases in graduate students in recent years acted to push the religious preference curve downward.

** The broken line from 1947 to 1953 suggests a correction for the effects of the large numbers of veterans. From other studies we know that veterans indicate less traditional religious commitment than nonveterans. Also the high ratio of men to women in the postwar years had a lowering effect on the percentage reporting a religious preference.

*** The procedures for gathering registration data changed in 1960, and the new procedures probably account for some of the precipitous drop in religious preferences in 1960 and the years following. The new procedures made the religious preference data available to all offices receiving registration data, not just to the Office of Religious Affairs, and apparently some students did not like the new availability of the information. Our best estimate is that the changed procedure acted to depress the trend line after 1950 by about 4 to 10 percentage points.

The trends in reporting religious preference at the University of Michigan are somewhat different from those at the University of Illinois up to 1946:

That war may increase the religious interest of college students is indicated by statistics compiled recently at the University of Illinois. Last year, before the war ended, 92 per cent of all the students reported a definite religious preference. This year 90 per cent did so. The wartime figure was the highest since the university began keeping such statistics. In 1941—the last pre-war year—88 per cent indicated religious interest. The low was 76 in the depression year 1933. (*The New York Times,* Jan. 27, 1946, IV:9)

The Illinois trends in religious preference match quite closely the questionnaire trends analyzed above.

The Michigan data appear to support the Bryn Mawr replications in showing higher levels of commitment to the church in the 1900's and 1910's than in the 1920's and 1930's. One cannot be certain, for the statement of religious preference may have been a socially sanctioned act in those days and not a good measure of personal commitment. But some decline in church commitment during the decades from 1896 to the late 1920's seems probable.

We turn now to other studies in the literature. E. C. Hunter (1951) administered a "Social Attitudes Test" to all entering freshmen in Converse College, a small independent women's college in South Carolina, each year from 1934 to 1949. The test was scored in terms of percentage of liberal or conservative responses. The low point for religious conservatism was 1934, and the high point was 1948. Conservatism rose slightly but steadily from about 1939–40 to 1948. From 1935 to 1939 the scores changed little. The total rise in conservatism was about 8 percentage points, a weak trend over sixteen years.

A study by Paul Whitely (1938) using the Allport-Vernon Study of Values provides four-year trend data from 1931 to 1935. The mean Religious scores for juniors and seniors at Franklin and Marshall College declined from 33.83 to about 30.77, showing a decrease in traditional religious commitment.

At the University of Buffalo, Richard Bugelski and Olive P. Lester (1940) studied entering freshmen from 1927 to 1930 using a conservatism-liberalism scale including items on traditional religion. They found a mild liberalization of religious beliefs during those years.

Surveys made at Notre Dame University between 1921 and 1936 included several replications (Cavanaugh, 1939). One shows increased independence of students from parents between 1927 and 1936. Another shows an increase in those "going with a non-Catholic girl" from 1931 to 1936. The alumni surveyed reported a slight decline in frequency of Communion between 1931 and 1935. These data depict some liberalization during the early 1930's.

A perceptive study of morals, religion, and values at twenty-three colleges and universities[12] in 1924 provides some data and observations on a broad range of religious attitudes and values (Edwards *et al.,* 1929). It shows unmistakably the great decline in collegiate paternalism and regulation of students since 1924. A main theme throughout the book is the rising student individualism and the problems of collegiate "control" over students. A dean of a large university told the authors:

> I suspended a man for intoxication at the big game. Boys go to ――――
> and raise "Ned." This is made a matter of discipline if we get the facts.
> We say, "We are in the place of your parents. Your moral attitude
> wherever you are is what we are interested in." (Edwards *et al.,* 1929:29)

All college officials agreed that campus activities, fraternities, and social events must be carefully regulated to ensure that they exert a wholesome influence on the students. Thirteen of the colleges had some form of compulsory chapel. The emphasis of administrators was in "controlling" the students, with the clear assumption that students were not responsible on their own.

Two 1924 accounts of social events at large coeducational universities demonstrate the contrast between college society then and now:

> Every one of the sixty-nine fraternities has been allowed four dances a
> year. The inter-fraternity council has cut this down to two a year. Then
> there are four dance halls, two run by ―――― Union and the other two
> privately operated. Each class has two dances a year. All of these have to
> be chaperoned. I think the dean of women picks the chaperones. These
> affairs take up the time of the student, but are not bad otherwise. There
> seem to be a lot of "petting" parties at houses, whether sorority or not,
> "necking" as they call it, and lots of it. I do not know much of sex
> immorality. You seldom see a girl smoking. I have never seen a drunken
> man in this town. They take great precautions against this. ―――― is
> working against the liquor difficulty, and most fraternities have rules
> against drinking.
>
> This was a dance on a week night in a hall built for students who come to
> dance. There were about fifty couples present the night I went. The
> dancing was clean and the music not unusually "raggy." Girls wore simple
> afternoon dresses. There were no moonlight waltzes or softened lights.
> The custom of the students is to dance until ten, and then stop on the way
> home for refreshments. (Edwards *et al.,* 1929:186)

The students of the 1920's were questioning the traditional religious beliefs and practices. The main trend was toward greater individual freedom of thought and behavior. One faculty member in a women's college observed:

FIGURE 2.5

Schematic Summary Diagram of Trends in Orthodoxy
(In percentage points change on attitude items) *

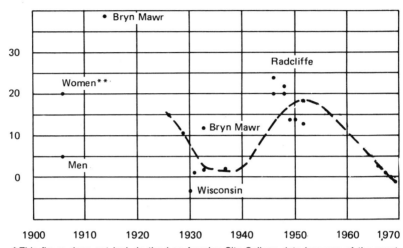

* This figure does not include the Los Angeles City College data because of the great
difference between L.A.C.C. and the other colleges studied. The vertical scale is average
percentage points of change on items measuring orthodoxy. The top of the figure
represents high orthodoxy and the bottom low orthodoxy. The results from the Thurstone
scales are plotted only in 1931, 1933, and 1937, when the data (Clark and Northwestern
studies) closely resemble the 1967 data. All scores are adjusted. Colleges departing
most from the overall trend line are identified. The zero line is set for 1968 data; 1966 and
1967 data are raised a percentage point or two and 1969 data are lowered a point to
conform to the declining orthodoxy in those years.

** The points in 1906 represent the nine-college study by Leuba, the least reliable
replication study. Probably they are within 10 percentage points of "true" positions.

[W]hile there is less professed religion than formerly, it is expressed in
different terms. There is no "piosity." The girls are very genuine. We are
experiencing a necessary transition in the change from traditional religion
to a new freedom. (Edwards *et al.,* 1929:15)

From the turn of the century until the present a major change in
American colleges has been the progressive freedom, autonomy, and
responsibility of the student and his voluntary groups. The development and maturity of students, or at least the collegiate and public
perception of their development and maturity, has gained. This
change has important implications for an investigation of trends in
religious attitudes and behavior. The student today is much freer of
college and parental influence than early in the century. He faces less
organized opposition and sanction when he raises the most searching
questions about norms and traditions. He is freer to form his own

views on religious beliefs and other matters, and he is in turn called upon to exercise that freedom responsibly.

All data and observations agree in several respects. They all suggest that a low point of orthodoxy occurred in the middle or late 1930's, and a high point occurred in the early 1950's. Levels of orthodoxy in the middle 1920's generally resemble those in the early or middle 1950's. Levels in the middle 1930's generally resemble those in the late 1960's. Figure 2.5 is a schematic diagram of overall trends in orthodoxy.

As Figure 2.5 shows, the data agree reasonably well in the 1930's, 1940's, and 1950's, but they do not agree in the period prior to 1926. Indeed we have only two studies prior to 1926, both replications of Leuba's work. The decline in orthodoxy at Bryn Mawr from 1914 to 1933 seems atypically great. Leuba's study of American scientists and the Michigan census data suggest that orthodoxy indeed was higher in the 1900's and 1910's than in the 1920's, so probably the trend line should show some decline in those decades. Perhaps we can conclude from the Bryn Mawr and Radcliffe results that liberalization in elite women's colleges has proceeded faster in the last three decades than in other colleges.

THE CHANGING RELATION
OF SCIENCE AND RELIGION

Several items in our studies ask about perceptions of the relationship between science and religion. Most important is an item replicated at Harvard-Radcliffe, Williams, and Los Angeles City College. See Table 2.9.

In twenty years there was minimal change at Harvard but a considerable shift toward perception of greater conflict at Williams and Los Angeles City College. In 1966–67 the item had a second part, asking those who perceived a conflict whether religion must give way to scientific formulations or whether science must give way to religion. At Harvard-Radcliffe and Williams about 95 percent said that religion must give way. At Los Angeles City College, 71 percent of the men and 80 percent of the women said so. In summary, at Harvard-Radcliffe and Williams the present students are divided roughly half and half—one group seeing no conflict and the other seeing a conflict in which science must prevail.

Those who see no conflict tend to have more orthodox beliefs. When the responses to the item are scored 5, 4, 3, 2, and 1, the item

TABLE 2.9

"How do you feel about the frequently mentioned conflict between the findings of science and the principal (basic) contentions of religion?" *

(*In percentages*)*

| | HARVARD | | | RADCLIFFE | | | WILLIAMS | | LOS ANGELES CITY COLLEGE | | | | | |
| | | | | | | | | | Both Sexes | | Men | | Women | |
N =	1946 386	1966 352	Adj.**	1946	1966 86	1948 87	1967 198	Adj.	1948 386	1967 245	1967 245	Adj.	1967 215	Adj.
To my mind religion and science clearly support one another.	21	16	50		18	38	16	50	29	21	21	35	18	38
The conflict is negligible (more apparent than real).	32	37			42	32	35		24	15	15		22	
The conflict is considerable, but probably not irreconcilable.	17	17	49		13	21	21	50	20	27	27	65	29	62
The conflict is very considerable, perhaps irreconcilable.	14	19			15	7	16		14	21	21		18	
The conflict is definitely irreconcilable.	16	11			12	2	12		13	16	16		13	
	100	100	99		100	100	100	100	100	100	100	100	100	100

* The Radcliffe results in 1946 were never reported, and the L.A.C.C. reports were never broken down by sex. The Williams men in 1948 are nonveterans only; elsewhere the 1946 and 1948 men include veterans.

** For information on adjustments, see Table 2.1.

correlates with the Conservative Belief Index at between .43 and .51 at Harvard, Radcliffe, and Williams. At Los Angeles City College the correlation is .27. Students with Jewish and liberal Protestant backgrounds perceive more conflict between science and religion than do those with Protestant or Catholic backgrounds. For example, at Williams, 73 percent of the liberal Protestants and "ethical Christians" perceive a conflict (responses 3, 4, 5) compared with 41 percent of the Jews, 54 percent of the Protestants, and 22 percent of the Catholics.

Lenski asked a very similar question to a sample of the adult population of Detroit. He found that 46 percent perceived a conflict. Fewer Jews than Protestants and Catholics did so (Lenski, 1963:281). The Catholics were most likely to perceive the conflict as "very serious" or "somewhat serious." In all except the Jewish group, *young* adults were much more likely to take the position that a serious conflict exists. Lenski conjectured that

> [t]his is probably a reflection, not of any trend, but only of the more recent exposure of young people to the school system. Older people are likely to have moved on to other problems and to have set aside any earlier difficulties which may have troubled them in this area. (Lenski, 1963:282)

He found that the sense of conflict is more pronounced among those persons who are doctrinally orthodox. In both the white Protestant and Catholic groups 19 percent of the heterodox thought that a serious conflict exists; this compares with 31 percent of the orthodox white Protestants and 34 percent of the orthodox Catholics. Glock and Stark found the same in a study of church members in California (Glock and Stark, 1965:287).

Our findings differ from Lenski's in several important respects. Whereas he found that the *more* orthodox persons perceived a greater conflict between science and religion, we found that the *less* orthodox persons perceived a greater conflict. Similarly, whereas he found that the Catholics perceived the *most* serious conflict, we found that the Catholic students perceived the *least* conflict. The difference seems to be in the degree of acceptance of modern science. The Detroiters generally ranged from a rejection of science where it conflicts with religious truth to a sense of no conflict between the two. The Harvard, Radcliffe, and Williams students ranged from a sense of no conflict between the two to a rejection of traditional religion where it conflicts with modern science. The "middle position" is the perception of no conflict; the Detroiters by and large shade off in the traditional antiscientific direction and the students in the nontraditional scientific direction.

Leuba found that American scientists tended to decline in orthodoxy of religious beliefs from 1914 to 1933. Twelve percent fewer believed in God (according to his definition) and 18 percent fewer believed in personal immortality in 1933 (Leuba, 1934). This suggests that the sense of conflict between traditional religion and modern science grew throughout American society and especially on American campuses during those years.

The 1924 questionnaire study of college seniors in twenty-three colleges carried out by R. H. Edwards, J. M. Artman, and Galen M. Fisher included some items on science and religion:

> While scientific courses as now taught headed the list of obstacles to religious belief (men, 26 per cent; women, 27 per cent), science and religion were considered complementary rather than unrelated or antagonistic by large majorities of both men (78 per cent) and women (85 per cent). Belief in evolution was also expressed by large majorities of both men (83 per cent) and women (80 per cent). (Edwards *et al.*, 1929:247)

These figures of 78 percent and 85 percent compare with a range from 53 to 70 percent at Harvard, Radcliffe, Williams, and Los Angeles City College in 1946–68 and 36 to 60 percent in 1966–67. The sense of conflict between science and religion has grown from the 1920's to the late 1960's.

Perhaps we may visualize the three positions discussed above as a continuum:[13]

1	2	3
There is conflict and traditional religion must prevail (most orthodox)	There is no conflict	There is conflict and modern science must prevail (most unorthodox)

The Harvard-Radcliffe and Williams students are almost evenly divided between positions 2 and 3; almost none take position 1. The Los Angeles City College students are mostly in positions 2 and 3, but about 10 percent take position 1. The Detroit adult sample has more persons in position 1 than in position 3. Among students since the turn of the century the sense of conflict between science and traditional religion has increased, and orthodoxy has declined; these changes must be interpreted as a movement from position 2 to position 3. Positions 2 and 3 will dominate campuses in the future, judging from present trends, and they may also dominate all intellectual discussion in our society.

Most observers today say that the debate between science and religion has subsided. It is not accurate to say that the sense of a conflict has subsided; rather it has grown. Perhaps it may be said that public debate has subsided because the issues are progressively being decided in behalf of the claims of modern science. Our own impression of theological developments and intellectual currents in leading theological seminaries supports this suggestion. Those elements of traditional theology most obviously conflicting with prevailing scientific views are the most embattled.[14] In terms of our continuum, position 1 is being abandoned.

CHANGES IN RELIGIOUS BEHAVIOR

Church Attendance

Twenty-year trends in church attendance are available in the Harvard-Radcliffe, Los Angeles City College, Denver, Dartmouth, and Haverford studies. At Williams data are lacking because of compulsory chapel in 1948. Identical items were used at Harvard-Radcliffe and also at Los Angeles City College. (See Table 2.10.) In short, the decrease in monthly or oftener church attendance is about 18 percentage points at Harvard, 15 points at Radcliffe, 12 points among L.A.C.C. men, and 10 points among L.A.C.C. women (adjusted).

At Haverford those saying they go to church almost every week rose from 40 percent in 1945 to 50 percent in 1952 and 1956, then fell off rather constantly to 20 percent in 1968 (same when adjusted). At Denver those Protestants attending "at least once a week" decreased about 13 percentage points from 1948 to 1968. At Dartmouth those attending monthly or oftener declined 22 percentage points from 1952 to 1968 (adjusted). In 1952, 43 percent reported monthly or oftener attendance; in 1958 it was 30 percent, in 1961 it was 25 percent, and in 1968 it was 21 percent. At Michigan men students attending monthly or oftener declined 21 percentage points from 1952 to 1969 (adjusted).

In a 1927 survey at Dartmouth an item asked, "Do you regularly attend any religious services?" Thirty-two percent said yes, 66 percent said no, and 2 percent were undecided. Levels of church attendance appear roughly the same in 1927 and 1952, for in 1952, 20 percent

TABLE 2.10

"During the past six months I have gone to church:"

(In percentages)

| | HARVARD | | | RADCLIFFE | | | LOS ANGELES CITY COLLEGE | | | | | |
| | | | | | | | Men | | | Women | | |
	1946	1966	Adj.*	1946	1966	Adj.	1948	1967	Adj.	1948	1967	Adj.
N =	123	361		86	87		73	251		143	221	
About once a week	25	20	} 21	39	20	} 28	24	16	} 31	35	29	} 45
About every other week	7	7		9	5		6	9		9	8	
Average once a month	20	13	} 79	10	15	} 73	13	8	} 69	11	15	} 56
Once or twice only	28	30		26	38		36	19		26	21	
Not at all	20	30		16	23		21	48		19	28	
	100	100	100	100	101	101	100	100	100	100	101	101

* For information on adjustments, see Table 2.1.

reported attendance "once a week or more," and a total of 43 percent reported attendance monthly or oftener (*The New York Times*, March 31, 1927:20).

At Dartmouth those reporting monthly or oftener church attendance at home before coming to college changed very little from 1958 to 1968. Trends in church attendance on college campuses are not the same as in middle-class society. The recent trends on college campuses are much sharper than in the broader society.

Another indication of this pattern is found in the Purdue Opinion Panel findings. In samples of high school students throughout the nation no discernible change in frequency of church attendance was found between 1951 and 1965 (Purdue Opinion Panel, 74:6). However, weekly or oftener church attendance decreased 9 percentage points for those in the upper income group.

At the University of Texas, Young, Dustin, and Holtzman (1966) found no noteworthy change in church attendance from 1955 to 1958 but a decline from 1958 to 1964. In the six years the number attending weekly or oftener declined 12 percentage points. The lack of change until 1958 but the dramatic change thereafter suggests that declines in church attendance in Southern colleges may date from a slightly later period—maybe from 1955–58 rather than from 1952–55 as in the Eastern colleges.

We may summarize that the data unanimously show declining church attendance during the period 1952–69. The decline in monthly or oftener attendance (or in "occasional" attendance) is about 15 to 25 percentage points in the Eastern and Midwestern colleges and about 10 percentage points at Denver and Los Angeles City College. These are dramatic changes. If such trends persist, *no* students in these colleges will attend church even once a month after the year 2010.

Long-term trends are, however, not the same as the trend between 1952 and 1969. At Syracuse an item was asked in 1926 and 1968 about church attendance, and the decline in monthly or oftener attendance was 27 percentage points (adjusted). In 1950, Roy M. Hall (1951:123) surveyed freshmen and seniors at Syracuse University and found a level of church attendance between that in 1926 and that in 1968. If adjustment calculations were possible with the 1950 results, the adjusted level of church attendance in 1950 would rise to a level similar to that in 1926.

At Clark University freshman men were asked about average church attendance in 1931 and 1967. In 1931, 60 percent reported

TABLE 2.11

Church Attendance, Michigan Undergraduate Men
(*In percentages*)

	"Weekly"	"Monthly" or More	"Never" *
1924, Church attendance on campus	**	**	16
1941, Church attendance on campus	19	39	29
1952, Church attendance total	30	61	18
1969, Church attendance total	17	40	38
1969, Church attendance on campus	17	27	43

* The columns in this table do not include all questionnaire responses. Do not add up figures horizontally.
** In 1924, 17 percent of the men attended church "regularly" on campus.

attending two or three times a month or oftener; in 1967 the figure was 30 percent (41 percent when adjusted). The decline from 1931 to 1967 seems comparable to that found at Syracuse from 1926 to 1968.

Two studies at Northwestern provide comparable data in 1927 and 1966. In a spring 1927 survey 48 percent of the Northwestern freshman men and 65 percent of the freshman women reported church attendance at least "frequently but not every Sunday." In the fall of 1966 Northwestern freshmen reported their church attendance at time of entrance. Forty-nine percent of the men and 50 percent of the women said they attended church frequently or oftener. Since church attendance of freshmen is more frequent before entering college than during freshman year, there is some decline from 1927 to 1966, especially among women.

Comparison of several studies at the University of Michigan provides some information on church attendance in 1924, 1941, 1952, and 1969. The items used were only partly comparable, and so only fragmentary data may be used for assessing trends. In Table 2.11 three discrete responses are compared over five surveys. Of the five, three asked about church attendance on campus, and two asked about total church attendance both on and off campus.

These data show that church attendance was more frequent in 1952 than in 1924, 1941, or 1969. The level of regular church attendance on campus was fairly similar in 1924, 1941, and 1969, but the number of persons who *never* attended increased from 1924 to 1941 and from

1941 to 1969. The overall picture is one of gradually decreasing church attendance from 1924 to 1969 with the exception of 1952, when the level was abnormally high. The adjusted scores do not change this overall trend pattern.[15]

In summary, our long-range trend data from four colleges depict a decrease in church attendance from the 1920's to 1968–69. At Syracuse the decrease in monthly or oftener attendance is about 27 percentage points; at Clark the decrease from 1931 to 1967 among men is about 20 or 25 points; at Northwestern the data are vague, but probably the decrease is less than 10 points. In these colleges the decrease, however, has not been continuous. At Michigan there was a clear increase in church attendance between 1941 and 1952, so that the level of attendance in 1952 was higher than in 1924. At Syracuse and Northwestern the data in the early 1950's are unclear, but the most reasonable conclusion at Syracuse is that the level of attendance in 1950 is not much different from that in 1926.[16]

Trends in church attendance have a rise-and-fall pattern beginning in the early 1940's much like the pattern in orthodoxy trends (cf. Figure 2.5). In addition, they seem to have a long-term gradual decline somewhat independent of the rise-and-fall pattern. This long-term decline must be explained by factors separate from those producing the short-run rise-and-fall. It is probably related to the long-term decline in those registering a "religious preference" at Michigan.

Bible-reading, Prayer, and Devotions

An item in the Harvard-Radcliffe, Williams, and Los Angeles City College studies asked about frequency of prayer, and the results are shown in Table 2.12.

Those reporting prayer frequently or oftener have diminished by 17 percentage points at Harvard, 27 points at Radcliffe, 15 points at Williams, 8 points among L.A.C.C. men, and about 3 points among L.A.C.C. women (adjusted).

A similar item asked about frequency of feelings of reverence, devotion, or dependence upon a Supreme Being. The percentage in 1966–67 reporting such feelings "occasionally" or oftener was 42 at Harvard, 43 at Radcliffe, 42 at Williams, 49 among L.A.C.C. men, and 72 among L.A.C.C. women. The trends over two decades were a decrease of 14 percentage points at Harvard, 23 at Radcliffe, 10 at Williams, 6 among L.A.C.C. men, and an increase of 2 among L.A.C.C. women (adjusted). The changes are almost identical to

TABLE 2.12

"During the past six months I have prayed:"
(In percentages)

	HARVARD			RADCLIFFE			WILLIAMS			LOS ANGELES CITY COLLEGE Men			Women		
	1946	1966	Adj.	1946	1966	Adj.	1948	1967	Adj.	1948	1967	Adj.	1948	1967	Adj.
N =	123	359		86	87		92	205		73	251		143	221	
Daily	22	12	} 19	35	13	} 26	19	9	(same)	19	10	(same)	36	29	} 74
Fairly frequently	14	10		18	11		20	15		10	11		16	22	
Occasionally	14	17		8	21		23	18		17	20		15	25	
Rarely	26	21	} 81	12	16	} 74	23	23		21	27		17	13	} 25
Never	24	40		27	39		15	35		33	32		16	10	
	100	100	100	100	100	100	100	100		100	100		100	99	99

changes in the frequency of prayer. Indeed the two items seem to measure the same dimension, for they correlate between .62 and .81 in the five groups studied.

The Denver study included two items on religious behavior, and the declines from 1948 to 1968 resembled those at Radcliffe. The Protestants who reported prayer occasionally or oftener declined 29 percentage points, and those who read the Bible occasionally or oftener declined 14 points (adjusted).

The Haverford study included two items on religious behavior: "I pray several times every week" and "I read in the Bible several times a week." The item on prayer received 34 percent "yes" responses in 1945, then rose to a high of 55 percent in 1952. Thereafter it fell off considerably. In 1968 it was 19 percent. (Adjusted scores reduce the decline by several percentage points.) The item on Bible-reading rose from 3 percent "yes" in 1945 to a high point of 15 percent "yes" in 1952, followed by a gradual decline to 3 percent "yes" in 1966.

Over a span of three or four decades we have fewer data. Three items were asked at Syracuse in 1926, 1932, and 1968. One asked about frequency of reading Scriptural or devotional writings, and those reporting they never read them increased about 20 points. The second asked about frequency of prayer, and those reporting prayer occasionally or oftener declined about 17 points. The third asked about frequency of feelings of reverence, devotion, or mind receptive to guidance, and those reporting such feelings occasionally or oftener declined about 20 points (all scores adjusted). These changes over forty-two years are comparable to the twenty-year changes at Harvard-Radcliffe and Williams.

At Michigan a 1924 item asked about Bible-reading. Five percent of both sexes read it regularly, 67 percent read it occasionally or seldom, and 28 percent never read it. In 1969, 5 percent of the nonveteran men read it regularly, 26 percent read it occasionally or at least once in recent months, and 68 percent never read it. The level of Bible-reading thus fell greatly over forty-five years.

To summarize, in the two decades between 1946 and 1967 the number who reported prayer at least frequently and feelings of reverence at least occasionally declined about 15 or 20 percentage points at Harvard-Radcliffe and Williams. At Los Angeles City College the decline was less than 5 points. At Denver and Haverford prayer at least occasionally declined about 30 percentage points. The forty-two-year declines at Syracuse in occasional prayer and devotional life were about 15 to 20 points. The levels in the early 1950's appear similar to those in 1926.

Bible-reading declined after 1952. Occasional Bible-reading fell about 14 percentage points at Denver, and Bible-reading several times a week declined about 12 points at Haverford. At Syracuse the decline from 1926 to 1968 appears similar to the two-decade decline elsewhere, but at Michigan the 1924 to 1969 decline seems greater. Probably Bible-reading in 1926 was a bit more frequent than in the early 1950's.

CHANGES WITHIN EACH TRADITION

To this point we have studied changes in attitudes and behavior in overall student populations. Now we look at the relative amount of change within each religious tradition.

Seven studies asked both for family religious background and present religious preference. A cross-tabulation of these two items produces an index of loyalty to one's home religious tradition. The index is the percentage of those students reared in each tradition giving that tradition as their present religious preference. It may be considered the "holding power" of each traditional group. See Table 2.13.[17] In general there was little switching from one religious group to another. By far the most important switching was from home religious tradition to "none" (or, in the Allport questionnaire, to "a substantially new type of religion is required").

In four studies over the last two decades the indices for the Catholics consistently fell. The indices for the Protestants fell considerably at Harvard-Radcliffe and Williams but remained constant at Los Angeles City College. For the Jews and liberal Protestants they rose. As we shall see later, on most items the Catholics and Protestants tend to be more orthodox than the Jews and liberal Protestants. The data thus support the general proposition that the more liberal the students at the time of testing, the weaker will be the holding power of orthodox groups and the stronger will be the holding power of liberal groups. The reverse is also true. Apparently the religious situation in middle-class American society in 1966–67 was more favorable to Judaism and liberalized Protestantism than it was in 1946–48. The indices increased remarkably among the Jews at Williams and Los Angeles City College. In 1946–48 it was the Jewish group which had the least holding power, but in 1966–67 it was the Protestant group.

TABLE 2.13

Percentage of Those Students Reared in Each Tradition
Giving That Tradition as "Preference"

		Catholic	Protestant	Jew	Liberal Protestant*
Allport questionnaire form**					
Harvard-Radcliffe					
Both Sexes	1946	±.69***	±.42	±.35	±.28
	1966	.48	.28	.36	.31
Williams College					
	1948	±.73	±.58	±.22	±.36
	1967	.65	.34	.50	.53
Los Angeles City College					
Men	1948	±.65	±.44	±.16	
	1967	.42	.43	.49	
Women	1948	±.71	±.57	±.34	
	1967	.65	.58	.65	
Ripon College					
Men	1968	.51	.52	.40	.40
Women	1968	.56	.54	(both sexes)	
Parallel questionnaire form**					
Dartmouth College					
	1968	.80	.71	.78	
Syracuse University					
Both sexes	1968	.75	.70	.84	
Bryn Mawr College					
	1968	.63	.74	.79	
University of Michigan					
Men	1969	.66	.61	.68	

* Includes "Liberalized Protestantism" and "Ethical but not theological Christianity."

** The questionnaire form probably affects the responses. The Allport questionnaire has more response categories and a more elaborate form. The "Parallel" form has two simple items asking religious background and religious preference.

*** Estimated figures are indicated by "±." They are probably accurate within ±.05 for all the groups.

We turn to changes in attitudes and behavior. In the 1946–48 Harvard-Radcliffe, Williams, and Los Angeles City College studies the researchers compared beliefs and behavior within each religious *preference* group (not each religious *background* group). This information helps depict the characteristics of those "loyal" to each traditional group. At Harvard the Protestants and Jews had no noteworthy change from 1946 to 1966 on five main items about attitudes and behavior. The Catholics declined an average of 11 percentage points on the orthodox responses. The greatest changes since 1946 are not in the characteristics of the persons loyal to each traditional group but in the *numbers* of those who are loyal. Thus, at Harvard, Protestantism lost in loyalty since 1946 but did not liberalize. Catholicism lost in loyalty and also liberalized. Judaism gained in loyalty but did not change. At Williams both the Protestants and the Catholics lost loyalty since 1948. The Catholics liberalized considerably, but the Protestants remained unchanged. The liberal Protestants and Jews gained in loyalty and slightly liberalized in beliefs. At Los Angeles City College since 1948, Catholicism declined in loyalty and liberalized slightly. Protestantism remained unchanged in loyalty but liberalized slightly. Judaism gained in loyalty and remained unchanged.

At Denver the decline on the Conservative Religious Scale from 1948 to 1968 was slightly greater in the Catholic background group than in the Protestant background group. Among the Protestant denominations the declines were greatest in those generally more conservative—the Lutherans and Baptists declined most and the Episcopalians and Congregationalists declined least. Similarly at Haverford the more conservative Protestants declined more than the Episcopalians and also more than the Jews.

At Dartmouth and Michigan the background group changing most from 1952 to 1968–69 was the Catholics; the group changing least was the Jews. The same was found at Syracuse between 1926 and 1968. Similarly, at Clark from 1931 to 1967 the decline in orthodoxy among the Jews was slightly smaller than among the Catholics and Protestants. At Northwestern, however, the changes from 1944 to 1967 were about the same among Catholics, Protestants, and Jews.

At Ripon College the pattern of change from 1929 to 1949 was different than from 1949 to 1968. From 1929 to 1949 the Catholics gained most in orthodoxy (5 to 7 points average on the belief items). The Lutherans, Methodists, and Congregationalists changed little, and the Presbyterians lost a few points. From 1949 to 1968 the Catholics lost most in orthodoxy (21 to 23 points average), the Episcopalians, Congregationalists, Presbyterians, and Lutherans lost an average of about 15 to 18 points, and the Methodists lost a mere 2 points on average. The Jews were too few in number to analyze.

At the University of Texas, Young, Dustin, and Holtzman (1966) found that the falloff in orthodoxy varied in the "religious preference" groups from 1958 to 1964. The Catholics declined least, followed by the Baptists and the Presbyterians. The Jews declined most, followed by the Methodists and the Episcopalians. This pattern is the *opposite* of that in the other colleges studied.

The main conclusion from these data is that the various religious groups *change together* in directions and in distance, suggesting that the major factors producing the changes are *common to all the groups.* They are external to the particular groups and not unique to any one of them. Our best data are from a period of declining orthodoxy. For this period we can summarize that *the most orthodox groups changed most.* The Catholics liberalized most, the Jews least, and the Protestants were arrayed between. The more conservative Protestants changed more than the liberals. The unusual pattern at the University of Texas runs contrary to this generalization, and the reason is unclear; perhaps our summary statement does not apply to Southern colleges. For periods of rising orthodoxy our data are meager. Only at Ripon have we information for a period of mildly rising orthodoxy, 1929 to 1949. There the Catholics rose in orthodoxy more than other groups, suggesting that the summary statement above is not valid in reverse form.

During the whole period of time covered by our research the Catholics have changed the most, and today the changes in the Roman Catholic Church are constantly in the headlines. It is a good bet that the Catholics will continue changing the fastest in the years immediately ahead.

SUMMARY

Available data agree rather well on trends in religious orthodoxy back through the middle 1920's. Beyond that point the data are thin and unclear. The trend line was summarized in Figure 2.5: the level of orthodoxy declined from the 1910's to the 1920's at an unknown rate. Starting in the late 1920's, it declined more rapidly until the middle 1930's. A low point was reached in the middle and late 1930's. Then starting in about 1940 the level of orthodoxy rose and continued rising throughout the 1940's to a high point in about 1952–55 which resembled the situation in the middle 1920's. After about 1956 it fell rapidly until 1969. The studies done in 1966–69 had results similar to the studies done in the middle and late 1930's. In short, the middle 1920's resembled the early 1950's, and the late 1930's resembled the late 1960's.

This orthodoxy trend line represents changes on items asking about religious beliefs and strength of commitment. The trend data on church attendance are slightly different. Trends in church attendance have a rise-and-fall pattern beginning in the early 1940's much like the pattern in orthodoxy, but in addition they seem to have a long-term gradual decline from the 1920's to the late 1960's. It is apparently a separate phenomenon which must be explained by factors separate from those producing the shorter-term changes after 1940. It is probably a product of long-range trends toward greater freedom and autonomy of college students. Because of the long-term decline, the levels of church attendance in the late 1960's were lower than those in the middle and late 1930's, even though levels of orthodoxy were similar.

The fluctuations in the trend lines are quite dramatic. The decline in orthodox attitudes from 1946–48 to 1966–69 in the various colleges (excepting Los Angeles City College) was about 13 to 23 percentage points on the orthodox responses to attitude items. Thus, for example, if 50 percent of the students in a certain college reported a certain orthodox belief in the late 1940's or early 1950's, the equivalent students in 1966–69 would report between 27 and 37 percent belief. In general the fluctuations are greater at the higher prestige colleges: the greatest declines over two decades occurred at Radcliffe, Williams, and Haverford.

Insofar as we can discern them, it seems that the aspects of religious orthodoxy declining most over the last two decades have been attitudes of exclusivism or particularism. Put in another way, the major change has been in increased tolerance of other religious views and of religious pluralism in society. Sentiments favoring *mergers* of Protestant denominations, however, have weakened since 1946–48. In almost all the studies, favorable attitudes toward the church varied along with orthodoxy of beliefs.

From the 1920's to the late 1960's there has been continually increasing perception of conflict between science and religion. In 1966–67 almost no one expressed views opposed to modern science. The more orthodox students perceive no conflict between science and religion, and those who perceive a conflict say that religious formulations must give way to scientific findings.

Most of the studies asked for religious preference as well as religious background group. One half to two thirds of the students gave their religious background group as their present preference. Most of the rest said that they had no religious preference or that a new type of religion is needed. If the "holding power" of each tradition is defined as the number preferring that tradition divided by the number reared in it, then in the late 1940's Catholicism had the highest holding power of any religious group. In the late 1960's it remained the highest but was closely followed by Judaism. From the late 1940's to the late 1960's the holding power of Catholicism fell, the holding power of Judaism and liberalized Protestantism rose, and the holding power of Protestantism fell a small amount. The evidence suggests that in liberalizing times the holding power of liberal groups increases and that of conservative groups decreases.

The students of Catholic background have liberalized more in their attitudes than any other group over the last two decades. Also they have changed more than any other group over the total time span of this research. The Jews changed least. Our only data on a conservatizing period is from Ripon College in the years from 1929 to 1949. There the Catholics gained most in orthodoxy, suggesting that the rise-and-fall pattern in the 1940's and 1950's was more pronounced in the Catholic group than in any other. The changes common to all religious groups were greater than those unique to any one, suggesting that the causes for the changes should be sought outside of the various groups and not within any of them.

CHAPTER 3

Changes in
Students' Values

In the last chapter we saw that religious change has occurred somewhat similarly in all religious groups, responsive to forces common to all. Also religious changes were related to broader social changes, both short-run as in the case of rising and falling orthodoxy in the 1940's and 1950's and long-run as in the case of gradually declining church attendance and declaration of religious preference. The search for explanations must include a study of broader values and commitments. In this chapter we look into some value changes documented by research and assess their relation to religious changes.

Several hypotheses mentioned in Chapter 1 will orient the discussion. First, is there support for the Durkheimian notion that religious commitments are associated with national commitments and that both will intensify during time of war or threatened war? Second, is it true that religious attitudes are closely related to political attitudes but not to economic attitudes or economic conditions? Are traditional religious commitments more responsive to social and political affairs than to economic affairs? Is attention to politics inversely associated with commitment to salvation religion, as Weber said? Are traditional religious commitments and political commitments functionally related or equivalent so that they have a sort of fixed-sum relation to each other? Third, have students been changing from inner-direction to other-direction in the 1940's and 1950's, and is this an explanation for the religious upswing in those years? Are other-directed students more traditionally religious than others, especially in public participation? Fourth, is it true that at any time an individual's religious attitudes will be similar to his political attitudes in terms of openness to change, optimism, individualism, tolerance of diversity, defensiveness, and so on? And were the increases in traditional religious commitment in the 1940's and early 1950's a product of the same forces causing the intense fears of Communism and totalitarianism? We begin with an initial review of evidence on value change among students.

ALLPORT-VERNON VALUES TEST SCORES

Probably the most widely used standard values test has been the Allport-Vernon Study of Values (1931) and its revised version, the Allport-Vernon-Lindzey Study of Values (1951, 1960). It measures relative emphasis on six areas—interest in scientific thought and philosophy (Theoretical), interest in practical affairs of business and commerce (Economic), emphasis on beauty and harmony in experience and creation (Aesthetic), concern with social welfare and justice (Social), emphasis on gaining power, influence, and political leadership (Political), and concern with religious teachings and experiences (Religious). The test has a total score of 180 (240 in the revised version) with a realistic fixed-sum structure. A gain in one score forces a loss in others. The Religious score may be considered a measure of general commitment to and interest in traditional religion, especially worship, communion, and church life (Hunt, 1968).

Three studies using the Allport-Vernon Study of Values depict changes over a number of years. First is our 1968 replication of studies of Dartmouth seniors in 1940 and 1956 (Bender, 1958). Irving Bender's 1940 sample was representative of the entire senior class, but his 1956 sample was not. Therefore we coded the backgrounds of all members of the sample and weighted their scores to compute a "1956 Construct" score more representative of the entire 1956 senior class. See Table 3.1.

The main changes are a constant decline in Economic scores and a rise in Theoretical scores after 1956. Religious scores had a prominent rise-and-fall pattern matching our other data on religious orthodoxy. From 1940 to 1956 the students' interest in business affairs and social problems declined as they turned more attention to traditional religion. From 1956 to 1968 interest shifted from traditional religion and business affairs to theoretical science, philosophy, and aesthetics. The changes after 1956 are quite dramatic.

The second study is at Haverford College, where all entering

freshmen since 1944 have taken the test.[18] The main trends from 1944
to 1966 are increases in Theoretical and Political values and decreases
in Economic values. Aesthetic values remained constant. Religious
values rose until 1952, then fell to 1966. The greatest single changes
were the increase in Theoretical scores from 1944 to 1964 and the
decrease in Religious scores after 1952.

TABLE 3.1

Allport-Vernon Mean Scores, Dartmouth Seniors

		1940	1956	1956 Construct	1968
	N =	107	67		68
Theoretical		28.7	30.4	28.8	33.6
Economic		31.8	28.3	28.3	24.6
Aesthetic		30.2	28.3	27.5	32.5
Social		31.2	29.2	29.6	31.3
Political		33.4	32.2	32.8	30.6
Religious		25.0	31.9	33.9	27.6

Third, C. William Huntley administered the Allport-Vernon test to
all entering freshmen at Union College (all men) at intervals since the
fall of 1952, and he very kindly furnished us the data through 1967.
The main trends were increases in Aesthetic and Social scores and a
decrease in Religious scores. Political scores rose slightly, and
Economic scores fell slightly. Huntley cautions that the admissions to
Union College have not been constant over the fifteen years. Since
about 1963, Union College has been accepting more students from the
metropolitan areas and more Jewish students. Judging from other
data, these new types of students probably do not account for very
much of the trends in Aesthetic, Social, and Religious scores. The
main trends in the data indicate value trends.

A fourth study was done in the 1930's. Paul Whitely gave the
Allport-Vernon test to a sample of juniors and seniors at Franklin and
Marshall College in the fall of 1931, then he followed the class of 1936
through four years (Whitely, 1933; 1938). This produced a comparison of juniors and seniors in 1931 with seniors in 1935. The only
noteworthy changes were a rise in Social scores and a fall in Religious

scores. The latter was larger, a difference of about 2.5 in the mean.

In these studies we see that Allport-Vernon Religious scores closely matched the attitude trends in Chapter 2. The loss in Religious scores after about 1955 was replaced mostly by gains in Theoretical scores and secondly by gains in Political and Social scores. Aesthetic scores appeared unrelated to the others.

VALUE CHANGES AT DARTMOUTH, 1952–1968,
AND AT MICHIGAN, 1952–1969

The data on value changes come mainly from four studies: the 1952–1968 Dartmouth replication, the 1952–1969 Michigan replication, the 1930–1968 Wisconsin replication, and the 1926–1968 Syracuse replication. Since the first two are almost identical, we review them together. In both cases about fifty items from the 1952 nationwide study by the Cornell Values Study group were repeated. Because 1952 was a high point of religious orthodoxy among students, these two replications are useful for understanding changes in values from then till the late 1960's. We discuss the data under six headings.

1. *Personal Commitments.* Probably the most eloquent single item on students' commitments was written by Gordon Allport (Gillespie and Allport, 1955), used in the Cornell Values Study (Goldsen *et al.,* 1960), and replicated at Dartmouth and Michigan. By asking for estimated future life satisfactions it assesses students' personal commitments. And like the Allport-Vernon study, it has a realistic fixed-sum structure. See Table 3.2. Most students ranked family first and career second in both surveys. The main change is the switch from emphasis on leisure activities to political involvement at Dartmouth and the switch from religious involvement to leisure activities and political involvement at Michigan. The change at Dartmouth is greater and more dramatic.[19] It shows a new political commitment with a national, not a local, focus. At Michigan the changes since 1952 are less dramatic, but they also include a new politicization. At Michigan commitment to religious involvement dropped markedly.

Other uses of this item show that the pattern we found is quite widespread among middle-class youth. In 1952 Dartmouth and Michigan were two out of eleven colleges studied, and their response patterns were quite typical of the eleven. In the fall of 1967 we included the item in the Clark University study, and the responses of

TABLE 3.2

"What three things or activities in your life
do you expect to give you the most satisfaction?"
(Three responses ranked; men undergraduates)

	DARTMOUTH				MICHIGAN			
	First Rank		1st, 2d, 3d		First Rank		1st, 2d, 3d	
N =	1952 349	1968 360	1952	1968	1952 386	1969 384	1952	1969
Your career or occupation	26	25	97	92	29	25	96	94
Family relationships	64	63	97	93	62	60	95	92
Leisure-time recreational activities	6	3	64	50	4	7	63	66
Religious beliefs or activities	2	1	11	13	3	3	18	9
Participation as a citizen in the affairs of your community	1	1	21	21	*	1	15	14
Participation in activities directed toward national or international betterment	1	7	11	30	2	5	13	23
	100	100	301	299	100	101	300	298**

* Less than ½ percent.
** Several respondents failed to rank all three.

the Clark men were within 3 points in each category of the 1968
Dartmouth responses.

One can discern changes in privatism and politicization from 1952
to 1968–69. The best indicator of privatism seems to be the responses
to the first three categories (career, family, and leisure) as opposed to
the last two (community participation and broader political participation). The data show increases in politicization and decreases in
privatism at both Dartmouth and Michigan; the change is greater at
Dartmouth than at Michigan. This new politicization is also shown

by an item asking, "Do you ever get as worked up about something that happens in politics or public affairs as you do about something that happens in your personal life?" In 1952, 39 percent responded "yes" at Dartmouth and 37 percent did so at Michigan. In 1968 the figure was 68 percent at Dartmouth, and in 1969 it was 71 percent at Michigan.

2. *Government, Social Constraint, and Anti-Communism.* Table 3.3 includes six items on political and international attitudes. The students in 1968–69 favor government requirements ensuring equal opportunity more than the 1952 students, yet the 1968–69 students agree with the 1952 students that "the best government is the one that governs least." Here is a curious pattern that is possibly traced to themes in the New Left ideology. The New Left sees government programs as necessary for social justice, yet at the same time it fears big bureaucracy in government. All big bureaucracy is seen as oppressive and dehumanizing (Lynd, 1969).

The last four items show greater pessimism about world peace, very much decreased faith in military service as being worthwhile for our country, and increased rejection of national ideology calling for sacrifice of human lives. The students in 1968–69 have lost faith in the American military system and the ideology supporting it.

Two items on Communism were included in the Dartmouth study only. One asked which was worse, Russian Communism or German Nazism. In 1952 the students judged them equally bad, but in 1968 only one percent said that Russian Communism was worse.[20] Another item stated, "Communism and Fascism are basically similar." In 1952, 37 percent agreed, but in 1968 only 11 percent did so. These items plus those in Table 3.3 show that fears of Communism have receded since 1952.

A series of items concerning social constraint of various groups is shown in Table 3.4. Several of the items are quite contrary to the American Bill of Rights. All six show a decreased anxiety about deviant or suspect groups. The year 1952 was in the McCarthy era, and public anxieties about disloyal leaders and internal subversion were running high. By 1968–69 such anxieties had virtually disappeared on these campuses.

3. *Economic Attitudes.* Table 3.5 shows four items on economics. There is some change away from laissez faire economic ideology but no greater support for organized labor. On the contrary, the support for organized labor declined at Michigan.

4. *College Studies and Experience.* One item stated, "I think college

TABLE 3.3

Six Items on Political and International Attitudes
(In percentages)

	DARTMOUTH						MICHIGAN					
	1952			1968			1952			1969		
	A	D	?	A	D	?	A	D	?	A	D	?*
The best government is the one that governs least.	26	58	16	27	56	17	29	57	14	28	51	21
The Federal Government should require all employers to hire people without regard to their race, religion, color, or nationality.	52	40	8	76	19	5	47	47	6	80	15	5
In spite of all our efforts for peace, nations just can't live together peacefully, so we might as well expect a war every few years.	15	73	13	21	68	11	13	80	7	20	67	13
An insult to our national honor should always be punished.	14	66	20	8	79	13	9	73	19	8	78	14
Anyone who serves in the Armed Forces is doing something worthwhile for our country.	62	22	15	43	37	20	60	22	18	35	44	21
Human lives are too important to be sacrificed for the preservation of any form of government.	11	79	10	17	73	10	13	75	12	27	57	16

* A = "Agree"; D = "Disagree"; ? = "Uncertain."

TABLE 3.4

Six Items on Social Constraint

(*In percentages*)

	DARTMOUTH						MICHIGAN					
	1952			1968			1952			1969		
	A	D	?	A	D	?	A	D	?	A	D	?*
It is unwise to give people with dangerous social and economic viewpoints a chance to be elected.	36	48	15	12	77	10	42	47	11	18	73	9
Only people whose loyalty to the government has been proved should run for public office.	42	43_	15	15	76	10	52	39	9	12	78	10
People who talk politics without knowing what they are talking about should be kept quiet.	31	61	7	14	80	6	27	67	6	20	72	9
Religions that preach unwholesome ideas should be suppressed.	18	62	21	5	85	10	19	63	18	5	83	12
Steps should be taken right away to outlaw the Communist Party.	30	56	15	5	85	10	36	50	13	11	77	11
Americans must be on guard against the power of the Catholic Church.	30	56	14	8	86	7	20	68	12	13	76	11

* A = "Agree"; D = "Disagree"; ? = "Uncertain."

TABLE 3.5

Four Items on Economic Attitudes
(In percentages)

	DARTMOUTH						MICHIGAN					
	1952			1968			1952			1969		
	A	D	?	A	D	?	A	D	?	A	D	?*
Labor unions in this country are doing a fine job.**	30	55	15				23	55	22	15	62	24
Government planning almost inevitably results in the loss of essential liberties and freedoms.				15	72	13	30	58	11	24	56	20
If people are certain of a minimum wage, they might lose their initiative.	38	53	9	22	65	13	35	56	9	26	64	9
Democracy depends fundamentally on the existence of free business enterprise.	59	30	11	52	34	15	67	25	7	51	34	15

* A = "Agree"; D = "Disagree"; ? = "Uncertain."
** Not asked at Dartmouth in 1968.

teachers are afraid to say what they really believe these days." In 1952, 21 percent at Dartmouth and 23 percent at Michigan agreed; in 1968–69 it was 7 percent at Dartmouth and 16 percent at Michigan. A second item stated, "Most of what I am learning in college is very worthwhile." In 1952, 67 percent at Dartmouth and 74 percent at Michigan agreed; in 1968–69 it was 58 percent at Dartmouth and 55 percent at Michigan. The anxieties of the McCarthy era have receded, and the students feel increased freedom to criticize higher education.

In an April, 1938, survey at the University of Michigan an item asked, "In general are you satisfied with the education you are getting from your courses?" Of the total undergraduates, 54 percent said yes, 41 percent said no, and 5 percent had no opinion. In 1969 the item was repeated but in statement form: "In general I am satisfied with the education I am getting from my courses." Of the men, 57 percent agreed, 33 percent disagreed, and 11 percent were uncertain. The two sample groups are not directly comparable, but probably the students were more critical of their college education in 1938 than in 1969. Apparently satisfaction with college education (or the fear to express criticism) had a rise-and-fall pattern, rising from 1938 to the early 1950's and then falling again to the late 1960's. Is this pattern related to the rise-and-fall pattern in traditional religious commitments? Correlations show that indeed the lack of criticism of college education has a mild association with orthodox religious attitudes and behavior. Also Goldsen and her associates show (Goldsen *et al.,* 1960:177–180) that traditionally religious students were less critical of their college education than others. In general such students expressed more conformity to many dominant social values than others.[21]

At Michigan an item was replicated in 1969 asking the students to select the educational goals the ideal college or university ought to emphasize. The greatest change from 1952 to 1969 was increased emphasis on providing "a basic education and appreciation of ideas," and the second greatest was an increase on providing vocational training which would "develop skills and techniques directly applicable to your career." Choices that lost in emphasis were "help develop your moral capacities, ethical standards and values" and "prepare you for a happy marriage and family life." There was no change on "develop your ability to get along with different kinds of people." The students in 1969 were considerably more "academic" or "vocational" and less "collegiate," using the terms of Burton R. Clark and Martin

Trow (1966). This change is confirmed by the smaller number of extracurricular activities per student reported in 1969. The Michigan students in 1969 were more intellectually oriented and more intent on a basic intellectual and vocational education.[22]

5. *Group Embeddedness and Other-direction.* The 1952 researchers developed an item to assess the embeddedness of individuals in groups, based on the Durkheimian notion that persons closely identifying with groups will gain a sense that the group has a personality of its own (Goldsen *et al.*, 1960:155). The item asked the students which groups they feel have their "own personality, something over and above the individual members" (see Table 3.6, first item). When a student check-marks any group it means either that he is emotionally embedded in it or that he somehow identifies with it. In both 1952 and 1968–69 the college is the group seen most strongly as having its own personality, and the immediate family ranks second. In 1952 "your church or religion" ranks third, but in 1968–69 "your nationality" ranks third. From 1952 to 1968–69 the students checked all the groups less frequently except for "your nationality," which gained, and "your clique or group of friends," which remained constant. The groups losing most were "your church or religion" and, at Michigan, "your fraternity." The total decline in group embeddedness was greater at Michigan than at Dartmouth. Group identification remained strong with respect to smaller and intimate groups, but it weakened with respect to larger and more formal groups.

The second item in Table 3.6 shows a dramatic change in perceptions of what is needed for social mobility and success. The main change is a decrease in the perceived importance of "having a pleasant personality" and an increase in the perceived importance of "brains (ability)." However, at Michigan "hard work" decreased slightly and "knowing the right people" increased slightly. The overall change may be interpreted as diminished emphasis on group acceptance and group embeddedness as a means to social success.[23] The third item in the table shows a decline in the importance of having "different kinds of people like you."

The authors of the 1952 study used the second and third items in Table 3.6 to measure levels of "other-direction" as defined by Riesman (1950); in the second item the indicator is the response "having a pleasant personality." The data show that other-direction has declined markedly on both campuses from 1952 to the late 1960's. The students in 1968–69 were more individualistic, less embedded in groups, and less other-directed. By contrast the college men of the early 1950's were conformist and cautious.

It appears plausible that the decline in group embeddedness and other-direction is related to the decline in fears about national security and subversion. Lazarsfeld and Thielens (1958) concluded that in 1955 the anxieties about Communism, radicalism, and social criticism were definite contributors to the political quietism and conformity of college students.[24]

6. *Anomie, Faith in Human Nature, and Alienation.* The 1952

TABLE 3.6

Three Items on Group Embeddedness and Other-directedness
(In percentages)

	DARTMOUTH		MICHIGAN	
	1952	1968	1952	1969
N =	366	367	406	387
"This group has its own personality"				
Your immediate family	51	50	50	42
Your college	77	69	52	48
Your fraternity	29	24	32	16
Your church or religion	40	26	40	24
Your nationality	38	44	29	31
Your team (s)	25	21	19	14
Your "clique" or a group of friends you go around with	27	27	25	25
Your club (s)	9	8	12	6
Two qualities that get a person ahead the fastest				
Hard work	63	68	66	57
Having a pleasant personality	59	33	65	32
Brains (ability)	32	53	29	57
Knowing the right people	29	28	30	38
Good luck	4	9	3	7
Being a good politician	5	7	3	8
How important is it to you that different kinds of people like you?				
Very important	54	28	48	26
Fairly important	37	54	42	50
Fairly unimportant	8	14	9	19
Very unimportant	0	4	1	4

questionnaire included three items measuring anomie and three measuring faith in human nature. On the anomie items no discernible change occurred from 1952 to 1968–69. On the faith in human nature items there was evidence of slightly lessened faith at Michigan but no change at Dartmouth.

Items on anomie or faith in human nature stated in general terms had little change, but other items asking about specific institutions and groups indicated distinct changes in levels of commitment or alienation. Four specific items were available. (1) In Table 3.3 we saw that agreement with the statement "Anyone who serves in the Armed Forces is doing something worthwhile for our country" decreased 19 points at Dartmouth and 25 points at Michigan, showing greatly increased alienation from the American military system. (2) Also in Table 3.3 agreement with "Human lives are too important to be sacrificed for the preservation of any form of government" increased 6 points at Dartmouth and 14 points at Michigan. Fewer students in 1968–69 had deep commitment to the American national ideology. (3) On an item stating, "Most of what I am learning in college is very worthwhile," we have seen that agreement fell 9 points at Dartmouth and 19 at Michigan; expressed faith in the higher education system had weakened. (4) Agreement with "There's little use writing to public officials because often they aren't really interested in the problems of the average man" dropped 11 percentage points at Dartmouth but remained unchanged at Michigan; apparently faith in the political process had strengthened among the Dartmouth students. This finding lends some support to the earlier discussion of new politicization in the 1960's. To summarize, in all these areas except the political process, alienation increased from 1952 to 1968–69. Below we shall see also that graduates were less willing to enter business careers in 1969 than in 1952. By "adding up" these specific items we conclude that social alienation of the students increased, even though the general items testing anomie and faith in human nature had little change. Future research on alienation must be more specific in its measures; it must utilize measures of specific alienation from each of several institutions in society in addition to general measures of feelings about society and humanity. These measures vary quite independently (for a similar argument, cf. Keniston, 1965:453).

To test the interrelatedness of these areas of institutional alienation we intercorrelated the four items at Dartmouth and at Michigan in 1968–69 and also included in the correlations the item asking whether or not the student had a religious preference. At Dartmouth the strongest correlation was .26 between alienation from American national ideology and alienation from the American military system. Also having no religious preference correlated .24 with alienation from the American national ideology. At Michigan the strongest correlation was .31 between having no religious preference and alienation from the American military system; next strongest was .27 between alienation from the American national ideology and alienation from the political process. At both Dartmouth and Michigan the corresponding correlations in 1952 were much weaker. The new alienation in 1968–69 revolved around lost faith in the American national ideology in general and the American military system in particular. Apparently both were associated with traditional religious commitments.

Finally, two items in the 1968 Dartmouth questionnaire asked about closeness to parents. From them a Closeness to Parents Index was created, and it correlated positively with having a religious preference but with none of the other indicators of alienation. Apparently traditional religious commitments and family commitments are associated in the students' total meaning-commitment systems.

Adjusted Scores

A selection of items in the 1968–69 Dartmouth and Michigan studies was adjusted. At Dartmouth the adjusted scores show slightly smaller changes in values and commitments since 1952 than did the raw scores. On most items the adjusted and raw scores were within 3 or 4 percentage points. The single change in students' background characteristics most responsible for the changes in responses was the rise in college board scores. Apparently the new students with higher college board scores in 1968 tended to bring with them a more cosmopolitan orientation, less religious commitment, less other-direction, and more criticism of college education.

At Michigan the adjusted scores diverged at times farther from the raw scores than at Dartmouth. For example, if the backgrounds had remained constant since 1952, agreement that dangerous persons should not have a chance to be elected would have fallen 18 points instead of 24. Agreement that the Communist Party should be outlawed would have fallen 17 points instead of 25. Agreement that human lives are too important to be sacrificed for any government would have gained 4 points instead of 14. Agreement that "what I am learning in college is very worthwhile" would have fallen 14 points instead of 19. As at Dartmouth, the single background change most responsible for the changes in responses was the rise in college board scores. The new type of student seems to have brought a lower anxiety about deviant social groups, less identification with national ideology, less orientation to leisure activities, and a stronger commitment to political participation.

From these calculations we conclude that not more than one third of the changes in values at Dartmouth and Michigan are the result of changes in recruitment of students. Most of the changes we found are actual value changes among middle-class youth.

Interrelation of Values

We created and intercorrelated indices from the 1952 and 1968–69 data. From the 1969 Michigan data nine indices were constructed: (1) A Social Constraint Index was constructed from the first five items in Table 3.4, each scored Agree = 3, Disagree = 1, and Uncertain = 2. (2) A Fear of Communism Index was constructed from four items (not discussed above). (3) A Free Enterprise Index was constructed from the last item in Table 3.5 and another stating, "The 'welfare state' tends to destroy individual initiative." (4) A Small Government Index was constructed from the first item in Table 3.3 and the second in Table 3.5. (5) An Orthodoxy Index was made up of the item on belief in a divine God and another item on belief in individual immortality. (6) A Church Commitment Index was made up of items about church attendance, Bible-reading, the item asking if your church or religion has "its own personality," and the item asking if religious beliefs or activities are a source of life satisfaction. (7) A Faith in Human Nature Index was constructed from three items. (8) An Other-direction Index was constructed from the second and third items in Table 3.6. (9) An Intellectualism Index was constructed from items asking about amount of reading outside of class requirements, the number of lectures attended outside of class, and whether the respondent thinks of himself as an "intellectual." On all indices high scores indicate strong or favorable attitudes on the topic in question. The intercorrelations of these indices are shown in Table 3.7, with the exception of the Other-direction Index and the Faith in Human Nature Index, whose correlations with all others never exceeded ±.17 and so were deleted. Most of the correlations in the table are weak, discouraging us from interpreting the various value changes reviewed above too easily as multiple indicators of a single overall change.

Several relationships, however, should be noted. Religious orthodoxy is weakly associated with advocacy of social constraints, support for a free enterprise economic system, and fear of Communism. The last correlation is .34, moderately strong. Also three indices are moderately interrelated, suggesting that they form a cluster—the Fear of Communism Index, the Free Enterprise Index, and the Social Constraint Index. From the 1952 Michigan data we constructed a similar matrix and found similar relationships, with the exception that traditional religious orientation and anti-Communism are a bit more strongly associated. And from the Dartmouth 1952 and 1968 data we constructed equivalent matrices and found weaker correlations than at Michigan.

TABLE 3.7

Intercorrelation of Indices, Michigan, 1969*

	Social Constraint	Fear of Communism	Free Enterprise	Small Government	Orthodoxy	Church Commitment
Fear of Communism	.39					
Free Enterprise	.30	.47				
Small Government	−.07	−.07	.24			
Orthodoxy	.22	.34	.24	−.06		
Church Commitment	.08	.24	.17	.03	.53	
Intellectualism	−.24	−.27	−.20	.13	−.13	.05

* N = 386. Correlation coefficients stronger than ±.10 are significant at the .05 level and stronger than ±.13 at the .01 level.

Are traditional religious commitments and political commitments functionally equivalent with each other so that they have a sort of fixed-sum relationship within the total meaning-commitment system? To check this hypothesis, we correlated the traditional religious indices in 1952 and 1968–69 with two items serving as indicators of political commitments—the item asking about "getting worked up about politics" and the item in Table 3.2 asking about anticipated life satisfactions. In both 1952 and 1968–69 the correlations were weak, suggesting that the two vary quite independently of each other. A simple functional equivalence producing a fixed-sum situation does not seem to exist. If traditional religious and political commitments are meaningfully related, it is in another, less direct manner.[25]

Are the determinants behind the rise in other-direction in the 1950's the same as those behind the rise in religious orthodoxy and commitment in the same years? Impressionistic evidence would suggest so. To check on the association, we correlated the Other-direction Index with the religious indices within each religious background group in 1952 and in 1968–69. The correlations are generally weak, but several noteworthy relationships appear in the Catholic and Jewish groups. Parsons has noted that social and political sentiments of McCarthyism were more intense in the recent immigrant groups, especially the Catholics, than among older and more socially established Protestant groups (Parsons, 1963a:222 ff.). Our data suggest that a mild relationship between traditional religious commitment and tendencies toward other-direction was present among the Catholic and Jewish students. Probably the relationship is traceable to social class factors or to the experiences of minority status in American society.

VALUE CHANGE AT WISCONSIN, 1930–1968, AND AT SYRACUSE, 1926–1968

Besides the Dartmouth and Michigan studies our main data on value change are from Wisconsin and Syracuse. Already we have reviewed five items on traditional religion in the Wisconsin study. In addition, five items were on economic issues, five were on political issues, and five were on sex and family matters. Each item had five responses expressing a spectrum of attitudes, scored from 1 to 5. For details, see Appendix B.

On the five economic issues (items A–E), changes from 1930 to 1968 were generally small. Item A asked about the advisability of government control on profits of industry. The change from 1930 to 1968 was a mean of .28 away from a strict laissez-faire position and toward profit controls. This is a rather small change.[26]

On two items the shift was in the conservative direction. Item C asked whether the inheritance of great wealth from generation to generation should be permitted or whether the government should curtail it. The change since 1930 was .38 toward permitting more inheritance of wealth. Item D concerned the benefits or evils of fashion change. The alternatives ranged from approval of fashion change because of stimulation of trade to condemnation because of wastefulness. From 1930 to 1968 the change was .85 toward greater approval of fashion change. On both of these items the 1968 students tended to check moderate and noncritical responses, suggesting that the issues being debated in 1930 have mostly disappeared.

On two of the economic items there was no noteworthy change from 1930 to 1968. Item B asked if the traditional capitalistic system of wealth distribution is wise and sound or if it is unjust and backward. Item E asked whether advertising benefits the standard of living or whether it exerts a harmful influence through creation of false desires and wastefulness.

On the five items on political issues (items F–J) the amount of change varied. Item F asked whether the American practice of democracy was wise and adequate or whether it was a failure because of its mediocrity, impracticality, aggressiveness, and lack of appreciation for culture and education.[27] Attitudes changed .29 toward greater support for American democracy. Item G asked if schools should increase emphasis on patriotism or if patriotism should be de-emphasized in schools and public life because it encourages militarism and war. Attitudes shifted .83 toward greater support for patriotism in schools and public life. This remarkable shift shows the intense criticism in 1930 compared with 1968. Item I asked if public expressions of opinion hostile to the government, to morality, or to sacred institutions should be prohibited or if all speech should be free without restriction. Attitudes shifted .60 toward greater freedom of speech. On the last two political items no noteworthy changes occurred since 1930: one dealt with the propriety or morality of nonobedience of certain laws as a means of changing them, and the other asked about the practicality or necessity of socialism as a form of government.

As in the areas of economics and politics, the items on sex and family (items K–O) showed mixed changes. On item L dealing with birth control the change since 1930 was very dramatic. At one extreme the item stated that birth control is a matter with which man has no business meddling, and at the other it stated that birth control is an urgent problem demanding immense attention. In 1930, 34 percent agreed that birth control is one of the important problems facing us and that it needs much study and research (responses 4 and 5). In 1968 the figure was 93 percent. The mean shifted 1.74 points, a change *almost twice as great* as any other in the study.

Two items asked about sex norms. Item N asked whether a young woman should engage in premarital sexual experimentation, and since 1930 the responses shifted .54 toward greater liberalism. This amounts to an increase of 22 percent choosing the two most liberal responses. Item O asked if sexual morality is a fixed and unchangeable code or if it is relative and elastic, depending on persons and circumstances. Attitudes changed .60 toward greater liberalism and contextualism.

Item M asked about the special value of the family unit. At one extreme it asserted that the family is the sacred and permanent unit of our society and must be kept inviolate; at the other it criticized the family as inhibitory and frustrating of human welfare and happiness. Attitudes changed .97 toward greater support of the family structure. Criticism of the traditional family structure has virtually disappeared since 1930. If the family was a topic of debate in 1930, it was certainly not in 1968. Item K questioning the value of strict monogamy changed little from 1930 to 1968.

All twenty items in the questionnaire were intended to have a conservative-to-liberal structure. From 1930 to 1968 the changes were not uniformly in one direction or the other. Some items in each of the four areas changed in one direction, some in the other. If all changes are averaged, the result is a slight change in the conservative direction. However, certain emphases have changed since 1930. There was in 1968 more support for existing institutions but a greater call for individual freedoms within those institutions. The 1968 students showed more support for American democracy and patriotism but called for more freedom of speech within them. They gave more support for the traditional family but called for more freedom of sex behavior and more birth control. They gave more support to the church but asked for less supernaturalism and dogma. Whereas the 1930 students stressed *basic reforms,* the 1968 students seemed to stress *freedoms.* This coincides with several analyses of radicalism in the 1930's and 1960's which contrast the sense of total rejection of the evil capitalist society among radicals in the 1930's with the more specific attacks in the 1960's (Allen, 1967; Harrington, 1965; Draper, 1967).

A leading historian of student activism holds that participation in American student political movements, proportionate to enrollment,

TABLE 3.8

Intercorrelation of Indices, Wisconsin, 1968

		Religion Index	Sex and Family Index	Political Index
Men:	Sex and Family Index	.58		
	Political Index	.48	.52	
	Economic Index	.27	.26	.46
Women:	Sex and Family Index	.57		
	Political Index	.50	.54	
	Economic Index	.17	.23	.36

was greater in the middle 1930's than in 1967 (Draper, 1967). Our Wisconsin data depict the depth of that radicalism already in 1930. Since the high point of student political activism came in the years 1934 to 1937, it was probably greater then than in 1930 or in 1968. The University of Wisconsin has been a liberal campus for decades and may not serve well as a representative example of broad student opinion in 1930. But it was not alone, for a 1930 survey at Columbia University shows just as much radicalism as at the University of Wisconsin.[28]

We factor-analyzed the 1968 Wisconsin responses of each sex to study the interrelation of the twenty items, and in the principal components solution one large factor appeared, accounting for about 31 percent of the total variance for each sex. It is the dominant conservative-liberal dimension built into the questionnaire. From four rotated factors we then created four indices: (1) a Religion Index composed of five items, (2) a Sex and Family Index of four items, (3) a Political Index of four items, and (4) an Economic Index of three items. The intercorrelations are shown in Table 3.8. The Religion Index and the Sex and Family Index are so strongly intercorrelated that they approach being the same dimension. This is another indication of the close relation between traditional religion and the family in most students' meaning-commitment systems. Also strongly related to the Sex and Family Index is the Political Index. The index *least* related to the others is the Economic Index, as Lipset hypothesized.

At Syracuse several items on higher education and political attitudes were asked in 1926 and in 1968. Perhaps the most important item asked about admired types of students. From 1926 to 1968, respect for the mediocre but industrious student rose considerably and respect for the "activities man" plummeted. Admiration for the capable but narrow scholar rose modestly. In 1926 it was the "activities man" who was the most admired type, but in 1968 it was the successful industrious student. Syracuse students placed much greater emphasis on educational and academic goals in college in 1968 than in 1926.

Six other items in the Syracuse replication help depict the value changes over forty-two years. The first asked how great the effect would be on Syracuse University if it sustained athletic losses. In 1926 the majority responded that athletic losses would lower the reputation of the University but not its merit. In 1968 the majority said athletic losses would affect neither Syracuse's reputation nor its merit. The shift in attitudes is large. On the second item no clear change occurred on reasons given why the respondent decided to go to college. The 1926 stress on vocational preparation, greater earning power of graduates, and intellectual enrichment changed very little. The third item asked about participation in student activities and organizations. Most noteworthy was the *lack* of change from 1926 to 1968. The only significant change was a decline in participation in women's government organizations and activities. This was a product of the greater integration of women into the total university life in 1968. In 1926 the men and women sat separately in classrooms, and the women had their own separate campus organizations.

The fourth item asked about the "double standard" of morality, i.e., whether certain acts were intrinsically worse for a woman to do than for a man. The responses in 1968 showed that the double standard has largely disappeared. The fifth item asked how much of the "supervision of morals" on campus should be in the hands of the administration and how much should be in the hands of student committees. The 1968 responses showed a large change toward rejecting any administration involvement and instead preferring either student control of "supervision of morals" or no organized control at all. The sixth item asked about freedom of speech for the faculty, and the 1968 responses advocated considerably greater freedom of speech than in 1926.

To sum up, over four decades there has been a major increase in the individual autonomy of college students. This is seen in the 1968 distaste of any "supervision of morals" and the insistence on freedom of speech for all persons. It was seen in the Wisconsin students' call for greater individual freedom and autonomy. It was seen in the Michigan students' beliefs that an individual can and must formulate religious meanings for himself, apart from any church. Also over four decades most colleges have seen considerable intellectual upgrading and restraint of the extracurriculum. Both changes are vividly seen in the account of how the 1926 survey was done. The 1926 Syracuse University administration supported the survey˚ and required all students to partake in the questionnaire study under the penalty of a "double cut" (in the class attendance enforcement system). The questionnaire administration was scheduled for a two-hour period on a Friday in May. Classes in the hour preceding this period were already dismissed at the standard time for the annual student class elections. Since then, enforced class attendance, enforced questionnaire surveys, dismissal of classes for student elections, and the whole round of organized student activities have departed the campus scene.[29]

From the 1968 questionnaire we constructed a Religious Orthodoxy Index, a Religious Behavior Index, a Student Autonomy Index, an Extracurricular Activities Index, and a political Hard Line Index. The intercorrelations between them, except for the two traditional religious indices, were all lower than $\pm .2$, too weak to be noteworthy.

Finally, at Clark University we were able to trace trends in militaristic or pacifistic attitudes from 1931 to 1967, using the Thurstone-Droba Scale on Attitude Toward War. Items measuring attitudes toward personal involvement in war showed rising militarism from the early 1930's to 1947–49, little change from then to 1954–56, and a decrease in militarism to 1967. The 1967 responses of Clark freshmen indicated less militarism than in 1931, but since we were unable to adjust the data, such long-range comparisons are precarious. Probably the rise-and-fall pattern, however, would remain in the adjusted scores. The amount of change on various items about war and militarism from 1954–56 to 1967 was about 6 to 16 percentage points (cf. Jones, 1970:56–62).

CHANGING CAREER CHOICES

Another indicator of changing personal commitments is career choice of graduating seniors. We secured trend data from Harvard, Dartmouth, and Michigan. At Harvard the percentage planning graduate work in the arts and sciences rose from about 18 in 1949 to 27 in 1967; those planning graduate work in business fell from about 12 percent in 1949 to 7 percent in 1967. Between 1948 and 1968 law increased in attractiveness by about 8 or 9 percentage points; teaching rose about 10 or 12 points; and business fell about 14 or 16 points.

At Dartmouth we were able to compare the class of 1966 with the juniors and seniors in the 1952 questionnaire survey. The major change over the fourteen years was a decline of about 11 or 12 points in business, with corresponding increases in law and teaching.

At Michigan an item in the 1952 survey was replicated in 1969. Students desiring to work in a private firm or corporation declined 10 points, and those desiring to enter a family business or a private professional office declined 5 points. Rather, students desiring work in the field of education rose 8 points, and those wanting to work in government offices or agencies increased 3 points.

It could be that changing career choices reflect changes in recruitment at these colleges. This suggestion is supported by an association at Harvard between higher scholastic aptitudes as freshmen and tendencies not to prefer business careers. Using data on rising scholastic averages at Harvard between 1949 and 1967 we calculated that this factor alone accounted for about 4 to 6 percentage points of the decrease in those desiring business careers and 4 to 6 percentage points of the increase in those wanting to teach. But most of the trends are traceable to value changes. The same conclusion is probably true for Dartmouth and Michigan. Shifts in career choices seem to coincide with changes in patterns of alienation found in the surveys at Dartmouth and Michigan since 1952.

OTHER STUDIES ON CHANGING VALUES OF STUDENTS

The literature includes several important studies of value trends. At Northwestern University in 1929, Crissman administered a "moral judgment" questionnaire to undergraduates, and in 1939 and 1940 he repeated the studies at the University of Wyoming. Then in 1958, Salomon Rettig and Benjamin Pasamanick repeated the study at Ohio State University (Rettig and Pasamanick, 1959). These studies provide a ten-year study at Wyoming and a twenty-nine-year study at Northwestern and Ohio State, probably reliable insofar as large differences appear. The questionnaire had fifty moral prohibitions which the subjects judged in degree of wrongness; then the fifty were ranked. From 1939 to 1949 the severity of antipolitical behavior, such as not voting, or antireligious behavior, such as not contributing money, increased. From 1929 to 1958 at Northwestern and Ohio State the items that intensified in moral stigma were suicide, "Testifying falsely in court when under oath," "Disbelieving in God," "Holding up and robbing a person," and "Not giving to religion when able." Generally the severity increased on those prohibitions associated with the sanctity of the individual life and the basic democratic form of government. The increased moral rejection of not voting may be due to the feeling that "democratic values are being challenged today more than at any other time" as the authors suggest (Rettig and Pasamanick, 1959:324). The increase in religious sentiments from 1929 to 1958 is probably also related to the cold war.

In a series of four studies Pressey and his associates studied changing moral disapprovals, worries, and interests of high school and college students in 1923, 1933, 1943, and 1953. All the studies were done in Ohio high schools and at Ohio State University, using the Pressey X-O Test (Pressey and Jones, 1955). It has three lists of words, and the respondents are asked to underline their moral disapprovals among the first list, their worries among the second, and their interests among the third. The main pattern was a decrease in the number of items considered to be "wrong." In each administration the number considered wrong decreased from high school to college and from college freshmen to seniors, but in addition the trend from decade to decade was one of decreasing wrongs. The items in the Pressey X-O Test are specific acts or tendencies which the researchers call "borderline moral acts"; it is clear that attitudes toward all such acts liberalized from 1923 to 1953. Change among the women was slightly greater than among the men. The change from decade to decade was somewhat uniform. Table 3.9 shows the "wrongs" and "worries" changing most from 1923 to 1953. Trends in "interests" are too bound to the particular fashions of each decade to be important to us. The decreases in moral disapprovals indicate a basic trend from strict and detailed moral codes to more reflective and internalized moral orientations. Both freedom and responsibility have increased over four decades. In the section on interests or likes were "prayer" and "church." Among the men the first increased 25 points from 1923 to 1953, and the second increased 9 points. Among the women "prayer" increased 32 points and "church" increased 8 points. These findings suggest that attention to church and religious observance was greater in 1953 than in 1923.

The many surveys by the Purdue Opinion Panel since 1942 include a series of replications producing data on value change among high school students (tenth through twelfth grades). One set of replications repeated a study of ethical values done in 1919. First a sample of students were asked to list the "worst things a person can do," then the responses were coded and the sixteen worst categories listed in

TABLE 3.9

Items Changing Most from 1923 to 1953, Ohio State University
(Percentage change)

			College Juniors and Seniors
WRONGS	Men:	craps	−44
		extravagance	−36
		flirting	−36
		silliness	−35
		slang	−32
	Women:	flirting	−37
		silliness	−36
		' overeating	−35
		immodesty	−33
		craps	−32
WORRIES	Men:	business	−20
		marriage	+17
		friends	−12
	Women:	marriage	+23
		popularity	+19
		money	+10

alphabetical order in the questionnaire. The subjects were asked to rate them according to "badness." Replications were done in 1954 and 1965. "Sexual misbehaving" slipped from second worst in 1919 to third in 1954 and to fourth in 1965. "Lying" dropped from fifth in 1919 to seventh in 1954 and 1965. Five from the 1919 list dropped out of the later studies entirely: gambling, swearing and vulgar talk, being selfish, idleness, and dancing. In their place came new practices mentioned in 1954 and 1965: using or selling narcotics, reckless driving, being undependable, being inconsiderate, and being cruel. The new "worst" categories tended to be traits of character rather than specific acts, and they tended to focus on interpersonal behavior rather than personal or individual acts (such as "idleness"). In the 1950's and 1960's morality was seen more in terms of character than in terms of following specific and discrete rules, and more in interpersonal than purely personal terms. These changes indicate gains in responsibility and autonomy of high school students over four decades (Purdue Opinion Panel No. 74).

Another Purdue survey item stated, "If I learned that some friends

TABLE 3.10

Replications in High School Samples, Purdue Opinion Panel

	Percent agreeing	
	1949	1963
The most serious danger to democracy in the U.S. comes from Communism and Communist-dominated groups.	76	68
Sending letters and telegrams to congressmen has little influence upon legislation.	41	28
Democracy depends fundamentally on the existence of free business enterprise.	57	53
Agitators and troublemakers are more likely to be foreign-born citizens than native Americans.	22	13
All Americans—Negroes, Jews, the foreign born and others—should have equal opportunity in social, economic, and political affairs.	74	78

of mine had not followed the morals or rules related to the behavior of unmarried people, I would not consider them good friends anymore." In 1952, 57 percent agreed, and in 1965, 30 percent agreed, the rest saying that it would make no difference to the friendship.

Several items resemble those used in the Dartmouth and Michigan studies, and the trends in responses are similar. See Table 3.10. The Dartmouth and Michigan findings can be generalized to many college and high school students.

Several Purdue replications show increased support for freedom of speech from the early 1950's to the middle 1960's. One item asked, "Should or should not high school teachers be free to criticize our government or our economic system?" In 1950, 62 percent said yes, and in 1965, 71 percent said yes. Another asked, "When a school board hires a teacher, do you think it has the right to ask the teacher about his or her political beliefs, or do you think that is the teacher's personal business?" In 1953, 33 percent said it has the right to ask; in 1965 only 21 percent said so.

Several items asked about religion in public schools. One asked, "Do you think that the public schools should teach religious

TABLE 3.11

"The ONE group of people I think can do the most
to promote peace in the world is:"
(High school students; in percentages)

	1959	1964	1967
Politicians	9	14	17
Religious leaders	40	30	26
Educators	15	25	25
Statesmen	6	9	10
Leaders in science	8	6	8
Military leaders	15	12	14
No response	7	4	0
	100	100	100

instruction—that is, teaching pupils to *live and believe* according to religious principles—as distinguished from teaching pupils to know about religion?" In 1953, 44 percent said it should be taught; in 1965 it was only 20 percent. This item suggests that during the height of the cold war and McCarthyism organized religion tended to become "established" and protected from criticism in American life. From 1953 to 1965 this "establishment" weakened. Another item asked if public schools should teach a course on the history and doctrine of world religions. In 1953, 45 percent said yes, and in 1965, 49 percent said yes. *Interest in* religion grew slightly.

Finally, Table 3.11 has an item asking about faith in various leaders in American life. Faith has shifted partially from traditional religion to political movements and education.

Several other studies in the literature are important but less extensive. In the years 1931, 1934, 1937, and 1939 a team of researchers administered Harper's Social Study to psychology classes at Purdue University (Breemes *et al.,* 1941). This test measured overall liberalism or conservatism based on the political, economic, educational, and religious issues then current. The researchers found a great increase in liberalism between 1931 and 1934, then little change through 1939. Bugelski and Lester (1940) found a very similar liberalization at the University of Buffalo from 1931 to 1934. Vernon Jones (1942) found little change in attitudes toward war between 1930 and 1936, but after 1936 a trend toward greater militarism and less pacifism, which continued through 1941. Theodore M. Newcomb (1943) found no change toward conservative or liberal attitudes between 1935 and 1938 at Bennington College.

Hunter administered a Social Attitudes Test to all freshmen entering Converse College (a women's college) in South Carolina during the years 1934 to 1949 (Hunter, 1951). On attitudes toward the Negro there was a major liberalization during those years. The changes were mostly before 1940. Pacifism rose from 1934 to a high point in 1937, then fell; after 1940 it fell precipitously. Attitudes toward economic and labor issues were unchanged between 1934 and 1946 but thereafter became more conservative. Liberal attitudes toward social welfare and social innovation were highest in 1940, then declined rather steadily till 1948. In general, liberalism was strongest in the late 1930's, and trends toward conservatism began about 1939 or 1940. After World War II, conservatism remained dominant.

In a history of student activism in the 1930's Draper comments on student movements and some survey results. He argues that the late 1920's was a period of depoliticization. This ended with the depression years and the threat of war in Europe. Involvement in war was the main political issue for students in the 1930's.

> In 1933 a sampling of 920 Columbia students included 31 per cent who considered themselves absolute pacifists—almost one-third; another 52 per cent stated they would bear arms only if the country were invaded; only 8 per cent said they were willing to fight for the United States under any circumstances. A national poll showed 39 per cent who said that they would not participate in any war, and another 33 per cent who would do so only if the United States were invaded. (Draper, 1967:168)

Social alienation among students was probably as deep in those years as in the late 1960's. Compare this with Goldsen's summary of college students' political and economic attitudes in 1952:

The investigator attempting to describe the political flavor of contemporary American campuses is immediately and forcefully struck by two themes. The first is what seems to be a remarkable absence of any intense or consuming political beliefs, interests or convictions on the part of the college students. The second is extreme political and economic conservatism. Both are in marked contrast to the radicalism usually attributed to American college students in the thirties, and said to be a traditional aspect of student culture in other countries. (Goldsen *et al.,* 1960:97)

The early 1950's, like the middle 1920's, was a time of privatism and economic conservatism, without significant student political activism.

INTERRELATION OF VALUES

The numerous surveys of the attitudes of college students have produced a large body of data on interrelation of values. Six summary statements can be made. First, all studies have shown that orthodox religious attitudes are associated with conservative political attitudes. In part the correlations of orthodoxy with political issues are dependent on definitions, for the particular attitudes considered "conservative" or "liberal" vary from decade to decade. Recent "liberal" attitudes have encouraged government social programs, regulation of industries and utilities, and strong defense of civil liberties. Jacob (1957) summarizes that orthodox religious beliefs tend to correlate with opposition to humanitarian public action. Rather, they emphasize individual initiative, personal virtue, and individual responsibility.[30]

Secondly, those students with orthodox religious attitudes tend to be strongly anti-Communist and tend to compromise civil liberties in the interest of anti-Communism. The correlations, when reported, tend to be between .2 and .3, similar to those we found at Dartmouth and Michigan. However, Theodore M. Newcomb and George Svehla (1937) found a correlation of .43 between attitudes toward the church and opposition to Communism among high school students, and Hilding B. Carlson (1934) found a correlation of .38 between belief in God and opposition to Communism among University of Chicago students. In 1938, Leonard W. Ferguson found a correlation of .22 between Thurstone scale scores on belief in God and a scale on anti-Communism; the data were from six universities (Ferguson, 1939:221; cf. Kitay, 1947).

Thirdly, the more orthodox students tend to express more racial and ethnic prejudice. This relationship is not found in every study, and it is less often found in recent studies. Jacob summarized that orthodox religious attitudes tend to be associated with greater prejudice (Jacob, 1957:20). The association is more complex when intervening variables are introduced into the analysis (cf. Argyle, 1958:83 f.; Young, Clore, and Holtzman, 1966). Also in recent studies such as Jeffrey K. Hadden's (1963) and our Dartmouth and Michigan studies the relationship appears weak or even absent. One reason is that self-consciousness about racial attitudes has heightened in the last decade. Probably we may conclude that the relationship between orthodoxy and expressed racial and ethnic prejudice is weakening.

Fourthly, before World War II the more religiously orthodox students tended to be a bit more conservative on economic issues such as organized labor or the controlled economy. The main evidence shows no such relationship today. We found at Dartmouth, Michigan, and Wisconsin that economic issues bore little relation to religious attitudes in the late 1960's. Norman Miller found the same in 1952 and concluded that "a probable reason for this is that organized labor today is by and large a theologically neutral subject" (Miller, 1958:164).

Fifthly, the more orthodox students are higher in authoritarianism. Among the religious background groups, the Catholics are usually found to be the most authoritarian and the Jews the least.

Sixthly, the more orthodox students tend not to approve of deviation from traditional morality and traditional roles. As Goldsen says, they "tend to be reluctant to countenance any kind of deviation or nonconformity" (Goldsen *et al.*, 1960:183). They are more conformist to group norms, even if the norms are morally ambiguous. They seem to feel more integrated in society. They express a desire more than others to have a cognitively structured universe and to know their future plans in advance. They tend to be more definite about college majors and career plans (Goldsen *et al.*, 1960:178 ff.).

To researchers in the 1930's the dominant dimension in student attitude systems was "radicalism-conservatism." Many investigators constructed omnibus radicalism-conservatism scales using items on political, economic, social, and religious issues. They reported single "liberalism" or "radicalism" scores. Others came to the same conclusion after studies using series of separate scales. For example, Carlson concluded that "an individual who is radical on one issue is somewhat more likely to be radical than to be conservative on another social question, and vice versa" (Carlson, 1934:208). Gardner Murphy and Rensis Likert concluded, "From our data it is clear that the desire for change is a somewhat generalized attitude, since radicalism in each of four scales is correlated with radicalism on all the others" (Murphy and Likert, 1938:66). The opposition of conservative and liberal value systems forms the basic structure of Newcomb's analysis of Bennington College (1943). This general picture of two attitude structures in opposition also coincides with descriptions of multiple social reforms advocated by student activists in the 1930's (Draper, 1967; Allen, 1967).

The liberal-conservative opposition disappeared with the onset of World War II. By the late 1940's the conservative attitude system was dominant because of the threat of world Communism. Whereas Americans had been more frightened by Fascism than by Communism before the war, now they were frightened above all by Communism. The effect was a shift to the right in political and economic attitudes. The leftists of the 1930's were in disrepute. The dominant attitude pattern on American campuses in the early 1950's was the Manichaean opposition of West versus East, of Americanism, "Free World" democracy, Christianity, and free enterprise versus godless Communism, world revolution, totalitarianism, and tyranny. Whereas students in the 1930's were on both sides of the issues, in the 1950's all were on the safe conservative side. The early 1950's were the years of caution and conformity. It was as if the radicals of the 1930's had been completely removed from the scene, and the conservatives had not only silenced the debate but also intimidated all the opposition.

With the events of the late 1950's and the early 1960's the cold war polarization collapsed, and popular anxieties eased. Serious social criticism and debate again became possible, and soon the civil rights movement and the anti-Vietnam war movement engaged thousands of students. A New Left emerged with a new analysis and criticism of American society.

In the late 1960's we could again speak of a polarization of two value clusters among college students, the "conservative-vocational" and the "liberal-intellectual." Students of the first orientation tended to be conservative on both religious and political issues. They tended to support the Vietnam war as necessary to contain Communism. They were found disproportionately in the fields of business, engineering, education, and other practical disciplines. They tended to stress occupational success, family life, and leisure as sources of meaning. They came from relatively less privileged families with less educated parents. They anticipated business careers, often in family businesses. Their futures were relatively well planned in advance.

The "liberal-intellectual" orientation is found more often among students in the humanities and social sciences. It stresses self-expression, aesthetic experiences, and social reconstruction as sources of meaning. It puts more faith in government programs, education, and international agencies for meaningful social progress. It is alienated from military leaders and from the Vietnam war. This group is less certain about future careers, but it looks forward to academic, scientific, governmental, or legal careers more than to business. Students with this orientation tend to come from more privileged and educated families. They are less oriented to fraternities, athletics, and leisure-time pursuits, and they are more individualistic (Lipset, 1971). The student activists in the late 1960's were usually in an extreme part of this second orientation—even more alienated from business, the military, the colleges, and government. Many of them were from families with a tradition of liberalism and Old Left political activism.

THE COLD WAR AND RELIGIOUS ATTITUDES

Our findings in this chapter provide some support for the hypothesis that the rise in religious orthodoxy and traditional religious commitment among students in the late 1940's and early 1950's was related to the anxieties and social pressures of the cold war and McCarthyism. In turn the decline in religious orthodoxy and commitment since about 1956 or 1957 may be seen as related to the weakening of cold war fears and anxiety about Communism. Do all available survey data support this hypothesis? Though we lack data on trends in students' attitudes toward Communism during the late 1940's and early 1950's, two social scientists have made analyses of the period. In 1957, Jacob argued that the sentiments in the general populace during those years tended to affect college graduates and college students as well:

> For instance, in the years from 1945–53 Americans became much less tolerant of Communists. The shift in opinion among the college educated was just as marked as among the less educated, even though a somewhat larger proportion of the college group started—and remained—tolerant. Among the college educated, those who would deny freedom of speech to a Communist increased from 31 per cent to 71 per cent; among the less educated from 42 per cent to 78 per cent. The tide of national opinion thus swept the college educated along just as easily. Their tolerance was just as volatile. (Jacob, 1957:48)

In a 1962 article Hyman showed that sentiments against Communists in the total population had intensified during the early 1950's, peaking in about 1954:

> At the height of McCarthyism, the earlier trend point had been established in January 1954, when 81 per cent of the national sample declared they would not allow Communist Party members to speak on the radio, a steady rise from a figure of 40 per cent in 1943. Three years later, in December 1956, the figure was 73 per cent, and in April 1957, it was 75 per cent. (Hyman, 1963:286)

Samuel A. Stouffer (1955) and Lazarsfeld and Thielens (1958) also place the high point of McCarthyism and anti-Communism in 1954. The same was true among high school students as determined by Purdue Opinion Panel surveys. Is the rise-and-fall pattern of fears of Communism closely associated with the rise-and-fall pattern of traditional religious commitment? The two trend lines match closely. Are the attitudes related, so that the two may be seen as dual products of common sources? For college students we have evidence from four studies. At Clark we correlated an item on trust or distrust of Russia with three Thurstone scales on religion for seven different surveys from 1947 to 1967. Most of the correlations were weak, but among the women in 1954 they ranged from .21 to .41. In each case the more traditionally religious students tended to express stronger distrust of Russia. In the 1955, 1956, and 1967 surveys, however, no noteworthy correlations appeared.

The 1968 Denver study included an eleven-item scale of attitudes toward Communism. The Catholics were the most anti-Communist and the Jews and "no religious preference" group the least so. Among all the men the Anti-Communism Scale correlated .40 with a Conservative Religious Scale; among all the women the correlation was .48. These quite strong correlations suggest that anti-Communism was intrinsically tied up with an orthodox religious orientation. The correlations were stronger among Protestants than among Catholics and Jews.

At Dartmouth and Michigan we correlated a Fear of Communism Index with an Orthodoxy Index and a Church Commitment Index. At Michigan in 1969 the correlations were .34 with the Orthodoxy Index and .24 with the Church Commitment Index. At Dartmouth in 1968 the correlations were very weak, .18 and .15. In the 1952 data no Fear of Communism Index could be created, but individual items suggest that the relationship between fear of Communism and religious orthodoxy was a bit stronger than in 1968–69.

In summary, the strong associations found by various researchers between anti-Communism and traditional religion in the 1930's have seemed to weaken in more recent years. Our own results are curious—the correlations are strong at Denver and Michigan but weak at Clark and Dartmouth. Perhaps it is significant that the first two are large Midwestern universities and the second two are small Eastern colleges. A possible sectional distinction is lent some plausibility by Parsons' analysis of McCarthyism, in which he clearly sees it as a Midwestern phenomenon, with strongest following in non-Anglo-Saxon groups of comparatively recent immigrant origin:

> There has been an important popular following (of Joseph McCarthy) of very miscellaneous composition. It has comprised an important part of those who aspire to full status in the American system but have, realistically or not, felt discriminated against in various ways, especially the Mid-Western lower and lower middle classes and much of the population of recent immigrant origin. The elements of continuity between Western agrarian populism and McCarthyism are not by any means purely fortuitous. (Parsons, 1963a:225)

It is possible that the strongest linkages between cold war sentiments and traditional religion were found in the lower middle rather than the upper middle class and in the Midwest rather than in the East. Available data are too meager for making definite statements.

SUMMARY

In this chapter we reviewed available data on value changes among students. At Dartmouth and Michigan our data compared 1952 with 1968–69. During those years the personal commitments of Dartmouth students switched somewhat from emphasis on leisure activities to political involvement and of Michigan students from religious involvement to political involvement. By 1968–69 the students had new emotional involvement in political affairs. Also they decreased their faith in the American military system and the national ideology associated with it. Their anxieties about Communism and deviant groups in American society largely disappeared. Support for civil liberties and criticism of higher education both increased. Group embeddedness and other-direction decreased. The other-direction and conformity so often noted among college students in the 1950's was apparently a short-lived phenomenon, not a basic long-term change in American values as Riesman suggested. It was a phenomenon of the 1940's and 1950's.

At Wisconsin we measured changes from 1930 to 1968. Changes in economic attitudes were slight. More students supported the American practice of democracy and patriotism in public life in 1968 than in 1930. More supported complete freedom of speech. With regard to norms of sex behavior the 1968 students called for greater flexibility and individualism than in 1930. They called for much greater attention to birth control. Criticism of the traditional family structure and of organized religion declined markedly from 1930 to 1968. Belief in immortality and the importance of God for meaning in life was stronger, yet emphasis on this-worldly concerns in religion was also stronger. There was evident a shift from emphasis on social *reforms* in 1930 to emphasis on individual *freedoms* within existing social institutions in 1968.

At Syracuse we found greater individualism in 1968 than in 1926. The 1968 students called for more individual responsibility and less regulation than those in 1926. They supported freedom of speech more strongly and emphasized athletics less than the 1926 students.

All studies show a basic change from the 1920's to the late 1960's in student freedom and autonomy. The student of today is much freer of parental and collegiate authority than in past decades. He faces less social sanction when raising the most crucial questions about norms, traditions, and practices. Paternalism and regulation have declined on all the campuses we studied. This change is one component of the trends we have found in religious attitudes and behavior. Most studies suggest that individualism and individual judgment are associated with more liberal religious attitudes. Individualism among students increased after the 1920's, but there is considerable evidence that it regressed during the late 1940's and early 1950's. It increased again in the late 1950's and 1960's. Studies of ethical norms depict a change over the decades from prescriptive codes of behavior among college students to more contextual and responsible orientations to ethical problems.

The hypothesis that religious commitments and political commitments are functionally equivalent in the personality and thus tend to exist in a fixed-sum relationship was tested and disconfirmed in three studies. Any relationship between commitments in these areas is apparently more specific than general, so that questionnaire items asking about political concerns in general or about religious concerns in general will fail to uncover them. Perhaps the level of specification needed in future studies of social alienation is also needed here.

The hypothesis that the rise and fall of orthodoxy and traditional religious commitment in the 1940's, 1950's, and 1960's is closely related to the rise and fall of cold war and McCarthyist sentiments was tested in various ways. The trend lines indeed coincide closely, but the correlations are of mixed strength. They are strong at Denver and Michigan but weak at Dartmouth and Clark, suggesting that social class of students or regionalism may be factors. In general the Durkheimian hypothesis, that changes in national sentiments and fears about the nation are a major source of religious change, finds considerable support in our research. But the particular variables and linkages require further specification before the causal interrelationships between national sentiments and traditional religious sentiments can be clearly seen.

Of all the attitudes studied in this chapter, those most strongly associated with traditional religious commitment are attitudes about sex norms and the family; we should expect to find changes in sex norms and family life accompanying the rise and fall of traditional religious commitments in recent decades. (We return to this question later.) By contrast, attitudes about economics proved unrelated to traditional religious commitment. Economics as a factor in religious change would appear rather unlikely unless the economic factor is mediated by family, community, or national changes.

For one crucial hypothesis we lack adequate data. We cannot assess how much religious attitudes are similar to political attitudes at any time in terms of openness to change, optimism, individualism, defensiveness, tolerance of diversity, and so on. We have, however, mentioned the rise of individualism among college students which had an effect on both religious and political attitudes. And we have discussed the intolerance of social deviance which issued in both the advocacy of social constraint on deviant groups and in attitudes of religious particularism in the early 1950's. A scrutiny of this important hypothesis in future research would help specify cognitive and affective inputs to religious change.

Earlier we said that the major source of religious change is not to be sought within any one denominational group. Now we add that the main source of religious change is not to be sought within the realm of religious practices, theology, and institutions but in events and experience impinging on and affecting a cluster of interrelated attitudes. And the most important attitudes in question are probably those closely associated with the family, community, and nation.

CHAPTER 4

Effect of
Background Variables
on Attitudes and Behavior

Several of the hypotheses guiding our analysis must be tested by studying the relation of students' backgrounds to their attitudes and behavior. In this chapter we review the data from the thirteen studies and the literature.

Three hypotheses are important. First, have changes in socioeconomic status or educational level among the students or their parents produced any of the changing religious attitudes and behavior we have found above? Are socioeconomic status and scholastic aptitude strongly associated with any of the religious attitudes and values we have measured? Second, are students from cities different than students from rural areas or suburbs in religious attitudes and values? Are there discernible differences within any of the main religious groups which can plausibly be assigned to the rural versus urban factor? And if so, what in the urbanization or suburbanization process appears to produce the differences? Third, is there evidence among more recently immigrated social groups of a "third-generation phenomenon" as described by Herberg, so that the third generation returns to the traditional religion after the ambivalent second generation had avoided it? Our practice of adjusting the actual responses in the 1966–69 replication studies was in effect to control these factors. Their effects, if noteworthy, must therefore be *added to* the other sources of religious change uncovered in the preceding chapters.

CHANGES IN THE BACKGROUNDS OF STUDENTS

For the thirteen colleges, we shall review changes in students' family religious background, socioeconomic status, scholastic aptitude, size of hometown, region of origin, and major course. First, the religious backgrounds of students in these colleges have undergone rather consistent changes over two or four decades. In most of the private colleges the percentage of Jews has risen considerably, and the percentage of Protestants has fallen; in the public institutions the changes are smaller.[31] In most colleges the percentage of Catholics rose a few points. The changes were greater in the 1930's and 1940's than in the 1950's and 1960's. Within Protestantism the shift has been away from the dominance of the old-line "establishment" denominations such as the Episcopalians, Congregationalists, and Presbyterians. Over the years the colleges have increasingly admitted students from a broader variety of social groups.

On socioeconomic status these colleges have experienced a kind of "leveling." Those colleges formerly educating only the social elite have had either a gradual lowering of students' socioeconomic status or no change. The other colleges have experienced rising socioeconomic status of students.

On scholastic aptitudes we have data from twelve colleges. In eleven they have risen sharply in the last ten or fifteen years. Only at Los Angeles City College have scholastic aptitude levels failed to rise. In the other colleges the increases over fifteen or twenty years have been between 60 and 156 points in mean or median Scholastic Aptitude Test scores. The increases have been greater in mathematical than in verbal scores. The main increases came after 1957 or 1958, and several people we interviewed traced the increases to the effects of Sputnik I on American higher education.

Available data on size of hometown and region of origin show that these colleges have enlarged the geographic range of their students. Colleges such as Northwestern, Clark, Denver, and Ripon, which formerly had mostly local students, have diversified greatly. At Ripon the percentage from the state of Wisconsin dropped from 90 percent in 1930 to 28 percent in 1968. At Denver the percentage from Colorado dropped from about 50 percent in 1948 to under 30 percent in 1968. Changes in sizes of hometowns are not significant. In general the trend is toward larger cities and suburbs, about the same as the overall demographic changes in America.

The data on trends in major course selection in these colleges include considerable diversity, but one summary statement can be made. Over the decades there has been an expansion of the social sciences at the expense of the humanities and natural sciences. Especially women students tend to major less often in the humanities today than in decades past.

SEX DIFFERENCES

Sex comparisons could be made in several of our studies. To sum up the findings, it is clear that women had more orthodox attitudes and more traditional religious behavior than men. The differences varied considerably but were on average less than 10 percentage points on attitude items. They were greater among Protestant students than among Catholics or Jews. These findings agree with those in virtually all other surveys of students.

Argyle reviewed available data and agreed that sex differences are greater in Protestant groups than in Catholic and Jewish groups (Argyle, 1958:76 f.). The differences are greater in private beliefs and practices than in public observances and institutional behavior. Argyle also cites three studies in the late 1920's and 1930's (including the 1926 Syracuse University survey) showing that Jewish men held more orthodox religious beliefs than Jewish women. This was not found in our 1966–69 studies except at Wisconsin. The reversal since the 1930's possibly represents an actual change in the Jewish group. Jewish men have declined in orthodoxy faster than Jewish women over three decades (Argyle, 1958:77).[32]

H. H. Remmers and D. H. Radler (1957) reported that in the Purdue Opinion Panel data high school boys have less orthodox religious attitudes and behavior than girls. Thirteen percent fewer boys reported at least weekly church attendance in a 1951 study. Generally boys are more independent, less inhibited by groups, more self-confident, and more autonomous than girls. They are also more superpatriotic, less internationalistic, and less liberal on most civil liberties questions.

Data on trends in sex differences are available in several studies. At Northwestern the difference between women and men increased slightly from 1940 to 1967. At Clark no change in the differences is discernible since the middle 1940's. At Syracuse sex differences increased in the Protestant and Jewish groups since 1926, but they decreased in the Catholic group. At Wisconsin the sex differences diminished considerably in all attitude areas from 1930 to 1968. In the University of Michigan religious censuses sex differences seemed quite constant ever since 1896—about 8 to 12 percent more women than men have "religious preference." In the face of the diversity of these data no summary statements seem possible.

RELIGIOUS BACKGROUND GROUP DIFFERENCES

The religious background groups differ systematically. The Catholics are the most orthodox and conservative in religious and political attitudes and the "no religious background" group is least so. Close to the latter are the Jews, and arrayed between the Catholic and Jewish groups are the Protestants. The lineup from orthodox to liberal is virtually always (1) Catholics, (2) Protestants, (3) Jews, and (4) no religious background. In the surveys where a Liberal Protestant and Ethical Christian group was large enough to be studied alone it was found to resemble the Jews.

At Haverford, Bryn Mawr, Syracuse, Wisconsin, and Ripon we were able to study the Protestant denominations separately. Also Bugelski and Lester gathered data at the University of Buffalo (1940), Carl H. Poit did so at Michigan State (1962), and Young, Dustin, and Holtzman (1966) did so at the University of Texas. The most consistent findings were that the Episcopalians and Congregationalists are the least orthodox, while the Lutherans and Methodists are the most orthodox. Presbyterians and Baptists were arrayed between, and other denominations were too small to study separately. At Wisconsin and Ripon the Lutherans were very conservative in religious, political, and social attitudes, often more so than the Catholics.

At Dartmouth and Michigan we compared religious groups on the Social Constraint Index and the Anti-Communism Index in 1968–69. No noteworthy differences were found on the Social Constraint Index, but on the Anti-Communism Index the Catholics were highest and the Jews lowest. In addition, we checked *change* in each group from 1952 to 1968–69. Four items are shown in Table 4.1.

The Catholics and the "Mixed and Other" students have changed more than other groups. The Jews have changed the least. Whereas the Catholics were the strongest advocates of social constraint in 1952 (cf. the second and third items in the table), by 1968 they resembled the other students. At Michigan the same pattern appeared—the Catholics and the "Mixed and Other" students changed most, and the Jews changed least. These data, just like the data on traditional

TABLE 4.1

Responses of Religious Background Groups, Dartmouth, 1952 and 1968
(*In percentages*)

	Protestant	Catholic	Jewish	Mixed, Other
Item on Life Satisfactions:				
Those ranking "National political				
participation" 1952	12	7	12	5
1968	31	30	22	34
It is unwise to give people with				
dangerous social and economic				
viewpoints a chance to be elected.				
Agree 1952	33	57	34	43
Agree 1968	12	16	11	10
Steps should be taken right away to				
outlaw the Communist Party.				
Agree 1952	29	47	21	32
Agree 1968	4	13	0	2
Qualities needed to get ahead				
today: "Pleasant personality"				
1952	61	65	53	55
1968	34	35	34	23

religious attitudes, support the general formula that in liberalizing times the formerly most conservative groups change most and the formerly most liberal groups change least. The change is an "assimilation to the liberal norm," with those groups having farthest to go moving the fastest.

In nine of the studies we calculated the variance in the religious attitudes and behavior accounted for by the religious background groups. They accounted for between 5 percent and 34 percent of the variance. Only in the Clark and Wisconsin studies was the figure higher than 20 percent.[33] They accounted for roughly the same percentage of the variance in religious attitudes as in religious behavior. On anti-Communist attitudes at Denver and Dartmouth religious background accounted for only 2 to 6 percent of the variance. At Wisconsin it accounted for about 20 to 23 percent of the Sex and Family Index, about 17 to 20 percent of the Political Index, and about 5 to 7 percent of the Economic Index.

Religious background group is the second most important variable for predicting religious attitudes and behavior. Most important is a measure of religious influence in the home.

RELIGIOUS INFLUENCE IN THE HOME

At Harvard-Radcliffe, Williams, and Los Angeles City College we replicated a 1946 item asking about religious "influence in your upbringing." Among Harvard men and L.A.C.C. women it increased over the two decades, but among the Radcliffe women, Williams men, and L.A.C.C. men it did not significantly change. The changes that occurred may be a product of changes in college admission policies or they may reflect the higher levels of religious participation in the society in the late 1950's as compared with the late 1930's. The responses are systematically related to home religious tradition—the more theologically conservative the religious group, the stronger was the religious influence during upbringing. The broader culture for these students appears not to be religiously orthodox, since lack of strong religious influence in the home is associated with nonorthodox attitudes and behavior.

In all our studies, religious influence in upbringing is the single strongest predictor of religious attitudes and behavior, but when it is studied within each traditional group it is roughly equal in predictive power to the differences among the main traditions. At Williams religious influence in upbringing taken alone accounted for about 8 to 14 percent of the variance in the Conservative Belief Index and in frequency of prayer. At Harvard-Radcliffe and Los Angeles City College the variance accounted for was a few points higher. At Clark religious influence in upbringing accounted for about 22 to 30 percent of the variance in the Influence on Conduct Scale and in church attendance. At Ripon and Bryn Mawr measures of home religiosity accounted for about 10 to 22 percent of the variance in two religious attitude indices and a bit more in religious behavior.

Past studies of the influence of home religiosity on students' religious attitudes and behavior have consistently supported two conclusions. First, home religious influence is the strongest and most important factor in the religious attitudes and behavior of students. Second, the influence of mothers exceeds that of fathers. A summary of the literature is in Argyle (1958:39–42). Correlations of students' religious attitudes with their parents' religious attitudes have been found to range from about .3 to about .5, usually stronger in lower socioeconomic status families (Kirkpatrick and Stone, 1935;

Newcomb and Svehla, 1937; Hirschberg and Gilliland, 1942; Vincent, 1956). Luther Ellis Woodward (1932), Marvin Nathan (1932), Philip M. Kitay (1947), and Donald Brown (1956) stressed that harmony and close relationships within the family are positively associated with loyalty to the religious tradition. Poor parent-child relations or even poor sibling-sibling relations tend to dispose children to depart from the home religious tradition. Family sentiments are an important component of traditional religious sentiments.

Three of the 1966–68 studies replicated items asking about comparison of the respondent's faith with that of his parents. See Table 4.2. All the students report less firm religious beliefs than held by their parents. All attribute firmer beliefs to their mothers than their fathers. Among the men the gap between themselves and their parents is greater in 1966–67 than in 1946–48, but among the women there is no noteworthy change. In 1968 we asked a similar question in the Denver study, and the results were much the same. The studies in the literature comparing students' religion with parents' religion generally agree with these findings (Horton, 1940; Newcomb and Svehla, 1937; Kirkpatrick and Stone, 1935; R. Smith, 1947).

We cannot infer anything about trends by comparing students with their parents, since strength of religious commitment is known to vary over the life cycle. Argyle (1958: Ch. 6) assembled data showing that, in the early 1950's in the U.S.A. and England, traditional religious commitment and participation tended to fall off from age sixteen to about age thirty, then to increase again at an accelerating rate. The fact that the *gap* between students and parents is greater in 1966–67 than in 1946–48 shows, however, that the life cycle alone does not determine changes in religious commitment but that current historical experiences also have some effect.

At Dartmouth an item used in 1958, 1961, and 1968 asked about the student's church attendance before college and during college, also about his parents' church attendance. Over the ten years the reported levels of parents' church attendance was unchanged, but the student's attendance after arriving at college dropped; the percentage attending at least monthly dropped 9 points from 1958 to 1968. These data support our conclusion, mentioned earlier, that the parents of college students have changed less over recent years than have the students themselves.

TABLE 4.2

"How, in general, does the firmness of your belief in religion compare with your mother's belief? with your father's belief?"

(*In percentages*)

	HARVARD				RADCLIFFE				WILLIAMS				LOS ANGELES CITY COLLEGE							
													Men				Women			
	1946*		1966		1946		1966		1948*		1967		1948*		1967		1948		1967	
	Mo	Fa	Mo	Fa	Mo	Fa	Mo	Fa	Mo	Fa	Mo	Fa	Mo	Fa	Mo	Fa	Mo	Fa	Mo	Fa
More firm	7	16	8	15	14	23	12	19	7	14	10	15	12	19	9	11	11	21	11	27
Less firm	51	27	54	34	41	27	40	20	39	20	55	37	44	24	49	33	34	21	40	21
About the same	32	36	26	34	27	24	34	33	30	33	19	35	32	37	22	25	41	37	31	21
Don't know	10	21	11	17	18	26	14	27	24	33	16	13	12	20	20	31	14	21	18	31
	100	100	99	100	100	100	100	99	100	100	100	100	100	100	100	100	100	100	100	100

* All men at Harvard and Los Angeles City College; nonveterans at Williams.

SOCIAL CLASS DIFFERENCES

In the 1966–69 studies we found either no relation between socioeconomic status (SES) and religious indicators or a weak association of higher SES with liberal religious attitudes and decreased commitment. About half of the possible correlations were strong enough to be noteworthy, and a few of the strongest reached .3 or .35. They are equally strong for men and women. They are weaker in the Eastern private colleges than elsewhere. And they tend to be stronger among Protestants than among Catholics and Jews, probably because of the greater diversity of Protestants. The main causal factor seems to be parents' education, not father's occupational prestige or family income; any relationships with the last two are usually traceable to parents' education. Evidence in the literature agrees with these conclusions (Harris *et al.*, 1932; Nelson, 1940; Ross, 1950; Havemann and West, 1952; Potter, 1953; Goldsen *et al.*, 1960; Hadden, 1963).

Probably the best study of socioeconomic factors in students' attitudes is by Miller, using the Cornell Values Study data (Miller, 1958). He found that attitudes toward civil rights were weakly related to SES differences, with the higher SES groups being more liberal. However, within each religious group the relation of SES and civil rights was different. In the Protestant group liberalism decreased as SES declined, in the Jewish group liberalism increased as SES declined, and in the Catholic group there was no change. Miller attributes this pattern to varying cultural emphases in each religious community. He found that in the Ivy League colleges SES was inversely related to civil rights, so that the poorer students were more liberal. In the state universities no pattern appeared.

If higher SES is associated with liberal religious attitudes and decreased commitment, it is plausible that rising educational levels and standard of living in future years will produce further liberalization and weakening commitment to churches. No reliable statement can be made, however, until it is clearer whether the association is with standard of living in an absolute sense or relative to the average levels in the society.

RURAL-URBAN DIFFERENCES

In our 1966–69 studies the relationships between type of hometown (city, suburb, or small town) and religious indicators were consistently weak. Table analysis was undertaken within each religious tradition. At Harvard-Radcliffe, Williams, and Los Angeles City College we found no relationships at all. At Dartmouth we found only one relationship, that suburban Jewish students have stronger church commitment than those from cities. At Syracuse, however, the opposite pattern occurred. At Bryn Mawr the Protestant and Jewish students from suburbs were less orthodox than those from cities and towns, but the differences were small. At Denver we found only that Catholics from cities attend church oftener and are more favorable to the church than other Catholics. At Wisconsin small-town students were more conservative on the Sex and Family Index than suburban and urban students, but other relationships were weak. At Clark the Catholics from the suburbs were more orthodox in attitudes but attended church less often than other Catholics; on the other hand, the Protestants and Jews from cities were more orthodox than others. At Ripon the Catholics and Protestants from suburbs were lower in orthodoxy than others, and at Haverford the Protestants from small towns were more orthodox than others. In summary, the only pattern is that suburban students are less religiously orthodox than those from large cities and small towns, but the differences are small. The differences that occur are unsystematic and probably the result of other factors.

Most studies in the literature have found no relationships between rural-urban origin and religious attitudes of students (Ross, 1950:242; Murphy and Likert, 1938; Harris *et al.*, 1932:331; Young, Dustin, and Holtzman, 1966). Young, Dustin, and Holtzman found no relationship in 1958 at the University of Texas, but in 1964 they found city students to be slightly less orthodox than those from small towns. The Purdue Opinion Panel studies found few urban-rural differences on social, political, or religious attitudes (Purdue Opinion Panel, 30:6). Ferguson, in a study of eighteen colleges (Ferguson, 1944), found that students from small towns and farms were more orthodox in religious attitudes than those from cities, but the differences were small. There was no difference in humanitarian attitudes.

In his analysis of the Cornell Values Study data, Miller found that urban students are more liberal with respect to civil liberties than those from rural areas. Of those from cities over 50,000, 47 percent were rated as pro civil rights; of those from towns under 2500, the figure was 39 percent (Miller, 1958:103). Miller pointed out the difficulty in distinguishing suburban areas from rural areas and concluded that upper-middle-class rural students are actually more

suburban than rural. High SES students from urban and rural areas
are very similar to each other. This parallels our findings in 1966–69,
since most of the students in the colleges we studied are relatively
affluent. Miller concludes that the main factor underlying liberal
attitudes is not urban residence so much as "cosmopolitan" orientation (as opposed to "local" orientation). This supports the Durkheimian theory that across-group contact and altered communication
patterns are the crucial factor in affecting attitudes, for "cosmopolitan" means in effect having communications across traditional group
boundaries.

One of the hypotheses underlying our research is that urbanization
is a source of "secularization." The data on college students do not
support it. How about nationwide poll results? The best nationwide
polls on religious attitudes have found that urban residents are on the
average less orthodox and religiously committed than those in small
towns and rural areas. A 1965 poll asked how important religion is in
the respondent's own life; of those in cities or metropolitan areas over
one million in size, 65 percent replied "very important," and of those
in rural areas it was 74 percent. Of those in cities over a million 54
percent attend church about twice a month or oftener; of those in
rural areas it was 57 percent. Of those in cities over a million 72
percent said that the Bible is the revealed word of God; of those in
rural areas it was 93 percent. In short, when no variables are
controlled, the rural residents report more orthodox attitudes and
slightly more religious behavior than the urbanites (Marty *et al.*,
1968). If one were to control for religious tradition, educational level,
and occupation, the original relationship would weaken and possibly
disappear.

One prediction of this weakening is found in our studies of college
students, which in effect control for educational level, age, religious
tradition, and (to an extent) occupational level of fathers. With all
these held constant the only difference remaining was that suburban
dwellers are slightly less orthodox than those from cities or rural
areas.

Another prediction of a weakening relationship stems from the
concentration of educated persons in cities. In a 1954 national survey
it was found that in metropolitan areas over 100,000 in size about 49
percent of the adults had finished high school; in cities between 2500
and 100,000 it was 45 percent; in towns under 2500 it was 43 percent,
and on farms it was 35 percent. The numbers graduating from college
were 10 percent, 9 percent, 7 percent, and 5 percent, respectively
(Stouffer, 1955:120). In the U.S.A. in metropolitan areas 55 percent

of the adults have had at least four years of high school; outside the metropolitan areas the figure is 44 percent (U.S. Bureau of the Census, 1968:111). If educational level were controlled in the nationwide poll data, rural-urban differences would be reduced.

Thirdly, the religious groups in the United States are unequally distributed in urban and rural areas. Argyle shows that Jews are concentrated in the large cities, Catholics are concentrated in the middle-sized and large cities, and the more conservative Protestant denominations are more often in small towns under 10,000 or farm areas (Argyle, 1958:136). If religious background is not controlled in a nationwide poll, the larger cities appear slightly less orthodox and the smaller cities slightly more so solely because of the religious groups in them.

The basic hypothesis that urbanization produces secularization must be recast into three more precise hypotheses. (1) Urban dwellers are no less orthodox than rural dwellers within each religious tradition and socioeconomic level, but they appear so in nationwide polls because of disproportionate numbers of upper-income persons and Jewish persons in large cities. This hypothesis could be tested with nationwide polls. The small differences we found between urban and rural students in each religious group support the hypothesis. However, Miller found that although affluent students from urban and rural areas may be alike, persons in lower SES levels are probably not. Also Stouffer found in 1954 that regardless of what controls he introduced, rural persons remained less tolerant of deviant groups than urbanites (Stouffer, 1955:122), contrary to the hypothesis. (2) Urban centers are less orthodox in nationwide polls because educated persons tend to move to cities—thus liberalization is not a product of urbanization, but it is a product of certain educational experiences and is merely "carried to" the cities. Studies have shown that college graduates, and especially the best-qualified college graduates, tend to move to large cities (Havemann and West, 1952:235). (3) Urban experiences have the effect of liberalizing city dwellers' religious attitudes and behavior. This is the Wirth-Cox hypothesis. It may also be applied to suburban areas. Immigrant subcultures in the inner cities may tend to preserve traditional religion, but as members move into the suburbs their commitment to the tradition may attenuate. As noted in Chapter 1, Lenski's study of Detroit does not support this third hypothesis but on the contrary shows that religious activity *increases* with length of urban residence of the family (Lenski, 1963:46).

We cannot test these hypotheses with our data. But the patterns among college students would appear to lend most support to the first of the three hypotheses. Miller's analysis of the Cornell Values Study data would seem to support the third hypothesis inasmuch as he emphasized differences in "cosmopolitan" versus "local" orientation in both urban and rural areas.

DIFFERENCES IN IMMIGRANT GENERATION

To assess Will Herberg's third-generation hypothesis (Herberg, 1960: Ch. 3), we asked about birthplaces of parents and grandparents in the Williams, Dartmouth, and Denver studies. Most of those with foreign-born grandparents or parents were Jewish, and the grandparents or parents were usually born in Eastern Europe. In each religious group we tabled the second, third, and fourth-plus generations with the religious indicators. We found only a few weak and unsystematic relationships. At Williams and Dartmouth we found no significant relationships at all. At Denver there was only one significant relationship. Among the Protestant men there was a weak but significant tendency for the second and third generations to be more conservative than the fourth-plus generation on the Conservative Religious Scale. Otherwise the generations both within the across-religious groups were indistinguishable.

These studies of college students are not in themselves powerful tests of verification. In his study of Detroit, Lenski (1963:44 ff.) found a pattern of increasing religious activity linked with increasing Americanization. The third generation was more church-oriented than the second, and the fourth-plus more than the third. In addition Lenski cited studies by Converse and Lazerwitz finding no third-generation phenomenon in survey data (Lenski, 1963:47–48; cf. Lazerwitz and Rowitz, 1964).[34] In view of these failures to find empirical support for Herberg's formulation of the third-generation hypothesis, we should abandon it as an explanation for religious change in recent American history. A more elaborate model must be developed, including educational factors, social mobility, and changing communication patterns.

DIFFERENCES IN SCHOLASTIC
APTITUDE AND ACHIEVEMENT

In the 1920's and 1930's many researchers studied the relation of liberal attitudes to intelligence. Gardner Murphy, Lois Barclay

Murphy, and Theodore M. Newcomb summarized the results as follows:

> Religious and political radicalism, at least as measured by numerous experimenters, and social and economic liberalism as measured, for example, by Harper's test, do show consistent though usually low positive correlations with the common measures of intelligence. (Murphy *et al.*, 1937:932)

The correlations found in the various studies varied from about .1 to about .4 (Howells, 1928; Carlson, 1934; Bugelski and Lester, 1940; Breemes *et al.*, 1941; Corey, 1940; Harris *et al.*, 1932; Pintner, 1933; Symington, 1935; Murphy and Likert, 1938; Moore and Garrison, 1932). Argyle reviewed all available studies and found that the most common correlations were between .15 and .30, with religious conservatism related to low intelligence. He also noted that authoritarianism was found to correlate with intelligence at −.2 to −.5 (Argyle, 1958:93). In recent years the relationship between intelligence or scholastic aptitude and attitudes is usually found to be weaker. Young, Dustin, and Holtzman (1966) found no relation between cumulative grade-point average and religious attitudes in 1958 but a weak relation in 1964, when high grades were associated with lower orthodoxy.

At Harvard-Radcliffe and Dartmouth we found no significant relationships between Scholastic Aptitude Test (S.A.T.) scores or grades and religious attitudes. At Dartmouth, however, those with lower verbal S.A.T. scores tended to advocate social constraint of deviant groups, with correlations ranging from .27 to .30 in the three religious groups.

At Michigan we found no noteworthy relationships between S.A.T. mathematical scores and any attitudes. On verbal scores the correlations with the Social Constraint Index were −.39 among the Catholics and −.36 among the Jews but very weak among the Protestants. On the Anti-Communism Index the correlation was −.25 with verbal scores among the Protestants but weak elsewhere. At Wisconsin academic standing in high school had no noteworthy relationships with any of the attitude indices. At Haverford no noteworthy relationships were found with S.A.T. mathematical scores, but in 1948–50 verbal scores correlated −.18 with religious orthodoxy and −.21 with the religious behavior index.

At Denver, S.A.T. verbal scores were mildly associated with lower religious orthodoxy. With anti-Communism they correlated −.24 for the Protestant women; the correlation with the mathematical scores was −.18. For the Catholic women the corresponding figures were −.38 and −.24, and for the Jewish women they were −.52 and −.41. In all cases higher S.A.T. verbal scores were associated with less fear of Communism. Among the Protestant men the correlation between verbal scores and anti-Communism was −.21; among Jewish men it was −.36; among Catholic men no relationship existed.

John Kosa and Cyril O. Schommer reviewed available evidence on the relation of intelligence to religious attitudes and practices, and they stressed the fact that most studies were done with students in secular or liberal colleges and universities.

> Social environment regulates the relationship of mental abilities and religious attitudes by channeling the intelligence into certain approved directions: a secular-oriented environment may direct it toward skepticism, a church-oriented environment may direct it toward increased religious interest. (Kosa and Schommer, 1961:90)

They carried out a study in a Catholic college and found an association between scholastic aptitude and higher religious knowledge and participation. They concluded that educational and social environment is decisive in the orientations of the better students. We would agree that the correlations discussed above are almost entirely due to educational influences or biases in the intelligence tests. Probably the influence of schooling is greater on the brighter students, thus producing liberal tendencies in those students enrolled in liberal and secular schools (cf. Newcomb, 1943).[35]

The weaker relationships found in the late 1960's are probably the result in part of the earlier intellectual development of students; we found that intellectual scrutiny of religious beliefs by students had begun earlier in the high school years than in 1946–48. The weaker relationships may also reflect the higher educational level in these students' homes, so that the long-discussed "shock" of freshmen encountering atheistic professors at college and the transition problems from childhood religious beliefs to intellectually defensible beliefs have been reduced in recent years. Today the shock comes earlier and with less force than in decades past.

DIFFERENCES IN MAJOR COURSE GROUPS

At Harvard, Williams, Bryn Mawr, and Los Angeles City College we found no noteworthy differences between major course groups in religious attitudes and behavior. At Radcliffe the natural science majors tended to be more orthodox than others. At Dartmouth the differences were not large, but on all indices taken together the most liberal were the humanities majors followed by the social science majors. The most conservative were the engineering majors.

At Michigan the engineering students were the most orthodox, and the social science and "other" (mostly business, journalism, education, and architecture) the least orthodox. On the Social Constraint Index and the Anti-Communism Index the engineers were again highest and the social science students lowest. At Denver among the women all differences were small, but among the men the business majors were the most orthodox and the humanities majors least so; the differences were rather great. Also the natural science, engineering, and business majors were the most anti-Communist and the humanities majors least so. At Wisconsin the most liberal on all indices were the humanities and social science majors. Most conservative were the business, natural science, and engineering majors. At Clark and Ripon the natural science majors tended to be the most orthodox and the humanities the least so; at Ripon differences among the women were slight. And at Syracuse the men in education and journalism were highest in religious orthodoxy; again differences among the women were slight.

It seems that in large universities the major course groups are comparatively more diverse than in smaller colleges, possibly because they attract more diverse students into the various curricula. In all cases the differences among students as entering freshmen were at least as great as differences attributable to college experiences; in some cases they were much greater. Differential recruitment is a more important determinant than college experience. In summary, the natural science, business, and engineering students are consistently more religiously orthodox than the humanities, social science, and psychology students. And in most cases the attitude differences between major course groups are greater for the men than for the women.

Differences in major course groups are studied in the review and analysis of the literature by Feldman and Newcomb (1969). They review a large number of studies and emerge with a series of generalizations, several of which we repeat here.

Most studies find a pattern in students' choices of major course. Those high in SES overchoose the major fields related to medicine, social science, arts and humanities, law, and other political and governmental ventures. The fields of education, engineering, and other technical areas are overchosen by those of lower SES. Jews are more likely to choose premedicine, prelaw, and social science, while Catholics are more likely to choose physical science, law, and business. Protestants tend to choose education and not to choose natural science, social science, premedicine, and prelaw (Feldman and Newcomb, 1969: Ch. 5).

In political, economic, and social orientations, students in social science tend to be liberal. Humanities students are mixed but are generally in the middle of the spectrum. Those in natural science and business are medium to conservative, and those in education, engineering, home economics, and agriculture are clearly the most conservative. In religious orientation the natural science (not applied science) students tend to be the least orthodox. Students in the humanities and social sciences range across the spectrum. Those in business administration, engineering, and education are the most religiously orthodox. On authoritarianism, students in the humanities are the lowest, followed by social science majors. Those in natural sciences and business range across the spectrum, and those in education and engineering are highest.

Feldman and Newcomb find that initial differences between major course groups tend to accentuate from freshman to senior year. Although they do not compare the strength of initial differences and differential effects of various curricula, the figures suggest that the former is greater. Most researchers agree (cf. Stern, 1965:45; Webster, 1956:41).

The only difference between our 1966–69 studies and those reviewed by Feldman and Newcomb is that in our studies the natural science majors tended to be *more* rather than less orthodox in religious attitudes. The reason for the discrepancy is not to be found in historical change, for Leuba's survey of scientists in 1933 (Leuba, 1934:296 ff.) also found that natural scientists are more religiously orthodox than social scientists or psychologists. Other attitude data also seem to agree with our 1966–69 findings.[36] The discrepancy is probably the result solely of the varying methods of categorizing the natural versus applied scientific disciplines (on the categorizing problem, cf. Feldman and Newcomb, 1969:163).

Since major course differences have been shown not to be the result, for the most part, of higher education in the various disciplines, major course is of only moderate importance in the study of the determinants of religious attitudes and behavior. The choice of one or another major course appears to be the product of certain home and community values plus school experiences. Future research should specify these values and experiences, for they, more than college learning, are the explanation for the differences we have found.

INDIVIDUALISM

The research literature on college students includes important discussions of individualism, autonomy, and other-direction as they are related to attitudes and values. Our own research touches on this topic only slightly in the Dartmouth and Michigan studies. In Chapter 3 we discussed several mild positive associations between other-direction and traditional religious commitment among the Catholics and Jews.

The earlier studies in the literature almost unanimously show that less religiously orthodox persons tend to have greater individualism and less dependence on others (Argyle, 1958:85 ff.). In one of the best studies Thomas A. Symington (1935) compared religious liberals and conservatives on a series of measures. He found that the liberals tended to be more individualistic, introverted, and bookish:

> Liberals claim that they (1) Prefer books to companions. (2) Understand problems better by studying than discussing. (3) Take a chance alone in situations of doubtful outcome. (4) Are considered radical in beliefs. (5) Stick to a tiresome task without prodding or encouragement. (6) Usually can make up their minds before time of action comes. (7) Are not touchy on certain subjects. (Symington, 1935:42)

The liberals demonstrated greater independence of mind. They were slightly more "cosmopolitan" in the sense that they could better fit into wider social circles, could understand others, and could better foster the spirit of social cooperation. They tended less often to express beliefs in a series of ready-made doctrines or dogmas; more often they attempted to integrate their own thinking. Woodward made a similar study and concluded:

> Fundamentalism has a larger measure of emotional dependence than liberalism. The fundamentalists feel that all has been determined and decided. God must give and forgive, protect and provide, heal and keep; man can only accept, submit, trust—all passive qualities, not entirely unlike a child's way of feeling toward the parent in the earlier dependent years. The liberals cannot accept so unquestionably; they have to see for themselves; they demand a more active part; they tend to emphasize man's aggressive efforts and trust less to the grace and providence of God. (Woodward, 1932:30)

Richard E. Peterson (1965) found that among students in sixteen colleges frequent attendance at religious services correlated $-.29$ with a Family Independence Index—the more church attendance, the less independence from the family (cf. Webster, 1956; Dreger, 1950). Richard Flacks found that religious and political liberals are more intellectual, more vocationally undecided, and less oriented to leisure-time recreation (Flacks, 1970).

Leuba, in his 1933 study of American scientists, found that the greater scientists in each discipline reported less belief in God and immortality than the others. He cited a statement of Sir Francis Galton that "the first of the qualities of especial service to scientific men is independence of character." To break with tradition and to set aside traditional authority requires great independence of thought, and this same trait causes the lower level of acceptance of religious doctrines (Leuba, 1934:300). Leuba used the same theory to explain the lower level of orthodoxy among college seniors as compared with freshmen.

In summary, the earlier literature uniformly shows that individualism and independent thought are associated with religious liberalism, and broad trust in authority is associated with religious orthodoxy. Our studies at Dartmouth and Michigan, in 1968–69, however, show only very weak relationships. Possibly if broader and more diverse groups of students were studied, the relationships would exist in the late 1960's just as much as in the 1930's. And possibly historical changes have made the research findings of the 1930's obsolete and no longer true. Our limited research is inadequate for deciding, but our hunch is that the latter is true.

COMPARISON OF COLLEGES

Although our research was not designed to make comparisons between colleges, several gross comparisons could be made. The men at Ripon and Los Angeles City College are the most orthodox, and those at Harvard, Clark, and Dartmouth the least so. The women at Ripon and Los Angeles City College are the most orthodox, and those at Radcliffe, Clark, and Bryn Mawr the least so.

All studies in the literature comparing colleges have found that students in secular colleges and universities are less religiously orthodox than those in denominational colleges (Nelson, 1940; Flacks, 1970; Lazarsfeld and Thielens, 1958). Colleges in the South are generally more orthodox than those in the North (Nelson, 1940;

Goldsen *et al.*, 1960). The better quality colleges are generally less religiously orthodox than those of lesser quality (Glock and Stark, 1965:276 f.). In general the least orthodox colleges are the Eastern private elite colleges (Goldsen *et al.*, 1960; Lazarsfeld and Thielens, 1958).[37]

SUMMARY

Religious background group and religious influence in the home are the most important determinants of students' religious attitudes and behavior. Family commitments are a very important element in traditional religious commitments.

The relationship between scholastic aptitude and religious attitudes was weak, with correlations typically weaker than .25. In every case higher S.A.T. verbal scores were associated with lower orthodoxy and religious behavior. Also higher S.A.T. verbal scores were associated with more liberal social and political attitudes. Mathematical scores were less related to the attitudes studied here.

Major course groups had systematic differences on religious and social attitudes. The natural science, business, and engineering students were consistently more orthodox and conservative than the humanities, social science, and psychology students. Major course differences were greater in large universities than in small colleges. It was found that major course group differences were as great among freshmen as among seniors, suggesting that higher education in one discipline or another is not a strong determinant of religious attitudes and behavior. Rather, major course choice (like religious orientation) is a product of home and community values and influences prior to college entrance. Major course group differences must be explained in terms of such values and influences more than in terms of higher education in certain disciplines. This finding supports the notion that the impact of modern science is not a major source of recent religious change. Not only is higher education in science not a strong determinant of religious attitudes and behavior, but also the natural science majors and engineers, who are the most exposed to high level science, are the most orthodox in religious attitudes. The impact of modern science appears to be indirect, not a frontal displacement of religious doctrines by scientific findings.

Two of the three hypotheses stated at the beginning of the chapter are unsupported by the available data. First, the theory that urbanization causes secularization is not supported. We found only slight differences between students from cities, towns, and suburbs, and the only pattern was that suburban students tended to be slightly less orthodox than the others. The relation between rural-urban residence and religious attitudes seems to be mediated by cosmopolitan versus local cultural orientation, and the two variables (rural-urban and local-cosmopolitan) are not the same. Changes from traditional religious commitments seem indeed to occur with cross-cultural contacts, but these contacts occur in many ways, and urban residence is only one possible way. Liberal education, cross-cultural experiences, and social mobility are others.

Second, the third-generation hypothesis failed to find any support. The data included no differences between immigrant generations. The hypothesis should now be abandoned or reformulated.

The hypothesis that religious attitudes and behavior vary by socioeconomic status was mildly supported. Higher SES was associated with less orthodox attitudes and behavior; in about half of the situations the association was strong enough to be noteworthy. If educational levels and standards of living rise in the future, one may expect, for this reason alone, slightly more liberal religious attitudes and reduced commitment to church life.

These data touch on a fourth hypothesis mentioned in Chapter 2. Individualism and independence of thought were rather strongly associated with liberal religious attitudes in the 1930's, and though the association is probably weaker today, it is not absent. We have seen that the history of American college students over recent decades includes increasing independence and personal autonomy. This trend, if continued, would have an effect on religious attitudes and behavior. One cannot guess with any confidence how much of a continuation of this trend is likely, for the new youth culture of the late 1960's includes some reactions to the extreme individualism and personal independence in American society, and the youth culture may have some influence on the future.

CHAPTER 5

Impressions of
Changing Students
Since 1900

The search for explanations for changes in students' religious attitudes and behavior must cast a wider net than just the available survey data. Especially in the earlier decades of the century the data are sparse and inadequate. Therefore we reviewed contemporary and historical accounts of college students, especially in the years prior to the middle 1950's.[38] The main focus was on political and religious attitudes and behavior in Eastern and Midwestern universities.

The years prior to World War I saw little political interest among college students. College education was still considered primarily for the children of the elite or moderately elite, and their political interests were weak. Students gave attention, rather, to issues of fraternity membership, athletics, school pride, and the ever-controversial campus rules. Colleges were still in the Victorian period in their moral outlook. Many forbade mixed dances well into the 1900's or 1910's. Coeds had to adhere to firmly enforced rules of modesty in dress. College life was under the tight control of the deans, and moral laxity (or, from another perspective, moral freedom) was perhaps the most important campus issue during these years.

Social snobbery intensified during these years at some of the Eastern colleges, with the formation of overtly exclusive eating clubs, fraternities, or secret societies. The fervor of school spirit, football, and drinking reached new heights and began alarming administrators. After 1910 several colleges attempted to regulate and restrain such

activities. Football was slowly put under faculty control and regulation, drinking was restrained at least in campus buildings and
fraternities, and various efforts were made to "clean up" the morals
(cf. Lee, 1970:9–11).

It is safe to summarize that student political activism prior to the
1930's was sporadic and weak, with no effect on national life. In the
nineteenth century and the first three decades of the twentieth there
was nothing at all comparable to the movements of the 1930's and
1960's. Two movements in the pre-World War I period, however,
deserve mention. First was the suffrage movement. It spread in the
years after 1910 especially in the women's colleges. Also a series of
socialist clubs sprang up in the 1910–15 years and formed an
Intercollegiate Socialist Society. By 1917 it claimed sixty chapters and
2200 members. It sponsored lectures, debates, and journals raising
issues of immigration, free speech, the labor movement, and American entry into World War I. However, the colleges in the 1910's were
too small and too elite to have any effect on mainstream American
politics and social life.

A wave of pacifism spread over several college campuses in the
1914–19 period. It introduced a new level of seriousness to college life
which a *New York Times* editor found unbefitting.

> Some of us whose lingering in academic shades was done a good many
> years ago are deeply mystified—and, to tell the dreadful truth, are more
> than a little disquieted—by the news, coming now from one American
> college after another, of students who gather in great numbers and draw
> up and sign petitions to the President that half implore and half command
> him on no consideration to let this country be dragged into war. . . . The
> college boys of other days were not given to demonstrations of just this
> sort. There was about them a certain pugnacity, a certain instinctive
> eagerness to get into any convenient trouble that took the form of combat,
> no matter what the kind. This was not wise, and it was not in all or even
> many ways commendable, but it was Youth, while petitions for peace, with
> a perilous implication in many cases of "at any price," that is, or used to
> be, Old Age. (*The New York Times*, May 15, 1915)

College students in the 1900's were not much interested in
traditional church life. Reports speak of the lack of interest among
college students in doctrinal matters but a strong impetus for social
service. The observers of the college scene tended to contrast the
present emphasis on social service with the earlier religious fervor
centered around revivals and saving souls for the Lord.

> The normal type of a serious-minded young man at the present time does
> not talk much about religion. Sometimes this reserve proceeds from

self-consciousness and ought to be overcome, but quite as often it proceeds from modesty and ought to be reverenced. At any rate, such is the college student—a person disinclined to much profession of piety, and not easy to shape into the earlier type of expressed discipleship. Yet, at the same time, this young man is extraordinarily responsive to the new call for human service. I suppose that never in the history of education were so many young men and young women in our colleges profoundly stirred by a sense of social responsibility and a passion for social justice. The first serious question which the college student asks is not, "Can I be saved? Do I believe?" but, "What can I do for others? What can I do for those less fortunate than I?" (Peabody, 1901:451)

College students were depicted as being above petty religious sectarian disputes, denominational narrowness, or doctrinal rigidity. Their interest was not in doctrinal questions or inward spiritual nurture. Rather, their religion was one of liberal humanitarianism, tolerance, and religious social concern. A 1903 article on college women's religion ended with these words:

> If a girl, as a result of college influences and her own choices, has gained a broader view of God, a better knowledge of service, and a wiser tolerance of her fellow-creatures, college religion has given her a working hypothesis for a useful future wherever it may be. (Fallows, 1903)

On all college campuses, and especially the less elite ones, the traditional Protestant evangelicalism remained in force, but it did not command the attention of the contemporary observers of the college scene and did not strongly affect the ethos at most colleges. At Columbia University a 1903 poll found that only 69 percent of the students expressed a religious preference (*The New York Times*, April 19, 1903).

The strongest religious movement in the first decade of the century was the Student Christian Volunteer Movement, a coalition of various Protestant religious groups including the Y.M.C.A. and the Y.W.C.A. Its main emphasis prior to World War I was on recruiting and supporting foreign missionaries. In 1906 an observer wrote of its recent growth:

> The Student Volunteer Movement is one of the most remarkable facts in modern academic history. No other organized effort has so got hold of the undergraduate imagination. In March, at Nashville, the annual convention brought together nearly five thousand students, three-fourths of them men. No assembly so representative both of States and of churches has ever met for such a purpose on this continent. The college man of a generation ago can hardly believe it. . . . And the greater part . . . has come about within the past few years. (Hodges, 1906:700)

In the 1920's a series of new influences converged to produce a cultural revolution among college students. The intellectual life was reshaped by the doctrines of Freud, Dewey, and Lenin and by the writings of Mencken, Hemingway, Fitzgerald, and Sinclair Lewis. They effectively challenged the Victorian and Puritan moral codes and proposed new visions of society and morals. It was a decade of prosperity and optimism, accompanied by the arrival of the automobile, radio, and movies. Women's skirts rose from ankles to above the knees. Coeds began using cosmetics, smoking cigarettes, going to movies unchaperoned, dancing hitherto prohibited dances, and even admitting to necking and petting. The public image of a college man included the raccoon coat, gaudy roadster, hip flask, and ideas of free love. The most discussed issues on campus were not political or economic, but were in the areas of sex, drinking, the new and exciting things to do, and the boorishness of conventional middle-class life.

> The bright young college graduate who in 1915 would have risked disinheritance to march in a Socialist parade yawned at Socialism in 1925, called it old stuff, and cared not at all whether the employees of the Steel Corporation were underpaid or overpaid. Fashions had changed: now the young insurgent enraged his father by arguing against monogamy and God. (Allen, 1931:189)

In 1919–1921 came the Great Red Scare, based on an overblown fear of a Bolshevist revolution and a series of bomb blasts traced to radical leftist groups. Millions of Americans seriously feared a revolution. The scare brought censorship, a growing mood of intolerance, and new patriotic societies setting out to uncover and battle the alien forces in society. The Ku Klux Klan grew immensely during 1922, 1923, and 1924. College professors were scrutinized for their radical ideas and generally intimidated. A mood of caution and conformity pervaded many campuses. Student political radicalism was impossible in this climate, and the socialist clubs died out.

The prosperity of the nation permitted students to have a good time in college. Football, fraternity parties, and school spirit took over. The mood was light, sophisticated, optimistic, and even superficial.

> It is not the profiteer and the capitalist who stirs college youth to critical expression in these days so much as George F. Babbitt, his Rotarian friends and the hosts of the "stodgy" and the commonplace. The Opposition in college today is not composed of the rigid economic dogmatists of yesterday with fixed ideas on the distribution of wealth, labor unions and the revolution, but rather it is made up of the carefree,

mentally and morally loose-jointed "flapper" whose twin passions are disrespect and personal honesty and whose favorite word is "moron." It is all very gay and most earnestly flippant. (*The New York Times*, June 7, 1925)

A discernible change occurred during the late 1920's. A 1928 writer described the decline in rah-rah spirit in many colleges, so that football, college spirit, and the nonserious paraphernalia of the extracurriculum were falling out of their former eminence. Fraternity hazing was being suppressed, and the athlete no longer paraded around in his letter sweater. Academic standards rose, and pressures for conformity seemed to weaken.

> Perhaps the colleges have more respect for individuality, in dress as in everything else, than they used to have, though in view of the rather rigid codes and patterns, which are still insisted upon in certain Eastern institutions, this generalization must not be taken too sweepingly. Certainly there is a far greater variety of collegiate types than there was fifteen or twenty years ago. (*The New York Times*, Jan. 22, 1928)

The 1920's were a time of political apathy among students, but toward the end of the decade some serious political movements arose, including the Student League for Industrial Democracy and the National Student Federation of America. They raised issues of internationalism, pacifism, support for the League of Nations and the World Court, and opposition to ROTC on campus.

The evidence about religious changes in the first half of the 1920's is unclear. Dr. Harry Emerson Fosdick said in 1923 that over the ten years he had visited Harvard never had he found the students so keenly alive to religion and religious problems as then. Attendance in the Harvard College chapel increased each year after the war until at least 1923. The many religious group meetings being held by students led the observer to say that "there is verily a renaissance of religion" (*The Outlook*, June 13, 1923:179). It seems that student interest in religion increased during the postwar years while support for organized churches remained unchanged or dropped off. The accounts include frequent statements of college students that whereas Christianity deserved their faith and commitment, the organized church did not. Such a viewpoint was found in a 1923 survey of Vassar girls.

> Religion is considered vital to happiness in life by 97 of the group (out of 200 surveyed), and churchgoing by 40. Many express a deep desire for a more live and useful religion than they can find in churches that they attend. They resent that "those who administer religion allow it so often to

surround itself with a shell." The impression drawn from many answers is that these girls are thoroughly spiritual and are anything but fundamentalists. (*The New York Times*, June 3, 1923)

A 1926 poll of college presidents, undergraduate newspaper editors, and college preachers asked about changing religion of students. The most common response was that religious interest had increased since the war, while formal religious participation had fallen away. One spokesman for this majority wrote:

> It is obvious that these years (1900–1926) have witnessed a large decreasing interest in creeds. But I am inclined to think that there has been, and particularly in the last few years, an increasing interest in the fundamental religious problems. . . . This shows itself in an eagerness to discuss the underlying problems of religious faiths and developments, and also in the responsibilities of services which the applications of religion usually entail. (*The New York Times*, May 2, 1926)

The split between religious interest and church participation was also seen in a 1933 survey of students west of the Rockies. An item asked, "Do you believe participation in some organized religious activity is vital to your religious life?" Only 19 percent said yes. (*The Christian Century*, April 4, 1934.)

In the latter half of the 1920's observers reported decreases in students' religious interest and participation. Several 1928 *New York Times* articles discussed a "weakening" of religion on campus. In 1929 the chaplain of Amherst College told of an "alarming decrease" in church affiliation, and in the same year a conference of Christian Endeavor agreed in perceiving a "religious slump among college students." An observer in 1930 stated that "without any question, religion is a real concern for very few college students."

> Not so long ago, the campus Christian associations would put on an annual "religious week" when, after months of prayer-meetings and special discussion groups, the imported speakers and "personal workers" made a frontal attack on student wickedness. Similar attempts since the war have been increasingly futile. Resenting such pressure, students keep on saying, "Religion is my own business." The technique of other days—mass meetings, signing life-purpose cards, membership drives, prayer groups, even voluntary Bible study classes—distasteful to most undergraduates, is probably gone never to return. (Chamberlain, 1930:1312)

He blamed the weakening of religious concern on the economic and social ease of college students, their lack of cares and pressures, the speed of American life, and the stress on the sophisticated, the sensational, and the practical among students.

Was there after World War I, during the Great Red Scare, an intensifying of traditional religion just as there was after World War II, during the McCarthy period? The available evidence on students is sparse, but it is possible that the gain in religious interest and participation at Harvard was paralleled elsewhere. A rise in religious commitment and participation in the total population during and after World War I has been noted by several observers (T. Smith, 1960:12; Leuba, 1934:297).

In 1925 and 1926 there was a wave of challenges to compulsory chapel on campus after campus, including Yale, Princeton, Dartmouth, Williams, Rutgers, Amherst, Dubuque, Brown, N.Y.U., Smith, Wellesley, and Vassar. The main arguments against chapel were not arguments against religion but against the element of compulsion in religious observance. The opponents of compulsory chapel argued that true religion is stifled by any regimented and perfunctory arrangement of such a sort. Several colleges liberalized compulsory chapel rulings during these years.

Whereas the 1920's were a period of prosperity and levity, the 1930's were a time of depression and apprehension. Starting in 1930 and 1931 a majority of college graduates went unemployed. With the hard times the frills of campus life were trimmed back. Campus activities, big dances, publications, and even fraternities were reduced or even eliminated. A new seriousness came into college life. Concern was increasingly directed to the economic and problems of the nation and the world.

> The new era on the campus began, it is now apparent, about 1930. It was manifest first in a marked drop in attendance at football games, a drop in the number of students trying out for teams, an increased registration in economics, history and social science courses, and a flare of interest in politics. (*The New York Times*, June 11, 1933)

Sex, drinking, and moral liberty were no longer salient issues to students. Now economic breakdown, the rising Fascism and Communism in Europe, pacifism, and the labor movement became new issues of discussion. The prevailing mood was somber.

> More than anything the most characteristic student of this generation is a skeptic. The self-assured young man with the flask on his hip has been replaced by a young man no less self-assured, but sure especially of his right to doubt. Frequent exposures of graft in politics and shadiness on a grand scale in finance have impressed upon him the idea that this is a cut-throat world, in which the clever and not too scrupulous man is

rewarded. . . . Underneath this hard philosophy is a deep sense of loss, and a determination to avoid trite illusions that constitute a far more significant revolt than the naughtiness of the Twenties. Many students are saying to themselves that "All the idols are broken. There is nothing left to believe in." (*The New York Times*, June 11, 1933)

The 1930's saw the first large-scale political activism by American students. It came and it went during the 1930's, arising in the 1931–32 period and then dying out with the beginning of the European war in 1939–40. The levels of participation were very high, higher in proportion to total college enrollment than the protests in the late 1960's. The concerns of the 1930's were generally not issues of college education or rules but broad political and economic questions. Unlike the 1960's, the generation gap rhetoric was not a part of the protest of the 1930's. Most of the student organizations were affiliates of more significant adult social and political organizations.

Until about 1935 the main issue was the need for national economic reform (if not socialist *revolution*) and the resistance to Fascism. A debate raged about the truth and merits of Marxism-Leninism. The proponents of radical economic change tended to be radical in other areas as well—political, religious, pacifistic, and others. After about 1935 the main issue came to be American involvement in the threatening European war. The largest student movements of the decade were united in an antiwar stance. The American Student Union was formed in 1935 as a coalition of left-of-center organizations on the antiwar position. Large numbers of students at the more cosmopolitan colleges and universities were deeply involved in the antiwar movement. The movement was strongest in the Eastern colleges and above all in New York City.

In 1934 the annual national Strike for Peace began. It took place for one hour on a day in April each year through 1939. Central to the Strike for Peace was the Oxford Pledge, imported from England. It stated that "this House will not fight for King and Country in any war." An Americanized version of this pledge was recited by those taking part in the strike. The biggest turnout was in 1936, when 350,000 students out of a total college population of one million took part. An anti-ROTC movement came alive at this same time, with the purpose of reducing or eliminating the drill requirements for male students, and it achieved a few successes.

Political attitudes radicalized during the early 1930's. A series of polls at Wesleyan University found a definite trend. "Comparing polls of the past which have dealt with political faiths in some form, the recent one shows a steady trend toward radicalism." (*The New York Times*, Jan. 13, 1935.) Students also turned out for political work. In the summers of 1936 and 1937 hundreds of volunteers for peace worked throughout the nation, spreading antiwar propaganda and being of service however they could. A *New York Times* article said that students' activities in the 1936 election were at a level unprecedented in America.

The antiwar movement broke down in internal division in 1938 and 1939. The pure pacifists opposed those willing to aid the European democracies against Fascism. Support for the Oxford Pledge weakened in 1937, 1938, and 1939, and by 1939 the collective security faction had clearly won over the radical pacifist faction. The American Student Union died in 1939 due to the division. By this time President Roosevelt was arranging lend-lease and assistance to Britain. The propaganda from Europe was frightening and disheartening. Idealism was replaced by pessimism and fear, and the draft was already a real possibility. The student movements collapsed.

During the early 1930's religious trends were a continuation of the decline in traditional religious participation in the late 1920's. A report by Dean Gauss of Princeton in 1932 stressed a new individualism and liberalism.

> There is really more individualism today, particularly in the intellectual sphere, than there was a few years ago. It is far less easy to indoctrinate (students) with ready-made views on political, social and economic questions than it was in the recent past. . . . It has been a matter of much concern for many years past that there is much less of sturdy old-fashioned religious sectarianism in the generation on the college campus than among their parents. The undergraduates are more latitudinarian and liberal. For good or for ill, this liberalism is beginning to be more strikingly in evidence on questions concerning the political and economic order as well. (*The New York Times*, June 5, 1932)

A 1933 report from Harvard said that the students were showing a new attitude in inquiry and hopefulness in regard to religion, "quite in contrast with the shoulder-shrugging rejections and blatant denials of the hard-boiled '20s." Interest in religion and religious questions was somewhat higher than in the recent past, yet participation in organized religion continued to be low. The students were searching for religious truth and meaning outside the walls of the churches. The religious interest was more philosophical and aesthetic than theologi-

cal in any traditional sense (cf. *The New York Times*, Feb. 5, 1933).
The radical political tendencies in the 1930's affected the religious
organizations as well.

> The Council of Christian Associations, the organization uniting the Y.M.
> and Y.W.C.A.'s, published a pamphlet in 1931 entitled "Toward a New
> Economic Society" in which collective ownership of natural resources and
> public utilities was advocated. Older national leaders of the Y's became
> disturbed at the Council's publication and disavowed its socialist position.
> The Student Christian Volunteer Movement placed less stress on overseas
> missionary work and paid more attention to domestic problems. Resolu-
> tions passed at the first National Assembly of Student Christian Groups in
> 1938 indicated religious students had become more radical. One resolu-
> tion, passed by a substantial majority, stated that capitalism and fascism
> were unacceptable and that the goals of the Cooperative Movement and of
> Marxian socialism were preferred. (Altbach and Peterson, 1971:7)

The Catholic student groups were at first nonpolitical, and when
they did organize for political action it was in opposition to the
antiwar movement.

A 1939 writer reported a greater interest in religion among college
students in that year than in the years previous. On many campuses
the reports of Religious Emphasis Weeks told of higher levels of
attendance. The writer speculated that the reason might be "the need
for understanding the problems of a troubled world."

During the late 1940's, after the close of World War II, the
returning veterans created a distinctive ethos which dominated college
life. In most colleges and universities veterans comprised over half of
the male enrollment. Emergency housing was erected and emergency
accelerated programs were set up to speed the veterans to their
degrees. The culture of the married student had its first big impact on
the colleges. Without doubt the veterans were more serious than the
other students, and they got higher grades. They paid less attention to
the extracurriculum and more to the bread-and-butter questions of
how to get a degree, what it would be worth, and how to get on in the
world. The mood of the campuses was businesslike, practical, and
job-oriented. *Fortune* reported that the Class of 1949 was "the
soberest, most trained graduating class in U.S. history."

The early 1950's were the beginning of the "silent generation." It
was silent in political affairs because of a desire for a return to
normalcy, an intense practical mood, and the fears of McCarthyism
and the anti-Communist witch hunt. During the Korean War fear of
the draft added to the apprehension.

Because of the uncertainty over military service and the generally unsettled atmosphere, college students are becoming jittery and have lost morale. Many have adopted a "what's the use" attitude. As a result, their grades have fallen off. . . . A number of colleges report that many students are rushing into marriage, to get as much as they can out of life until the husbands are drafted. (*The New York Times*, Feb. 13, 1951)

Later in 1951 an article reported that in seventy-two colleges surveyed, students and faculty were becoming wary of speaking out on controversial issues, lest they experience social disapproval, a label of Communist, criticism by friends or superiors, rejection for further study at graduate schools, or even personal investigation. Part of the silence was also a product of a sense of powerlessness in the midst of overwhelming international developments.

This censorship, wariness, caution and inhibition largely took these forms: 1. A reluctance to speak out on controversial issues in and out of class. 2. A reluctance to handle currently unpopular concepts even in classroom work where they may be part of the study program. 3. An unwillingness to join student political clubs. 4. Neglect of humanitarian causes because they may be suspect in the minds of politically unsophisticated officials. 5. An emphasis on lack of affiliations. 6. An unusual amount of serio-comic joking about this or that official investigating committee "getting you." 7. A shying away, both physically and intellectually from any association with the words "liberal," "peace," "freedom," and from classmates of a liberal stripe. 8. A sharp turning inward to local college problems, to the exclusion of broader current questions. (*The New York Times*, May 10, 1951)

The period of silence, caution, and conformity lasted through most of the 1950's. The mood of the campuses, as of the country at large, was decidedly apolitical. The adult leftist groups in the nation were in total disarray and constantly beleaguered by attacks. The argument was made that in the face of the international Communist threat any social criticism and protest would only play into the anti-American propaganda of the Communists. In 1955, Lazarsfeld and Thielens found that not only Marxism, but any topics in the realm of race, religion, or political criticism were taboo on campus as "too hot to handle." Like the 1920's, the early 1950's were a period of political disengagement. It is interesting that in 1955 the Ford Foundation established a unit to encourage political discussion groups on campuses.

By the end of the fifties, there was an almost total lack of any political activity on the left more fundamentally critical of American society than the Americans for Democratic Action or the American Civil Liberties Union. (Allen, 1967:99)

A few right-wing student groups organized during the 1950's and gained more prominence on campuses than they had for decades.

During the late 1940's and early 1950's religious participation on campus increased. Already in 1948 the dean of the chapel at Princeton noted that "the present-day college undergraduate, to a far greater degree than his pre-war counterpart, has a readiness to identify himself with religion." He reported increased attendance at chapel services, increasing enrollments in religion courses, and increasing support being given to the Student Christian Association (*The New York Times*, Nov. 25, 1948). A 1951 article noted further increases and suggested that the international crisis and the students' concern about their relation to it were the prime causes. A 1954 article told of increases in religious interest and participation at the University of Michigan.

> Student religious participation and affiliation has increased during the past few years, according to many of the leaders of local religious groups. . . . The conscious interest in religion can be shown by the small Bible and prayer groups that have formed in the girls' dorms during the past year.

> Rev. Robert Wittaker of Canterbury House noted, "Most noticeable on campus, however, is a general climate of fear. The effect of the Communist hunt has had a general reflection in discussions. For while many students are outspoken in theological discussions the student who is outspoken on political or social issues is rare today, though there are those who do." (*Michigan Daily*, July 29, 1954)

A 1955 article portrayed the new interest in religion on campus and said that religion was being studied more than ever and had become "intellectually respectable."

> Today's undergraduates are deeply concerned with religion, and sincerity of purpose is characteristic of this interest. Where students of the Nineteen Thirties were wrestling with social problems, students in the Nineteen Fifties are giving more and more time to a thoroughgoing consideration of what religion is all about. . . . The emphasis is on basic principles and theology. This interest in religion is more often evidenced by objective study and inquiry than by reverence. It does not necessarily mean a turning to the church. (*The New York Times*, Oct. 22, 1955)

In 1957 *Newsweek* reported that religious interest and church participation were higher on American campuses than they had been for decades.

Voluntary chapel attendance is booming. At Northwestern University in Evanston, Ill., where chapel attendance is not required, almost twice as many boys and girls now attend the university chapel as did a decade ago. At the University of Michigan, almost 5,000 of a total 22,000 students go to church at least once a week. . . . The Wednesday night voluntary candlelight service at Stanford, which attracted as few as ten students in 1947, now draws 150 to 200 regularly.

"In my Princeton class of '32," Mr. Kellogg (Episcopal chaplain at Harvard) recalls, "not one man out of 700 went directly from college into the ministry. In the Harvard class of '57, there are already twelve who have decided to go into the Episcopal ministry alone." (*Newsweek*, April 22, 1957:115, 120)

In the late 1950's the cold war attitude framework tended to break down on campuses. In 1957 President Eisenhower signaled the end to the worst hysteria by advising students in a speech to study the *Communist Manifesto* and acquaint themselves with the forces opposing democracy in the world. With the death of Stalin, the Khrushchev policy of peaceful coexistence, the Sino-Soviet dispute, and the increased communication across the Iron Curtain, the Manichaean view of the world became blurred. Serious domestic social criticism again became possible. With the beginning of the sit-in movement in 1960, the appeal of President Kennedy to the idealism of youth, the establishment of the Peace Corps, and the acceleration of the civil rights movement, a new liberalism and political interest returned to campuses.

The profound attitude shift in the late 1950's did not occur without great social dislocations. It is significant that in 1958–60, after the first relaxation of cold war anxieties, several forums of leading Americans (and even a Presidential commission) were convened to uncover "the American national purpose." By then the cold war framework had given way to a malaise about "what it means to be an American," a situation of drift that lasted until the first few years of the Kennedy presidency. During these years the Beat Generation made its appearance, and discussion of the "identity crisis" was fashionable among intellectuals. On May 23, 1960, *Life* magazine introduced a five-part series, "The National Purpose." The introduction quoted Walter Lippmann:

The critical weakness of our society is that for the time being our people do not have great purposes which they are united in wanting to achieve. The public mood of the country is defensive, to hold on and to conserve, not to push forward and to create. We talk about ourselves these days as if we were a completed society, one which has achieved its purposes, and has no further great business to transact.

The events of the 1960's issued out of the collapse of the cold war framework and introduced a new era. After the transitional period of the end of the 1950's the Kennedy presidency helped to bring a new focus and purpose to student culture, best symbolized by the Peace Corps. Also students gradually found a new sense of freedom to speak out in criticism of American society. The civil rights movement captured the imagination of many during the early 1960's, and it rose to a crescendo in the March on Washington on August 28, 1963.

The Berkeley revolt of 1964 is best interpreted as an extension of this newfound sense of freedom and political power among students. An analysis of its leadership discovered that most were veterans of long months of civil rights activity (Lipset and Altbach, 1966:322). It was an outgrowth of the civil rights movement, seeking the civil rights of students, both black and white.

The decision by President Johnson to escalate the Vietnam war in February, 1965, ushered in the era of student activism and counter-culture in the late 1960's. During 1967 and 1968 student political activism in opposition to the Vietnam war reached new peaks reminiscent of the middle 1930's. A New Left returned to campus with a new ideology based on "participatory democracy." It found abundant support for protests against the war and against the university. Student attitudes radicalized. In political attitudes and activities the later 1960's resembled the middle 1930's. But in the 1960's college students had the numbers and attention to gain sizable impact on national life. The main goal was an end to the Vietnam war, and secondary goals were university reform, black power, and action against injustice and poverty. Radical campus political groups such as Students for a Democratic Society had their greatest effect in 1967 to 1969.

May, 1970, was a turning point, for it represented a high point and climax of the activities of the late 1960's. The nation recoiled in shock when National Guardsmen shot four students at Kent State University during a protest against the Cambodian invasion, and police shot two black students at Jackson State College. Meanwhile, de-escalation of the Vietnam war, draft reforms, and numerous university reforms had taken the venom out of the protests. In late 1970 an eerie silence was noted on campus. The era of activism had ended. The

Students for a Democratic Society lost its power after 1970, partly due to the cooling of fervor and partly due to its inability to ally with the labor movement, the traditional liberals, or the blacks.

Some students turned to cultural revolution. They argued that meaningful social change in America is impossible at present, but a cultural revolution, by transforming consciousness, undermining American myths, and creating new love-centered communities, could usher in the desired change. A rather amorphous counterculture preached a variety of themes criticizing the individualism, competitive corporate systems, careerism, nuclear family living, hypocrisy, and militarism in American life. The main effect of the counterculture was felt after about 1967 or 1968. An early emphasis on drug experiences seemed to have passed by 1971.

Observers of the campuses in 1970 and 1971 wondered what to expect next. Was the new silence a move back to the climate of the 1950's? Most observers said no, that the calm was not a deep change in values but only a tentative change of mood and strategy. The students were just confused and disillusioned with political activism. Probably the Nixon Administration's strategy of defusing campus activism had worked, leaving students with some goals attained but no longer a focus for action. One student said, "I think people of my generation are beginning to learn that change is agonizingly slow." Another said: "It's a strain being politically conscious all the time. It takes a lot. And I guess most people don't have it. I guess people are a little tired out now." (*The New York Times,* Dec. 20, 1970.) The apocalypticism was gone. What political commitment remained went to work within the system.

In religion too, 1970 was a kind of turning point. Indications of a new personal spirituality began appearing about then on campuses. It took two general forms, either a revival of conservative Christianity or a turn away from all organized religion to new personal experimentation. Most conspicuous was the new Jesus movement, about which much is written (Knight, 1971; Streiker, 1971; Enroth *et al.,* 1972). By 1972 it made visible inroads on a large number of campuses, often in the form of the Campus Crusade for Christ. The Jesus movement is a loose classification of new groups with varying attitudes toward the organized church. Some groups embraced conservative churches of the Billy Graham mentality, and others rejected all organized religion as being cold and without the Spirit. Insofar as any of the Jesus movement voice social and political attitudes they are conservative, akin to those of fundamental Protestantism. Among the Catholics there has been a similar revivalism in the Catholic Pentecostals. Even among Jews some stirrings have been observed. Edward B. Fiske suggested that the new conservative mood in religion is a reflection of a more general conservatism in the nation. "The campuses as well as the big denominations have cooled down. College graduates are showing new interest in working 'within the sytem.' Nostalgia is 'in.' " (*The New York Times*, March 5, 1972.)

Much of the new spiritual revival turned away from the churches. There were signs of new interest on campuses in the occult, in Eastern religion, and in primitive practices such as witchcraft. Rock music took on religious themes, and rock festivals became a sort of liturgy for the new spirituality. The mood was private and experiential, concentrated on the individual and the intimate group. It tended to be antihistorical and anti-intellectual. Its only institutional form besides the rock festival was probably the commune, of which hundreds sprouted up around major universities. The appeal of the commune is in part the desire for a withdrawal from the pressures and competition of the larger society and a chance to put the love ethic into action in a small group. For these students the spiritual quest is an inner-directed search for meaning in intense personal and interpersonal experiences. It sees little relevance in theology or churches.

RESEARCH ON RELIGIOUS CHANGE
AND VALUE CHANGE SINCE 1968

The social research on recent religious changes among students calls for greater restraint by journalists. No spiritual renewal is visible. The Jesus movement, though commanding the attention of many writers, is not strong enough to show up on nationwide student surveys. Available indicators of traditional religious attitudes and commitment continue downward after 1968, more or less continuous with the trends we found since the middle 1950's.

The American Council on Education's annual poll of college freshmen found in the fall of 1970 that 9.8 percent of a national cross section of freshmen had no religious preference, up from 6.9 percent in 1968 (*The New York Times*, Dec. 20, 1970). In May, 1968, and November–December, 1971, the Gallup poll asked a nationwide sample of college students, "Did you, yourself, happen to attend church in the last seven days?" In 1968, 47 percent said yes, and in 1971, 37 percent said yes. The difference in the month of the survey may have affected the result, but most likely some decline took place over three years (Gallup Opinion Index, February, 1972, p. 30).

The Yankelovich poll asked a nationwide sample of college students two questions about religion in 1969 and in 1971. First, "What role does each of the following values play in your life—is it very important to you, fairly important, or not very important to you?" The percentage saying that "religion" was very important was 35 in 1969 and only 27 in 1971. Second, the poll asked for personal agreement or disagreement with a series of statements, including "Belonging to some organized religion is important in a person's life." In 1969, 42 percent agreed, and in 1971 it was 35 percent (Yankelovich, 1972:38,41).

These research findings suggest that the trend since 1968 is away from traditional religious commitment either inside or outside the church. If there has been a spiritual revival, it is not seen by the students as being "religion."

The Yankelovich studies between 1968 and 1971 provide rich data to support general conclusions about recent value changes. He summarizes that the students in 1971 have "pressed forward in their search for a cultural revolution while taking a step backwards from political revolution" (Yankelovich, 1972:7). Between 1969 and 1971 there was a decrease of student involvement in public affairs and decreased willingness to participate in political protests. The 1971 students surveyed thought they were less socially alienated than they had been a year before. Since 1968 there was a consistent erosion in the willingness of students to fight wars for any reason; those saying a war to contain the Communists would be worth fighting declined 16 percentage points over the three years. Between 1970 and 1971 the students' criticism of major American institutions fell. And generally the evidence shows that students in 1971 were withdrawing emotional involvement from social and political matters and channeling it into their own private lives where they experienced more control, less frustration, and greater contentment. In 1971, 61 percent of the students said that they were more involved in their own private lives now than in the previous year; 12 percent reported less involvement in personal matters; and the other 27 percent said their mood had not changed. Also the 1971 students reported that they were happier than a year before, were studying harder, and were more fearful about being able to get a job in the future. In short, the 1971 poll uncovered some movement toward privatism after the intense politicization of the late 1960's.

During the same time prominent themes of the cultural revolution gained more support. The students in 1971 believed more than in 1968 that marriage is obsolete and expressed interest in experimenting with communal living. They expressed greater acceptance of casual premarital sexual relations, extramarital sexual relations, and homosexuality between consenting adults. There was less and less readiness to abide with traditional forms of authority. In 1968, 56 percent of the students said that they did not mind the future prospect of being bossed around on the job. This number fell to 49 percent in 1969, 43 percent in 1970, and 36 percent in 1971. The desire for more sexual freedom was considerably stronger in 1971 than in 1969.

The Yankelovich studies suggest that the religious changes and value changes we have seen since the middle 1950's are proceeding farther, even though political activism and protest are now dead. The 1970's, in this view, will have some resemblance to the middle 1920's; the issues will be personal and cultural rather than political—sex mores, personal freedom, and life-styles. The coming period will not resemble the early 1950's because of the absence of a climate of political intimidation and caution. And one cannot foresee any strengthening of commitment to traditional religion or the organized church.

Finally, a study by Vreeland (1971) compared Harvard students' attitudes toward dating in 1960 and 1970 and drew contrasts between dating today and in the findings of researchers in the 1930's, 1940's, and 1950's. The main trends over the decades are diminished importance of "rating" among peers and with the opposite sex. The whole campus syndrome of "rating" and personal prestige is weaker in 1970 than at any time earlier, and dating today is no longer perceived as part of a competitive game of status-seeking. Rather, in the 1970's the emphasis is greater on fun and companionship conceived more privately. Students in the '70s relate to girls more as they would to members of the same sex—as people and potential friends.

The importance of sexual intimacy in dating was, interestingly enough, not studied until the 1960's, so statements about trends are precarious. Whether sexual intimacy is greater today or whether there is merely more openness about it is not clear.

The other overall trend has been the decreasing segregation of activities into same-sex and cross-sex peer activities. A greater range of activities is suitable for dating today, and the recent trend is toward informality. "In the last 30 years heterosexual relationships among adolescents have steadily become less formalized, less exploitative, and more like close same-sex relationships" (Vreeland, 1971:6).

CHANGING THEOLOGICAL EMPHASES

We interviewed sixteen professional Protestant and Catholic theologians and veteran campus ministers acquainted with theological currents among students. All of them had experience in Eastern and Midwestern colleges. The interviews focused on theological change at the level of students, not at the more rarefied level of scholarly journals or the less informed level of the general population.

The changing theological emphases depicted among Protestant students differed from those depicted among Catholic students, and the two must be discussed separately. Among Protestant students the informants agreed in discerning at least two turning points in the last five or six decades. One was seen in the middle or late 1930's, and another was seen in about 1960–63.

Prior to the middle 1930's Protestant college students generally adhered to either a pietistic orthodoxy or a liberal social gospel; both currents were strong throughout the 1910's and 1920's. The liberal emphasis stressed humanitarianism and progress toward the Kingdom of God on earth. It was allied with a kind of "ethical monotheism." The orthodox emphasis was a continuation of the evangelical pietism of late nineteenth-century Protestantism. In the 1910's and 1920's the foreign mission movement was very strong, partly because both theological emphases fed into it. The orthodox students set out to convert the non-Christians, and the liberal students set out to uplift the uneducated and oppressed. The Y.M.C.A. and the Student Volunteer Movement were also strong organizations. On economic matters the liberals tended to be leftists of one variety or other, and many were members of Communist groups. Most were strong supporters of internationalism, pacifism, and interracialism. The religious movements on campuses during these years tended to be ethical and action-oriented, not inward or spiritual. During the 1920's the fundamentalist-modernist controversy raged, but most college students of the liberal type took little notice.

Beginning in the early 1930's Reinhold Niebuhr gained influence among students, and by the middle 1930's he was widely heard and read. By about 1940 Niebuhr was at the forefront of a new theological era, variously called "neo-orthodoxy" or "Christian realism." Niebuhr was adopted as the intellectual leader of the main religious student movement of the time, the Student Christian Association. He traveled from campus to campus delivering powerful lectures and chapel sermons. He reintroduced classical Reformation theology into the college scene, stressing political realism, the innate sinfulness of man, the limitations of human nature, and the ambiguities of personal and social life. He attacked the ideologies of utopianism, progress, and pacifism. Rather, he stressed the transcendence of God and the judgment of God on man's pretenses. By the 1940's this neo-orthodox orientation had supplanted the older liberal social gospel on most campuses. For students of evangelical background the neo-orthodox theology sounded familiar and eminently true.

The thought of Barth and Brunner also came into popularity on campuses during the 1940's, and Tillich, Buber, and Bultmann appeared during the 1950's. Probably the neo-orthodox theology was strongest during the early and middle 1950's. Thereafter it took some new emphases and directions but remained quite strong until the early 1960's. One new emphasis was existentialism and the search for personal meaning; it sought meaning in man's individualism and despair, and it gave comparatively little attention to social structures. It couched ethics in individual terms. Another new emphasis was ecumenism, which was enthusiastic for a time until it weakened in the face of many frustrations.

All the experts agreed that neo-orthodoxy died at the end of the 1950's, and the period 1960–63 was a second turning point. With the decline in the cold war tensions and the appearance of the civil rights movement came an emphasis on social involvement and social relevance. Some said that this was not really a theological theme but rather an absence of any theology and a borrowing of ideology from non-Christian movements; social action was seen as good and as Christian even without a deeper theological structure. Others stressed that a respectable "secular theology" came alive during the early and middle 1960's, more optimistic of human possibilities than the neo-orthodoxy, more positive toward social change, technology, urbanization, and "secularity." It stressed man's "coming of age" and looked forward to significant social change through Christian inspiration and hard work. The main attention was devoted to civil rights and the opposition to the Vietnam war. Action was foremost; study and personal growth were legitimate only as they related to action. The "death of God" theology was a kind of outgrowth of this stress on secularity and human society. Insofar as theologizing was done it took social ethics as its point of departure. Often the guidelines for social ethics were borrowed as much from the New Left as from the New Testament.

The experts were divided in their interpretation of the last few years. Some said that the era of social relevance in college students' theology is over, while others were not yet ready to say so. Indications of a basic change in theological themes appear on every side, but how strong and lasting the forces for change will be cannot be known. To most of the experts the years 1967–69 represent a turning point in college students' theology as important as any other. It was a change that found little counterpart in the adult culture.

After 1967–69 there began new religious interest among college students, but it was on nonrational, esoteric, and intensely personal themes. The new religious emphasis was inward and immediate. Some concern remained for the social order, but few students dedicated much effort to long-range strategy and planning. There was a kind of retreat to the personal realm of immediate experience and an effort to work out a new counterculture. Some students tried ways of "turning on," from Eastern religious practices to drugs to rock festivals. There was also new optimism about the inherent goodness of man and a rather naïve utopianism about what is possible in human society; the moral ambiguities and limitations once stressed by Reinhold Niebuhr were now totally lost from sight. Some inclination to new mysticism was visible, a mysticism akin to existentialism and without social and political orientation.

In the last few years the more extreme manifestations of occult and nontraditional religious practices faded away. A high point seemed to have passed. Then in 1971 and 1972 the Jesus movement began catching everyone's attention. The new conservative fervor is so different from the ethical and socially relevant religion of most campus ministers that many find themselves at a loss to relate to it. It is seen as fundamentalism warmed over, uncritical of intellectual questions and lacking in social ethics. The old battles must be fought again. Several of the campus ministers adopted a wait-and-see attitude, hoping to engage conservative students in theological and ethical discussions.

The Catholic experts tended to divide the last few decades into two or three discernible periods, with the most important watershed at the Second Vatican Council from 1962 to 1965. The results of the Council have brought a thoroughly new mood to Catholic students, and the new mood has had several ramifications. First and most important is a new sense of freedom and individual voluntarism. Students have felt freer to act and to speak out, even if it involves criticism of the church. They now defend their thoughts and actions in the name of "freedom of conscience," arguing that conscience should be supreme over ecclesiastical directives. Contacts with Protestants, formerly ignored or even avoided, have been established at many points. The conscious identity of many Catholic students has shifted from "Catholic" to "Christian."

Second is a new wave of criticism of the church. Students are more critical of the church now than at any time in memory. The main criticisms stress irrelevance and hypocrisy. Students point out that the church has not been a leader in the civil rights movement or in popular political movements in the Third World. They point out that it has been in collusion with urban machine politics of the worst kind. They repeatedly ask, "What have you done?" And they charge hypocrisy, since the church has always taught a social responsibility and has exhorted its members to contribute in the name of human uplift. The students are especially critical of "religious practices" which they formerly carried out under a sense of obligation and fear of loss of grace or social favor. Many students say that the Mass is irrelevant and dead. The priesthood has also been increasingly criticized since Vatican II. Students ask, "What good has this done you?" or "Why is your thing important?" The number of candidates for the priesthood and for the religious orders has fallen precipitously since 1965.

Catholic students in the late 1960's became more involved in the social relevance movement around the colleges and universities. Martin Luther King and Eldridge Cleaver were read and admired. An articulate Catholic social theology, however, was generally lacking, and the Catholic activism borrowed about as much from the New Left ideology as from anywhere. In this sense recent theological emphases among Catholic students increasingly resemble those among Protestant students in the middle 1960's. New theological directions since Vatican II are not very clear or unified at present. Beginning in 1971 and 1972 the new Catholic Pentecostalism caused some reevaluation of attitudes about informal worship, celebration of Mass in homes, glossolalia and other fruits of the Spirit, and understandings of religious authority.

No one should think, however, that the Vatican Council was the sole event that unleashed these new developments among Catholic students. The new feelings and criticisms were building up among Catholic thinkers all during the 1950's. Hence one must see the 1950's as a period of ferment. In the 1940's and 1950's the Catholic ethnic communities were opened up to mainstream American culture by war experiences and increased secular higher education. The result was many questions and many calls for change.

In the decades prior to 1950 the experts could discern little important change in Catholic students' theological emphases. Scholastic apologetic theology, emphasis on Catholic community and Catholic higher education, and defensiveness over against the mainstream American Protestant culture characterized Catholic thought all during the 1920's, 1930's, and 1940's.

We asked the experts to speculate about the causes of the various shifts in students' theological emphases, and they generally pointed to national and community events as the crucial factors. Among the Protestants the emphasis was on events in national and international life; among the Catholics it was on events and developments within the Catholic Church and the Catholic community life. The cause of the Protestant turning point in the 1930's was seen as being the depression, the rising Fascism in Europe, the threat of Communism, the failure of the League of Nations, and finally the European war. In the early 1960's it was the end of the cold war anxieties, the new freedom for social criticism, the civil rights movement, and then the war in Vietnam.

The immediate cause of change among Catholic students was seen in the Vatican Council and the events surrounding it. The underlying change was the long-range increasing participation in American culture by means of more frequent attendance at secular colleges, entrance into many new occupations and institutions, greater geographic mobility, upward social mobility out of the ethnic neighborhoods, and the impact of the mass media.[39]

From the interviews we conclude that changing theological emphases among students are largely the product of historical events and reflection on them. In this respect theological thought resembles secular political and social thought. In addition, theological emphases are responsive to experiences of certain communities. For example, the greater participation of Catholic communities in American secular culture had an effect on Catholic students, and prominent themes in American youth culture had an effect on many students, especially seen in the Protestant group.

Can it be said that theological tendencies caused the trends in attitudes and behavior which are outlined in Chapters 2 to 4 above? Statements about alleged causation must be made circumspectly, for the causal interrelations and feedbacks are complex. Probably the safest statement is that historical events were the impetus for

short-range trends in theological thought, in attitudes, and also in
religious behavior. The latter are interrelated to each other in
complex ways. Langdon Gilkey ventures a summary statement:

> The evidence indicates that the intellectual shape of recent American
> theology has been determined in each decade by the character of the crises
> then current in the wider secular milieu. (Gilkey, 1967:94)

Gilkey contrasts American theology in this respect with most European theology, which is less oriented to secular thought and more
confined to church walls and classical theological traditions.

This review of impressionistic reports on students leads us to several
conclusions. First, the information reviewed here seems to fit the
attitude data quite well. The available information on the early
decades of the century remains inadequate for making conclusions
about religious trends. In Chapter 2 we concluded from questionnaire
data that orthodoxy was probably higher in the 1910's than in the
middle 1920's, but the amount of difference was impossible to know.
The impressionistic evidence seems to suggest that no great change
occurred, at least not in the prominent Eastern and Midwestern
universities on which we have reports.

The changes in students' theological emphases generally coincide
with the trends in measured attitudes. The change in the late 1930's
and the high point of neo-orthodoxy in the early 1950's are both
visible in the questionnaire data. The weakening of neo-orthodoxy in
the late 1950's is probably depicted in the lowering of orthodoxy in
the questionnaire data, but the theological developments of the 1960's
are otherwise not visible.

Second, the periods of greatest political activism were the periods of
lowest traditional religious orthodoxy and participation, and vice
versa. As noted above, this relationship is best seen in terms of similar
pressures on political and on religious realms at any one time. At any
time a radicalizing of both realms will cause a withdrawal from the
religious institutions and also organized resistance to the prevailing
political parties. Also at any time pressures toward conservatism and
conformity will increase traditional religious participation and sup-
press leftist student political movements.

Third, the 1920's resemble the 1950's in several respects, including
the pressures toward political caution and anti-Communism in the
early years and the relaxation of the pressures in the later years.
These parallels would predict that, as in the 1950's, students'
traditional religious commitments would be stronger in the early years

of the 1920's than in the later years. Unfortunately the information for the crucial years 1920–25 is sparse, but probably the political and social climate encouraged a higher level of traditional religious commitments during those years.

Fourth, it is clear that any analysis of religious change among students must distinguish levels of *interest in* religious problems from levels of traditional religious orthodoxy and practice. And it must analyze the determinants of each. Our research is more helpful in analyzing the determinants of traditional religious attitudes and behavior than the determinants of religious interest; indeed the conceptualization of the latter is unclear. We return to this problem later.[40]

Finally, these impressionistic accounts may help shed some light on the reason for the association between fear of Communism and higher levels of traditional religiosity. In Chapter 4 we established a statistical association between the two and concluded that the principal causation was from attitudes about Communism and America to religious attitudes. The accounts of college students' intensified religiosity in the early 1950's all mention the world and national political situation as a foremost cause. The explanation for the association remains unclear, but three hypotheses have been mentioned. (*a*) Due to the fear of appearing controversial or suspect and due to the fear of social disapproval, students during the McCarthy years strongly conformed outwardly to accepted conservative American religious beliefs and practices. They attended church often and portrayed themselves in questionnaire studies as proper conservative religious Americans. (*b*) Due to a feeling of anxiety and personal powerlessness amid the momentous forces of the cold war, students tended to withdraw from social and political concerns to the safer and more manageable realms of family, occupation, and friendship groups. That is to say, the cold war led to privatism. Traditional religion is an element of the privatistic value system due to its close association with family and subcommunity patterns. Also at the same time organized religion turned its attention to problems of personal meaning and authenticity. Hence there resulted increased religious interest and participation. (*c*) Because of the perceived threat of international Communism, students looked increasingly to their religious traditions and groups as a source of strength, support, inspiration, and direction for the hard battles lying ahead. Religion was seen as a weapon against Communism. The threat of Communism thus intensified the social interaction in religious groups. Churchgoing increased, and religious concerns intensified.

All three hypotheses appear in the literature. Without further research we cannot specify the degree and scope of the validity of each hypothesis, but available data and accounts may be helpful. The first hypothesis sees the increased traditional religious participation as being more outward than inward, more intended to gain protective coloring or to demonstrate one's solid Americanism than to answer an inner need. The contemporary accounts speak often of the conformity pressures felt by college students in the early 1950's, but whether the new religiosity should be explained in this way is left unclear. The accounts also stress the genuineness of the new religious interest and participation and leave no doubt that it was more than just outward behavior for the sake of appearance (e.g., *The New York Times,* Oct. 22, 1955). Probably the first hypothesis should not be considered important as an explanation.

The second hypothesis enjoys the support of the Dartmouth and Michigan data showing a decline in privatism from 1952 to 1968–69 and inferring a rise from the 1930's to 1952. There is little doubt that the 1952 students were relatively privatistic and apolitical. The question remains whether privatism encourages greater religious commitment and participation. We have seen in the Dartmouth, Michigan, and Wisconsin data that religious attitudes and behavior are closely associated with family attitudes and behavior. We have also seen that theological attention shifted to personal meaning and personal authenticity during the middle 1950's, largely ignoring questions of the meaning of national life and broader community life. Probably there is no necessary relationship between traditional religion and privatism, but certain theological themes have an affinity with a privatistic orientation and may facilitate greater traditional religious commitment and participation. There is evidence that this occurred in the middle 1950's. To summarize, the second hypothesis seems sustained; the increased religiosity was partly a result of the shift to privatism.

The third hypothesis is the obverse of the first; it asserts that the new religious commitment was the result of an inward need felt by students. It differs from the second in that the new religious concerns were responses to the international Communist threat and not just a result of withdrawal from all political concerns. It is not clear from the historical accounts to what extent religion was looked to as a resource in the cold war battles lying ahead; this theme is less prominent than the theme of conformity, privatism, and withdrawal of political interest. Also the particular religious emphases among students did not seem to relate very directly to the war against Communism. Consider, for example, a 1955 report:

> A five-day conference of the Student Christian Association at Princeton in December will deal with "The Relevance of the Christian Faith to the Individual in a World of Power." A number of educators and religious counselors agree that student concern for religion is a serious attempt to find a spiritual basis for action in the modern world. (*The New York Times,* Oct. 24, 1955)

The focus is on the individual and his meaning more than on social or political action against the threat of Communism. It seems that the third hypothesis is less powerful as an explanation than the second. The new religious commitment and participation was born out of political frustration, the demise of the campus left, and the shift to privatism.

CHAPTER 6

Interpretations
and Conclusions

Our attempt to interpret and explain the changes described in the preceding chapters begins with the assumption that the sources of the changes lie outside any single religious group. Also the same sources will explain more than just religious changes; they will explain broader patterns of changes in attitudes. Attention is thus drawn to some indicators of change over past decades related to religious and value changes. First we look at indicators of religious *interest*. Religious interest is clearly distinguishable from orthodoxy, traditional commitment, and participation. The distinction between religious interest and traditional religious commitment is analogous to that between political interest and commitment to a particular political party.

Religious interest is difficult to conceptualize and measure. In three questionnaires we included items asking the students to estimate their own religious interest (or "interest in the problems religion seeks to answer"), thus in effect leaving the definition and conceptualization up to them. Religious interest, measured in this way, proved to have no relation to political interest. Orthodox students and those with greater religious influence in childhood reported stronger religious interest. The correlations between religious interest and orthodoxy in the three studies ranged between .2 and .4. It is unclear to what extent the respondents conceptualized "interest in the problems religion seeks to answer" apart from traditional religious attitudes or commitments. Perhaps they were unable to do so.

It is also difficult to justify attempts to measure religious interest in such an omnibus way. Religious problems and concerns are diverse, and attempts to study or measure them must be aware of the plurality. Religious interest appears to be a product of the total state of the individual personality system and social system. These systems encounter *various problems* giving rise to religious "needs" and "interests." Max Weber analyzed "needs for salvation," which he tended to see as needs for finding meaning for suffering, injustice, psychic conflict, group conflict, and so on. They are of various types. Weber stressed that religious needs are not the same as material needs, for even the wealthy experience them, as for example in the problem of legitimizing their wealth. Weber said that ultimate religious questions tend to arise in times of social change, especially when the change brings social breakdown or distress (cf. Weber, 1963:151–201; 1946:267–301). An analysis of religious needs of systems has been stated in cybernetic terms by Deutsch (1963:214–244).

In spite of these difficulties, it seems of value to look at two indicators of possible usefulness in the study of religious interest—enrollment in religion courses and applications to theological seminaries.

ENROLLMENT IN RELIGION COURSES[41]

An article by Braden (1948) provides an overview of trends in enrollment in religion courses prior to World War II. Most of the colleges reporting data in his study were private liberal arts schools. In them the percentage of the student bodies enrolled in religion courses increased mildly from 1920 to 1925. After 1927 or 1928 a sharp decrease occurred, so that the levels in 1930 were lower than in 1920. From 1930 to 1940 there was little change. From 1940 to 1945 there was a distinct rise, but Braden could not discern to what extent the war and institutional factors had caused it. An analysis of emphases in specific fields found no noteworthy changes over the twenty-five years.

Data could not be found for the late 1940's and early 1950's, but these were years of great growth in religion departments. Between 1954 and 1969 the percentage of total student bodies which enrolled in religion courses remained generally constant according to a survey of 200-odd institutions (Welch, 1971). This overall picture changes, however, when particular types of institutions are scrutinized. The Roman Catholic institutions decreased markedly, especially since the early 1960's, and the decrease was partly a result of liberalizing course

requirements. The Protestant denominational institutions also decreased, partly for the same reason. The private nondenominational
institutions and public institutions gained somewhat after the early
1960's. Part of the gain is due to the improved offerings in the
expanded departments, but probably not all. The best conclusion
from the data is that, if institutional factors are controlled, trends in
voluntary enrollment in religion courses from 1954 to 1969 are mild
increases. It is very unlikely that the overall trend is a *decrease.* And
comparisons of the Braden data with recent data show that the
enrollment levels were higher in the 1950's than the 1930's. A 1955
report in *The New York Times* suggested that the levels of enrollment
in religion courses in Eastern colleges were higher then, as a
percentage of the total student body, than in the 1930's (Oct. 22,
1955:12).

Some indication of types of religious interest may be inferred from
trends in course enrollments in various types of religion courses. In
1960, Milton D. McLean and Harry H. Kimber commented on the
trends.

> A review of courses added to the curriculum since World War II indicates
> that greater emphasis is now being placed upon courses concerned with
> theological content and specific religious traditions and less emphasis, or at
> least not more, on courses concerned with the psychology and philosophy
> of religion, social issues, and religious education. (McLean and Kimber,
> 1960:115)

A study of fifteen-year enrollment trends in nine colleges shows some
evidence of different trends in the 1954 to 1964 period than in the
post-1964 period. Before 1964, courses that showed marked growth in
enrollment had to do with religion and society, religion in culture,
history of Christian thought, Christian ethics, religious ideas in
literature, religion in American life, and philosophy of religion. In the
post-1964 period the courses which seemed to enjoy greatest growth
were in the areas of history of religions, comparative religions, religion
in culture, and religion and literature. After 1964 the courses
specifically in Christian thought and tradition and courses in religion
and society seemed to have lost some appeal. Several persons
commented to us that interest among students in 1970 and 1971
seemed especially high in the experiential and even esoteric aspects of
religion. The concerns were personal and existential. The counterculture has also stimulated some interest in Eastern religions. Welch
found that the first priorities for new appointments in religion

departments in 1970–72 were in the fields of history of religions, comparative religions, and phenomenology of religion.

Probably the popularity of such religion courses demonstrates a personal search among students for bases of personal meaning and answers to the "big questions," a search that finds little satisfaction in the increasingly technical social sciences and philosophy.

> [R]eligion courses provide this generation, or seem to provide them, with a chance to study questions that interest and concern them—questions about morality and meaning. These courses appear to deal with "real" issues and not to be just engaged in word games or the mastery of some highly technical language which, while necessary perhaps, does not "speak" to the student's deepest concern. Perhaps in such courses they come to see how through history men have been motivated by religious convictions and how societies have achieved relative levels of meaningfulness in the context of religious systems. (Michaelsen, 1967:6)

If this analysis is accurate, then the increasing enrollments in religion courses should be interpreted not as indicating increasing interest in "religious problems" but as indicating a decreasing desire of other disciplines such as social sciences, history, and philosophy to speak to such problems in undergraduate courses. Whether this "retreat of other disciplines" explanation accounts for the entire rise in religion course enrollments remains doubtful; it seems that certain kinds of religious interest are increasing among students in recent years. A 1966 report argues that this is so.

> Not unlike the student rebellion, the revival of interest in the study of religion appears to have its roots in an intellectual search for direction and identity—not in sectarian or theological motives or in personal piety. The mood most generally reported is one of groping for answers, not of search for—much less acceptance of—dogma. (*The New York Times,* May 1, 1966)

In the present state of knowledge we may conclude that religious interest among undergraduates, as indicated by voluntary religion course enrollments, has either remained generally constant or has intensified since the middle 1950's. Unlike the indicators of orthodoxy, church commitment, or traditional religious behavior reported in Chapter 2, it has *not* declined since that time. We may also conclude that trends in enrollment in specific types of religion courses resemble trends in theological emphases in the last decade or two, as outlined in Chapter 5.

APPLICATIONS TO THEOLOGICAL SEMINARIES

Trends in applications to seminaries may be a useful indicator of certain types of commitment to traditional religion. Insofar as the applicants are intent on preparation for a professional ministry, the trends could serve as an indicator of commitment to the organized churches. Insofar as the applicants desire theological training for personal or academic reasons, the trends could serve as an indicator of broader or more personal religious interest. Data on applications are unfortunately impossible to find except for scattered reports and counts in several seminaries. The researcher must be content with reports on *enrollments*, realizing that institutional and financial factors also affect enrollments and render enrollment trends less reliable as an indicator of students' values and interests than application trends. Inferences from the data must be very carefully made.

For Protestant seminaries enrollment data are available after 1920.[42] A 1923 study found an enrollment of about 10,750 in 161 seminaries in the United States and Canada; a roughly comparable 1930 study found an enrollment of about 10,000 in 224 seminaries; and a 1955 study found an enrollment of approximately 25,000 in 178 seminaries (Niebuhr *et al.*, 1957:10). The variation in number of seminaries studied resulted not only from the founding and closing of schools but also from difficulties in the definition of a "seminary" for inclusion in the analysis.

A series of reports from the United States Office of Education gave figures for both Protestant and Roman Catholic seminaries but not seminaries affiliated with secular universities. They reported 8,216 students in 109 seminaries in 1920, 13,074 students in 164 seminaries in 1930, and 28,760 students in 114 seminaries in 1954. Finally, Niebuhr and his associates selected thirty-two seminaries representative of all the Protestant institutions and checked their enrollments in 1935, 1940, 1945, 1950, and 1955. They found growth of 151 percent over those twenty years, with 89 percent growth from 1935 to 1950 and 62 percent growth (based on the 1935 figure) in the 1950–55 period.

In summary, Protestant seminary enrollments in 1955 were about two and a half times as high as in 1935 and in 1925. Growth in enrollment was much faster during the late 1940's and early 1950's than during the 1920's and 1930's. A more detailed picture of trends is available in one denomination, The United Presbyterian Church in the United States of America. The enrollment in its schools increased

32 percent from 1920 to 1930, then decreased 19 percent to 1940; from 1940 to 1950 it increased again by 14 percent, and from 1950 to 1954 it increased by 31 percent (Niebuhr *et al.*, 1957:12).

The strong interest in the ministry during the early 1950's is shown in a 1950 report.

One of the larger universities (in the Ivy League) has a preministerial club with 150 members—which is at least ten times the number usual before the Second World War though enrollment in the undergraduate college is less than twice as large. A denominational college in West Virginia has 60 preministerial students—again, ten times as many as ten years ago. An engineering college in Pennsylvania has approximately 30 men who expect to shift to the ministry, though the traditions of the school have been antithetical to any such purpose for decades and the college chapel went unused from 1920 to 1945. Other comparable situations could be cited, but no comprehensive study is available.

Reasons for an enlarged interest in the ministry are doubtless numerous and varied. Probably the war caused many men to think more seriously about what they would do with their lives. Certainly the postwar period has led many students to conclude, oversimply, that the world struggle is between Christianity and communism, and has nudged them toward the side of the angels. Other causes are more specific, such as the improved caliber of campus religious leadership and the vigorous programs staged on many campuses by the Federal Council's commission on the ministry and by denominational counterparts of it. Not to be overlooked is the fact that certain other professions, such as engineering, are becoming seriously overcrowded. (Liston Pope, in *The Christian Century*, April 26, 1950:520)

The trend figures should be seen in the perspective of rising population, church membership, and education levels during the period. Whereas the enrollment in Protestant theological seminaries rose by about 150 percent from 1923 to 1955, the total enrollment in graduate education in the United States in the same period rose by over 800 percent; whereas the enrollments in the thirty-two representative Protestant seminaries rose 151 percent from 1935 to 1955, the total enrollment in graduate education in the same period rose about 216 percent, and the total population of the United States rose 30 percent.

Beginning in 1956 the American Association of Theological Schools calculated an index of enrollment each year, based on the enrollments in thirty representative Protestant seminaries. The 1956 level had an index score of 100. Until 1960 the index of enrollments was quite steady, and then it dropped to a low of 92.8 in 1964. It rose slowly thereafter, reaching 97.9 in 1967 and 103.6 in 1968. During the same twelve years the total enrollment of graduate students rose 200 percent in the United States, the number of total members of Christian churches rose about 21 percent, and the total population rose 19 percent.

The overall trends in Protestant seminary enrollments, seen in proportion to overall population trends, indicate mild gains during the 1920's and 1930's, then rapid gains between World War II and the middle 1950's. Thereafter the seminary enrollments fell slightly and then gained again, resulting in little change in total enrollments from 1956 to 1968. In a time of population growth this constituted a loss in percentage of the total population. Interest in theological education seemed to decline during the 1960's. The sustained interest of college students in religion courses did not carry over to the more vocational and traditional commitments of theological seminaries.

Data for Roman Catholic seminaries are taken from *The Official Catholic Directory*. Table 6.1 gives the enrollment figures, broken down by diocesan students and members of religious orders. The trends show rather steady increases from 1945 to 1962, when the members of religious orders began leveling off. Then in 1965 and 1966 the number of diocesan seminarians leveled off. In the last several years the number of seminarians in all categories declined sharply. The cause for the dramatic turning point in the figures is doubtlessly Vatican Council II and its ramifications throughout the Catholic community. In Chapter 5 we discussed several experts' speculations about the causes and ramifications.

CHANGE AMONG STUDENTS
AND CHANGE IN THE TOTAL SOCIETY

It is helpful to compare the attitude changes we found among students with changes in the total American society. Several replications done by nationwide polls enable us to make the comparison. In Chapter 4 we said that changes in students' religion do not appear to be the same as changes in their parents' religion, based on the students' reports. The trend data in nationwide polls confirm the conclusion that changes among students are not the same as in the total population.

At six different times the American Institute of Public Opinion (Gallup organization) asked about belief in immortality. The results are in Table 6.2. There is little overall change from 1944 to 1968, but

TABLE 6.1

Number of Seminarians Enrolled from
the American Catholic Church, 1945 to 1972

	Total Seminarians	Diocesan Students in Diocesan Seminaries	Diocesan Students in Other Seminaries	Members of Religious Orders
1945	21,523	7,433	3,610	10,480
1948	23,701	7,549	3,432	12,720
1949	26,215	7,877	3,845	14,493
1950	25,622	8,200	4,264	13,158
1952	32,692	9,230	6,204	17,258
1955	34,055	10,020	6,627	17,408
1957	36,468	11,340	7,052	18,076
1958	36,980	11,569	7,519	17,892
1959	38,105	12,169	7,433	18,503
1960	39,896	12,763	7,515	19,618
1961	41,871	13,834	7,486	20,551
1962	46,189	15,242	8,420	22,592
1963	47,574	16,356	8,891	22,327
1964	48,750	17,061	9,640	22,049
1965	48,992	17,464	9,268	22,230
1966	48,046	17,747	8,505	21,862
1967	45,379	15,859	8,434	21,086
1968	39,838	14,718	7,514	17,604
1969	33,990	12,772	6,801	14,417
1970	28,819	11,356	5,961	11,589
1971	25,710	9,672	5,315	10,723
1972	22,963	8,759	4,795	9,409

Source: *The Official Catholic Directory*, published by P. J. Kenedy & Sons, 1945 to 1972 issues.

belief in immortality seems stronger since the 1930's than in 1936. There is also a possible weakening in belief from 1960 to 1968.

Each year the American Institute of Public Opinion asks a nationwide sample if they had attended church or religious services within the past week. The trends in responses are shown in Figure 6.1 and Table 6.3.

It appears that the high point of church attendance was sometime in the middle or late 1950's. The increase from about 1940 to the middle 1950's appears to be about 9 or 11 percentage points, and the decrease from the middle 1950's to 1971 is 9 percentage points. It is possible to locate the particular group in American society accounting for most of the recent decline in church attendance. By comparing the breakdowns of the data in 1955 and 1970 we see the changes in each category. See Table 6.4.

Table 6.4 shows that the decline in church attendance was greater among Catholics than among Protestants and Jews. And more important, most of the decline occurred among young people. The trends in the total population are not as sharp as among the college

TABLE 6.2

"Do you believe there is, or is not, a life after death?"
(Nationwide samples; in percentages)

	1936	1944	1948	1957	1960	1968
Yes	64	76	68	74	74	73
No	36	13	13	13	14	19
No opinion	*	11	19	13	12	8
	100	100	100	100	100	100

* The response "no opinion" was not offered.
Source: Erskine (1965:147); *The New York Times,* Dec. 26, 1968.

students in our research, but the trends among affluent young people in the total population resemble the trends we found among college students.

The most illuminating replication study among the nationwide polls was the 1965 *Catholic Digest* survey, replicating a 1952 survey. Breakdowns of changes on five items are shown in Table 6.5. Since the number of undecided persons changed little, the table shows only the changes in percent reporting belief.

All five items showed slight declines in orthodox belief and behavior. The religious group declining the most was the Jews, and the group declining least was the Protestants.[43] The young people reported more drop in orthodoxy than any other age group. Those persons with college education declined in orthodoxy much more than others; the same is true of income groups—the upper-income group declined most, and the lower-income group remained virtually unchanged. Those in large cities declined most in orthodoxy attitudes and beliefs, but the rural persons dropped off most in church attendance and in estimated importance of religion in life. The 25,000 to 100,000 city populations gained the most on all items. The regions declining most were New England, West South Central, and Pacific states. The Mountain states gained most. The men averaged 2 or 3 points more decline on all items than the women (not shown in Table 6.5).

Table 6.5 demonstrates again that the trends among college students resemble the trends among all well-educated young adults

FIGURE 6.1

Percentage of Adults Reporting Church Attendance
During Week Preceding Inteview

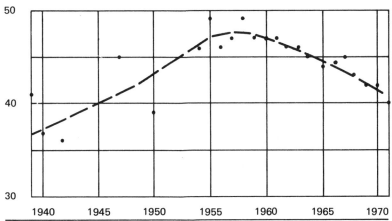

Source: Erskine (1965) and A.I.P.O. release, Jan. 7, 1972. Broken line fitted by hand.

from upper-income families. Indeed, most of the college students in our research represent this group. The present finding supports our conclusion in Chapter 2 that the trends found among students are not just the product of college experience but exist more generally among middle-class youth.

Tables 6.4 and 6.5 suggest either that (*a*) the causes of religious change should be sought in factors especially affecting the young, the college educated, and the higher-income groups, or (*b*) that the factors inducing religious change touch all groups equally but that the young, the college educated, and the higher-income groups are in some way freer to respond or quicker to respond than others. On hypothesis (*a*) the factors might be closer communications with American intellectual culture or closer communications with other religious and ethnic groups in the population. On hypothesis (*b*) the freedom to respond might be due to greater personal and family resources, greater security, greater mobility, or greater flexibility in behavior and commitments. For college students both hypotheses are probably true.

Tables 6.4 and 6.5 also have something to say about the future. If the cohort model of attitude formation has any substance, one may

TABLE 6.3

Percentage of Adults Reporting Church Attendance
During Week Preceding Interview in A.I.P.O. Polls

Year	Percentage	Year	Percentage
1939	41	1961	47
1940	37	1962	46
1942	36	1963	46
1947	45	1964	45
1950	39	1965	44
1954	46	1966	44
1955	49	1967	45
1956	46	1968	43
1957	47	1969	42
1958	49	1970	42
1959	47	1971	40
1960	47		

predict that young persons of today will "carry with them" through their adult lives the attitudes they formed during their twenties. The young people today are departing from traditional religious beliefs and commitments and will very likely remain about the same in the future. Also the college educated and the high-income groups, which have departed more than others from traditional beliefs and commitments, are likely to grow as a percentage of the total American population in the future. The effect of higher income is, however, not so clear if the standard of living of the entire society rises.

An item replicated several times by the Gallup polls asks, "At the present time, do you think religion as a whole is increasing its influence on American life, or losing its influence?" In 1957, 14 percent said "losing," and the figure rose steadily to 75 percent in

TABLE 6.4

Percentage Change in Adults Reporting Church Attendance
During Week Preceding Interview, A.I.P.O. Polls, 1955 and 1970

National Average	−7	College Graduates	−7
		High School	−8
Protestant	−4	Grade School	−6
Catholic	−14		
Jewish	−8	21–29 Years	−15
		30–49 Years	−7
Women	−8	50 or Over	0
Men	−5		
		Cities over 500,000	−10*
East	−9	50,000 to 499,999	−9*
South	−7	2,500 to 50,000	−5*
Midwest	−2	Under 2,500 or Rural	−2*
West	−5		

* Because of lack of 1955 data these comparisons are from 1958 to 1970.

1970 (A.I.P.O. release, March 5, 1970). When age, sex, and educational levels are studied separately no important divergences are found. It is interesting that the Catholics perceived less loss in religion's influence than the Protestants in each poll until 1969 and 1970, when the Catholics and Protestants converged in their estimates.

Two survey items in the 1930's are similar enough to the above item to permit some comparison of findings. In 1937 a *Fortune* poll asked, "Do you think religion is gaining or losing its influence in the life of the nation?" and 50 percent said "losing." Twenty-five percent said "gaining," and 25 percent had no opinion. In 1939 an A.I.P.O. poll asked, "Do you think the influence of religion in this community has increased or decreased during the last few years?" Thirty-two percent said "losing," 39 percent said "gaining," and 29 percent had no opinion (Erskine, 1965:150). In all these polls we see the same rise-and-fall pattern in attitudes toward religion noted several times above. At least the poll respondents *perceived* gains in the church's influence in the late 1930's and losses in that influence during the 1960's.[44]

In 1942, 1948, and 1957 the Roper polls asked respondents to rate the good done for America by each of several groups of institutional leaders. The responses are in Table 6.6. It is evident that public faith

TABLE 6.5

Percentage Change, 1952 to 1965, in Nationwide Polls

	Religion is very important in my life	Believe in God as a loving Father	Bible is revealed Word of God	Soul will live on after death	Church attendance twice a month or more
Total	−5	−6	−4	−2	−2
Roman Catholic	−7	−5	−6	−2	+3
Protestant	−2	−5	0	−2	−1
Jewish	−17	−20	−28	−18	−15
Other and None	−7	−9	−11	−6	−3
18–24 years	−7	−13	−14	−2	−4
25–34	−10	−12	−9	−2	−5
35–44	+1	−3	−3	−4	+3
45–54	−3	−1	−2	−3	+1
55–64	−3	0	+1	−4	+3
65 and over	−6	−7	−3	−2	−1
0–8th grade education	+2	+2	+2	+2	−3
1–3 years high school	0	−2	0	−1	−6
High school graduate	−3	−5	−5	−6	+1
1–3 years college	−7	−11	−8	−1	+4
College graduate	−10	−16	−13	−6	−3
Upper income	−10	−13	−11	−4	+1
Middle income	−6	−8	−4	−5	−1
Lower income	+3	0	−1	0	−3
Over 1 million	−3	−7	−4	−5	0
100,000–1 million	−2	−3	−5	−4	+6
25,000–100,000	+6	+3	+4	+7	+3
10,000–25,000	−6	−7	−11	+4	−2
Under 10,000	0	−2	−1	0	−2
Rural, farm	−10	−1	+3	+2	−5
New England	−13	−18	−14	−11	−6
Middle Atlantic	−4	−5	−2	−3	−1
South Atlantic	−7	0	+2	−2	−4
East South Central	+2	−5	−2	+6	+6
West South Central	−14	−5	−9	−7	−14
East North Central	+3	−3	+2	+1	+3
West North Central	+1	−5	−5	+1	+5
Mountain	+5	+17	+6	+3	−6
Pacific	−3	−16	−10	−11	+3

Source: Marty, Rosenberg, and Greeley, 1968: 184, 212, 220, 228, 246.

in religious leaders rose from 1942 to 1957. Unfortunately this item has not been used since 1957.

Other indicators of religious trends in the total American population tend to support the conclusion that commitment to traditional religion increased after about 1940, peaked sometime during the 1950's, then decreased until the most recent data. The increase after about 1940 was noted by Argyle (1958:34) and Herberg (1960:Ch. 4). Sunday school enrollment surged after 1940 but leveled off after about

TABLE 6.6

"Which one of these groups do you feel is doing the MOST good for the country at the present time?"

(Nationwide sample; in percentages)

	1942	1948	1957
Religious leaders	18	34	46
Government leaders	28	11	17
Business leaders	19	20	12
Congress	6	4	8
Labor leaders	6	12	4
No opinion	24	19	13
	101	100	100

Source: *The Public Pulse,* Elmo Roper and Associates, Dec. 21, 1957.

1955; in some denominations it declined after 1960. The value of new church construction rose sharply after World War II but tapered off in the middle 1960's. Demerath surveys these data and others, then cautiously concludes that American organized religion seemed to grow during the mid-1940's and mid-1950's but declined during the 1960's (cf. Demerath, 1968). Also during the middle twentieth century the relations between Protestants, Catholics, and Jews improved, and the Catholic subcommunity became increasingly assimilated into American middle-class society both economically and culturally.

The trends in the total population are less dramatic than among college students in the universities we studied. Whereas the students reported declines of about 13 to 23 percentage points in orthodox beliefs about God and immortality from the late 1940's to the late

1960's, the decline in the total population was not more than a few percentage points. Whereas the college students reported declines of 10 to 20 points in monthly church attendance from the late 1940's to the late 1960's, the total population declined no more than about 7 points in weekly attendance from the 1955 high point to 1970. We may also conclude that the trends among college students in our research are the same as broader trends among affluent young people.[45]

TABLE 6.7

"How great a danger do you feel that American Communists are
to this country at the present time—a very great danger,
a great danger, some danger, hardly any danger, or no danger?"
(Nationwide sample; in percentages)

	1954	1964
N =	4,933	1,975
A very great danger	19	17
A great danger	24	21
Some danger	38	39
Hardly any danger	9	12
No danger	2	7
Don't know	8	4
	100	100

Source: Stouffer (1955:76) and Survey Research Center, Berkeley, California, Nov. 1964 Survey.

From the area of religious attitudes let us turn to the areas of civil liberties and fear of Communism. Here again several nationwide poll replications provide an indication of attitude trends. In 1954 Stouffer asked about the danger of American Communists, and in 1964 the item was asked again. See Table 6.7. Those seeing a very great danger or a great danger decreased by about 5 percentage points.

In a recent thorough review of nationwide polls on freedom of speech, Erskine (1971) concludes that "acceptance of free speech for any kind of radical appears to be at a new low for the past three decades." The major increase in intolerance of radicals occurred in the late 1940's and early 1950's. Since then change has not been great one way or the other. The type of radicalism feared, however, has not been constant. Fear of Communists and Communist Party members fluctuated between 1940 and 1964. In 1940, 32 percent of a nationwide sample agreed that a Communist Party member should be allowed to speak on the radio. In 1943 the percentage agreeing that a Communist Party member could speak on the radio "in peacetime" was 48 percent. By 1953 the figure was down to 19 percent and in 1954 it hit a low of 14 percent. By 1964 it had risen again to 18 percent. Among the college-educated respondents, however, the liberalization after 1954 was faster. In 1954 only 20 percent of them would permit a member of the Communist Party to speak on the radio, but in 1957 the figure was 36 percent.

A similar item used in 1943 and 1954 asked, "In peacetime, do you think people in this country should be allowed to say anything they want to in a public speech?" Those saying yes fell from 63 percent in 1943 to 56 percent in 1954. Anxiety about Communists and other "un-American influences" rose during the period.[46] Hyman reports on a replication concerning freedom of the press:

> [W]e reported in 1954 that 45 per cent (of the adult population) would not allow Socialists to publish newspapers in peacetime, a rise from a figure of 25 per cent in 1943. In December 1956, 38 per cent still endorsed this policy and in April 1957, the figure was 39 per cent. (Hyman, 1963:286)

An item used frequently between 1939 and 1969 asked, "What do you think is the most important problem facing this country today?" Those saying "Internal Communism" ranged from 1 to 7 percent during the late 1940's. In 1954 they reached a peak of 14 percent. Since then they declined and never exceeded 3 percent after 1955.[47]

Several replications have been made using items about Russia and world Communism. One series of replications demonstrated increasing fear of international Communism as a military threat from 1946 to 1953.[48] An item used between 1955 and 1962 asked, "Would you say the United States or Russia is winning the 'propaganda war'—that is, doing the better job of winning the people around the world to its point of view?" Those saying "the United States" declined from 44 percent to 33 percent and those saying "Russia" increased from 23 percent to 40 percent during those years.[49] Between 1950 and 1969 the Gallup poll asked, "Do you think Communist China should or should not be admitted as a member of the United Nations?" Those saying "should not" were 79 percent in 1954; the figure decreased thereafter to 54 percent in 1969.[50]

These data on civil liberties and fear of Communism are a bit diverse, but several summary statements may be ventured. Attitudes about domestic Communism and individual freedoms seemed to remain more stable than attitudes about Russia, China, or international Communism; the former seldom varied over 10 percentage points over a decade or more. Also in the nationwide polls no attitude changes on domestic Communism and subversion occurred comparable to the sizable changes found among college students. Nothing in the nationwide polls comes close to the 24–26 point decreases from 1952 to 1968–69 at Dartmouth and Michigan on "Steps should be taken right away to outlaw the Communist Party" or "It is unwise to give people with dangerous social and economic viewpoints a chance to be elected." In the analysis of religious attitudes we concluded that changes among college students were much greater than changes in the total population. We concluded the same with respect to civil liberties and fear of domestic Communism. In the analysis of religious attitudes we also concluded that the college students' changes resembled those of young affluent people in the total population. Again we agree with respect to civil liberties and fear of domestic Communism. On a question asking if Communist Party members should be allowed to speak on the radio, the total adult population liberalized only 3 percentage points from 1954 to 1957 while those with college education liberalized 16 points. And on Gallup polls asking about American internationalism or isolationism the movement toward isolationism among young persons in the late 1960's greatly exceeded that among the total adult population (Gallup Opinion Index 45, March, 1969).

AN APPROACH FOR ANALYZING RELIGIOUS CHANGE

Personal Investment Model

Our task in this research is not only to trace trends in traditional religious attitudes and values among students but also to interpret those trends in general models and if possible to suggest explanations for them.

In Chapter 2 we stated that the main causes for the trends in religious orthodoxy lie outside any one religious tradition or group, but certain experiences particular to a single religious group have independent effects for that group, such as the effects of Vatican Council II in the Catholic group. We also stated that the causes are neither local nor regional, for the trends are similar throughout the Eastern and Midwestern colleges.[51]

We first looked for explanations in demographic factors and shifts in college admission practices. In several colleges we found considerable shifts in admissions, most notably the shift toward greater numbers of urban Jewish-background students at Syracuse and Clark universities. We tried to eliminate the effects of these shifts as thoroughly as possible in the "adjusted responses." The effects were usually small. Only in the Syracuse, Denver, Clark, and Michigan studies were they sizable. But even in the adjusted responses the trends remained clear, and Figure 2.5, summarizing orthodoxy trends, is constructed entirely from adjusted responses. Shifts in college admission patterns do not account for the overall trends in orthodoxy. It is possible that we overlooked some crucial demographic variables when calculating adjusted responses and therefore were prevented from finding some important demographic explanations. This is improbable, since our numerous interviews with admissions officers and our review of other research turned up no such demographic hypotheses. The trends are *within* the population groups supplying the students to the colleges. This conclusion is supported by the similar attitude trends found among high school students by the Purdue Opinion Panel (Chapter 3) and among young persons by nationwide polls (Table 6.5).

Secondly, we looked for explanations in terms of changes in college experience. Such explanations also fail. Three of our samples were composed largely of freshmen and sophomores, and four more were composed of freshmen beginning their first semester of study. The findings in the studies of freshmen are not significantly different from the findings in the studies combining both lowerclassmen and upperclassmen. Furthermore, both our data on freshman-to-senior changes and the data in other research show no noteworthy trends in recent decades in freshman-to-senior changes in religious attitudes. The trends exist already in the attitudes brought to the colleges by the freshmen.

Thirdly, the trends cannot be explained by economic conditions. We investigated a series of economic indicators for the United States which are plausibly related to religious attitudes, such as GNP per capita, personal consumption per capita, gross product per man-hour, disposable personal income, rate of savings as percent of disposable income, cost of living, expenditures for recreation, and unemployment levels (Sametz, 1968; Lebergott, 1968; Moss, 1968; U.S. Bureau of the Census, 1969). Over five decades we found no relation between them and the trends in religious attitudes among students. Argyle made a similar analysis in an attempt to explain rates of religious participation in the United States and England, and he similarly found no relationships at all (Argyle, 1958:139). Trends in student political activism have also been unrelated to economic indicators (Sampson, 1967; Allen, 1967). It is possible that economic conditions over *long* time spans are closely related to religious systems and religious change. It is also possible that more detailed analysis of economic indicators of urban upper-middle-class families may provide some plausible explanation for religious attitude trends among students. However, economic explanations for the trends seem very improbable.

Fourthly, we tested three hypotheses specifically put forth to explain recent American religious change and have found all three to be unsupported. The third-generation hypothesis by Will Herberg has been unsupported by any data in repeated studies. The hypothesis that urbanization leads to "secularization" cannot be accepted as an explanation for the trends in orthodoxy we found; not only did we find no important relationships between types of hometown of the students and their religious attitudes, but the urbanization trends in the nation in recent years have no discernible resemblance to the rise-and-fall pattern of religious orthodoxy among college students. The hypothesis that rapid social change which affects persons' usual roles and sense of identity brings about greater religious orthodoxy and commitment must also be declined. Such an explanation was put forth for the religious revival in the 1950's, but due to the continuing rapid social change and the downturn in religious orthodoxy among students in the 1960's it is rendered implausible. The trends we found among students are more short-run in nature and require more short-run explanations.

A promising source of interpretation for the orthodoxy trends is in the interrelation of attitudes and commitments within the individual's meaning-commitment system. We have noted that several attitude trends from the 1930's to the 1960's have a rise-and-fall pattern resembling the rise and fall of religious orthodoxy. We have also noted that the rise in religious orthodoxy and commitment in the late 1940's and early 1950's may be partly interpreted in terms of a shift to privatistic values. In searching for other possible indicators of privatistic values we found that the birthrate in the United States has the same trends. Figures 6.2 and 6.3 and Table 6.8 show the birthrates for the total white U.S. population and for white women 15–44 years old and 20–24 years old. The curves are very similar in pattern, and

FIGURE 6.2

United States: Birthrate of Whites per 1,000

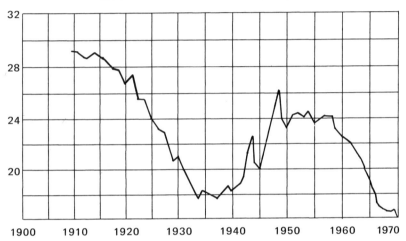

they closely resemble the trends for religious commitment among college students for as many years as we have data. This confirms the suggestions of both Herberg and Lenski that the birthrate is somehow related to changes in religious commitments. The rise in birthrate beginning about 1940 and continuing until the middle 1950's surprised demographers; this rise and then the sharp drop beginning in about 1957–59 were not predictable from economic factors. We would speculate that the birthrate is an indicator of commitments of young adults to family life as a source of life satisfactions. The rising birthrate, the rise of certain traditional religious commitments, and the lack of political activity were all components of the "privatism" of young adults of the upper socioeconomic groups during the 1950's.

The age-controlled birthrates show us that the main variation in birthrates is among the 20–24 age group. Its birthrate increased over 100 percent from the late 1930's to the late 1950's, while the birthrate for the 15–44 age group rose only about 50 percent. This seems to coincide with our finding that young persons vary more in their commitments than older adults. In both religious commitments and birthrates the young furnish most of the variation over time.

Several studies have inquired about the relation of fertility to religious preference. In 1956 the Princeton Fertility Study found that

FIGURE 6.3

United States: Birthrate of White Women, 15-44
Years Old and 20-24 Years Old, per 1,000

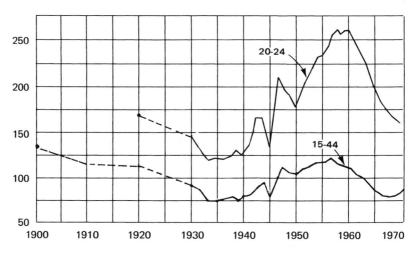

Catholics desired larger families than Protestants, and Protestants larger families than Jews. Religious preference was the "strongest of all major social characteristics in its influence on fertility" (Westoff *et al.*, 1961:180). Also a 1955 study found that the Catholic population had contributed disproportionately to the high birthrate in the United States since World War II (Kiser *et al.*, 1968:234). After the middle 1950's the fertility differences between Catholics and Protestants widened, as the Protestants declined but the Catholics did not. In the middle 1960's there began to be evidence of a decline in Catholic fertility so that the gap between Catholics and Protestants was narrowing again (cf. Demerath, 1968:420).

TABLE 6.8

United States: Birthrate of Whites per 1,000;
Birthrate of White Women 15–44 Years Old per 1,000;
Birthrate of White Women 20–24 Years Old per 1,000

Year	Whites*	WHITE WOMEN 15–44	20–24**	Year	Whites*	WHITE WOMEN 15–44	20–24**
1900		130		1939	18.0	74.8	125
1909	29.2			1940	18.6	77.1	131
1910	29.2	117		1941	19.5	80.7	143
1911	29.1			1942	21.5	89.5	165
1912	29.0			1943	22.1	92.3	164
1913	28.8			1944	20.5	86.3	152
1914	29.3			1945	19.7	83.4	138
1915	28.9			1946	23.6	100.4	184
1916	28.5			1947	26.1	111.8	211
1917	27.9			1948	24.0	104.3	198
1918	27.6			1949	23.6	103.6	195
1919	25.3			1950	23.0	102.3	190
1920	26.9	115.4	167	1951	23.9	107.4	207
1921	27.3			1952	24.1	109.8	213
1922	25.4			1953	24.0	110.6	220
1923	25.2			1954	24.2	113.1	231
1924	25.1			1955	23.8	113.8	235
1925	24.1			1956	24.0	115.6	251.3
1926	23.1			1957	24.0	117.4	257.6
1927	22.7			1958	23.3	114.8	255.1
1928	21.5			1959	23.1	113.9	257.5
1929	20.5			1960	22.7	113.2	258.1
1930	20.6	87.1	139	1961	22.2	112.2	—
1931	19.5	82.4	131	1962	21.4	107.5	243.7
1932	18.7	79.0	126	1963	20.7	103.7	231.2
1933	17.6	73.7	118	1964	20.0	99.9	219.9
1934	18.1	75.8	122	1965	18.3	91.4	196.8
1935	17.9	74.5	121	1966	17.4	86.4	185.9
1936	17.6	73.3	121	1967	16.8	83.1	174.0
1937	17.9 ·	74.4	124	1968	16.6	81.5	167.4
1938	18.4	76.5	128	1969	16.6	81.5	—
				1970	15.5	83.1	—

* Figures prior to 1935 are calculated estimates based on figures reported in the ten original registration states. Source: *U.S. Vital Statistics,* 1968.

** Available data for the 20–24 age group include all racial groups after 1955. The effect on overall trends is minimal. For example, the figure for all races in 1950 is 196.6, compared with 190 for whites; in 1955 it is 242.0, compared with 235 for the whites. Also the data through 1955 are for native women only. Sources: *Historical Statistics of the U.S., Colonial Times to 1957; Statistical Abstracts of the U.S., 1972.*

Studies of the relation of fertility to religious attitudes and behavior have found the strongest relationships among Catholics. There church attendance has been found to be directly associated with preferred family size. Also two other measures of traditional religious attitudes correlated between .2 and .3 with preferred family size among Catholics (Westoff *et al.*, 1961). Among Protestants the relationships are weak, but the more theologically conservative denominations have higher fertility than the liberal ones. It is not known to what extent socioeconomic factors can account for the difference (Kiser *et al.*, 1968:231). However, in 1958, Lenski found a positive association between church attendance and fertility in *each* religious subcommunity (Lenski, 1963:254). In short, available data show an association between traditional religious commitments and desire for a larger family.

Ever since about 1800 the fertility rate of Americans has been falling gradually and constantly. However, the rise during the late 1940's and early 1950's produced levels somewhat higher than the longer-range trend would predict.[52] The lower birthrates of the 1960's are closer to the overall trend line from 1800 to 1930 than were the higher rates of the 1950's. It would appear that the high rates in the 1950's represent more of a "special situation" than the lower rates of the 1960's. This fact may have implications for interpreting related social trends.

The above data suggest that short-range fluctuations in birthrate are related to the same factors producing religious attitude trends, especially in the Catholic community. Both in the Catholic community and elsewhere it seems reasonable to conclude that rising birthrates and rising religious orthodoxy were related elements in the shift to more privatistic commitments.

Joseph J. Spengler has put forth an analytic model for analysis of fertility trends based on values and costs (Spengler, 1966). He argues that fertility is one valid indicator of young adults' emphasis on family life as a source of satisfaction. He also agrees that the value commitments of young couples must be foremost in explaining the baby boom in the 1950's and the sharp decrease in fertility starting about 1957–59, since the prosperous economy during the 1960's would predict an increase, not a decrease in fertility.[53]

A model for interpreting religious change could begin on the level of the individual's meaning-commitment system. We would suggest a "personal investment model" based on the outlines of the meaning-commitment system given in Chapter 1 (also cf. Parsons, 1968). We have stated that the meaning-commitment system includes both cognitive and noncognitive elements. The term "commitment" includes both. The relation between the cognitive and noncognitive elements is a persistent problem reaching beyond our present capabilities for analysis, but we follow the judgment of M. Brewster Smith, Jerome S. Bruner, and Robert W. White (1956:Ch. 10) in stressing the importance and specific input of each. As to the relative overall importance of the two we would follow Daniel Katz (1967) in giving a bit more attention to the noncognitive.

Individuals "invest" personal commitments in certain institutions, ideologies, and leaders, and they expect some "returns" from the investments. A political leader delivering on none of his promises, a moral leader breaking faith, or a religious movement delivering no satisfactions soon loses the commitments of all followers. Except in a primitive society or rigid sectarian community, personal investments are plural and diverse. In American middle-class society this is clearly the situation. Individuals play multiple roles in multiple institutions and structures. For most middle-class Americans commitment to traditional religion is one component in a pluralistic system of commitments. Other important commitments may be to family, children, career, community participation, or political participation. We have seen in Chapter 4 that college men's dominant commitments tend to be to family and career. Since time, energy, money, and attention are limited, the total allocation of personal commitments resembles a fixed-sum system; as some commitments strengthen, others must weaken. The total commitments to social institutions and ideologies, however, need not be constant, for certain commitments may be withdrawn back into the self. Also the more conflict that exists in the total package of commitments, the less total energy will be available for them.

The analogy to a pluralistic financial investment portfolio is apt in several respects. The decisions about where to invest depend on both rational and nonrational factors, but ultimately they are based on faith. If any ego-investments fail to deliver the expected "return," the individual will withdraw from them. In Weber's terms this is "withdrawal of charisma."

Herberg has a kind of investment model in mind when he writes:

> The secular faiths of our culture have ignominiously collapsed under the
> shattering impact of the events of our time. Many of the "truths" by which
> "modern-minded" men lived in earlier decades have revealed themselves

to be little more than vain and fatuous illusions. We can no longer look to science, to "progress," to economics, or to politics for salvation; we recognize that these things have their value, but we also know that they are not gods bringing redemption from the confusions and perils of existence. (Herberg, 1960:63)

Adequate interpretation and explanation of religious change must work from the total meaning-commitment system of the individual. The reason is that investment in traditional religious doctrines or institutions may be affected indirectly by changes in other portions of the meaning-commitment system. For example, changing commitment to particular expressive styles, particular political programs, or particular community organizations, though apparently distinct from traditional religious doctrines and institutions, will affect the latter indirectly.

In our measurements of traditional religious attitudes we have found a fall-rise-fall pattern from the middle 1920's to the late 1960's. We have also seen similar patterns in other realms. Table 6.9 presents a schematic outline of seven variables and indicators appearing to tap elements of individuals' meaning-commitment systems. The seven are related to each other in varying degrees. We have seen that traditional religious orthodoxy is associated with fear of Communism, with commitment to family life, with commitment to military duty and patriotic war, and with commitment to dominant social norms. The extent to which it is associated with other-direction is not clear; our direct measures show little association, but historical accounts and other research suggest an association at least indirectly. We have also seen that religious unorthodoxy is associated with political action toward radical social change.[54] In the Michigan study we found that it was associated with criticism of college education. Not all these associations are strong; the strongest are the associations between traditional religious orthodoxy and fear of Communism, and between traditional religious orthodoxy and commitment to traditional family life. Also the associations are strongest among Catholics and in the Midwestern universities.

Table 6.9 necessarily oversimplifies the data and may lead to several misunderstandings. It does not say that the early 1950's resembled the middle 1920's in every respect but only in the overall allocations of those commitments measured by the indicators. It does not imply that the future will take on this same pattern of change or this same back-and-forth movement. It does not imply that these seven areas are closely interconnected so that a change in one will force a change in others. Rather, as we have seen in the correlation matrices in Chapter 3, the correlations between them are mixed in strength and sometimes weak. The seven are components of a loose

TABLE 6.9

Changes in Indicators of Personal Commitments

	INDICATOR, SOURCE	Middle 1920's	Middle 1930's	Early 1950's	Late 1960's
Traditional religious commitment and orthodoxy	Student surveys, Purdue polls	high	low	high	low
Fear of Communism or subversion	Dartmouth, Michigan surveys; nationwide polls; Purdue polls; historical accounts	high	low	high	low
Conformity to college social norms; other-direction	Dartmouth, Michigan surveys; historical accounts	high	low	high	low
Commitment to family life	Age-specific birthrate	high	low	high	low
Commitment to military duty and patriotic war	Clark surveys	—	low	high	low
Political activism toward social change (obverse of privatism)	Dartmouth, Michigan surveys; historical accounts	low	high	low	high
Criticism of college education	Michigan surveys	—	high	low	high

cluster of values.[55] Finally, it does not imply that the events were cyclical or that social change among college students is somehow intrinsically cyclical. The apparent cyclical pattern is accidental, due to specific events and social forces that will not appear again in the same configurations. Nothing in the social psychological analysis of meaning-commitment systems suggests a cyclical movement.

Is it possible to summarize the changes schematized in Table 6.9 in simpler terms? It might be said that the middle 1920's and early 1950's were conservative periods and the middle 1930's and late 1960's were liberal periods. The concerns of college students in the middle 1920's and early 1950's were relatively personal and privatistic, while in the middle 1930's and late 1960's they were more social and political, oriented to achieving social change or national policy change.[56]

One implication is that traditional religious commitment tends to be associated with (*a*) conservatism in all attitude realms and (*b*) personal and privatistic commitments not oriented to social change. Can this conclusion stand in the face of great diversity in theological emphases from decade to decade? During the middle 1930's and late 1960's campus religion tended to be liberal and oriented to social change; during the early 1950's it was more orthodox and oriented to problems of individual meaning and fulfillment, barely noticing the larger society. Traditional religious commitments are diverse, and they change in emphasis over time. Yet the data show that in the most global terms they were strongest in periods of conservative, personal, and privatistic emphases. In terms of the personal invest-ment model: as the dominant commitments in the total meaning-commitment systems shift (in the terms used above, "as religious interests shift"), commitment to particular institutions will also shift; the churches have tended to gain when commitments shifted to personal and private spheres and to lose when they shifted to social criticism and action for social change.

The approach to religious change via the use of the personal investment model has several theoretical advantages. The approach facilitates analysis of religious change in the context of broader changes in personal commitments. It permits analysis of the total meaning-commitment system almost in terms of Tillich's "ultimate concern" or Herberg's "religion of the American Way of Life." It also facilitates the inclusion of both cognitive and noncognitive elements in religious attitudes and behavior. A full analysis must include unconscious as well as conscious commitments. Questionnaire re-search based solely on theological or political doctrines will tend to be too limited to the conscious level. An approach to the unconscious level might be available through observations or reports of actual behavior or through decisions in conflict situations. A more thorough analysis would employ available measures of the unconscious level, such as the Thematic Apperception Test (T.A.T.) or other projective tests.

Several approaches to commitment allocation analysis have been shown above in Chapter 3. Another example is seen in Table 6.10,

TABLE 6.10

"How much confidence do you have in these institutions?"
(Nationwide student poll in 1965; in percentages)

	Great Deal	Only Some	Hardly Any	Not Sure
Scientific community	76	20	2	2
Medical profession	73	22	5	—
Banks and financial institutions	66	29	3	2
U.S. Supreme Court	65	28	6	1
Higher education	64	32	4	—
Big corporations	52	40	7	1
Executive branch of Federal Government	49	42	9	—
The arts	46	43	5	6
Psychiatric field	44	44	7	5
Congress	39	52	8	1
The military	38	43	17	2
The United Nations	35	49	14	2
Organized religion	34	46	18	2
Civil rights movement	33	47	19	1
The Democratic Party	22	63	10	5
The press	20	57	21	2
Advertising	16	38	44	2
Organized labor	13	55	29	3
Television	13	46	39	2
The Republican Party	12	53	29	6

Source: *Newsweek,* March 22, 1965:45, from The Harris Survey.

reporting on a 1965 nationwide poll. All these studies work from (or could be adapted to) a fixed-sum structure, and all ask for a comparison of commitments to traditional religious values or institutions with commitments to other values or institutions. A more complete analysis would ask not just about "expected satisfactions" or "confidence" but would distinguish attitudes about morality, competence, and openness. It would use a variety of approaches to assess strength, stability, and specificity of commitments. Within the realm of traditional religion it would seek to distinguish the particular pattern of religious interests underlying the commitments.

Historical Events

The personal investment model helps interpret religious change in terms of broader changes in commitments, but it does not help in the explanation of those changes. The task of explanation remains.

It is important to remember that trends in church attendance and registration of religious preferences, as noted in Chapter 2, were not the same as trends in orthodoxy. The former have not only the fall-rise-fall pattern from the middle 1920's to the late 1960's but also a long-range decline. We interpreted the long-range decline as a product of greater individualism and autonomy among students.

The evidence shows long-range changes and short-range changes in college students' religion and values. The two are quite distinct. The long-range changes are less reliably documented in our research, but they are visible in other research and in historical accounts. They appear to include at least three elements. First is increased individual freedom and personal autonomy of students. College students have more freedoms and more personal responsibility today than decades ago. They are treated by society more as adults than they were formerly. Social and religious authorities see them as more capable of, and more responsible for, forming their own views and guiding their own behavior. Second is a change in moral orientations. The overall shift is from detailed moral codes to more generalized and flexible moral orientations regarding personal and social values. There is greater tolerance regarding details of moral codes. Third is the rise of a self-conscious youth culture. This has occurred mostly in the past two decades, but it can be included with long-range developments. The youth culture has included diverse emphases, some encouraging further movement in the direction of the first two elements mentioned above, others opposed to further movement. But in itself it has embodied an exercise of freedom from the dictates of traditional culture.

We have looked at several possible explanations for the long-range changes. First we looked at possible effects of changes in students' backgrounds. Changes in socioeconomic status, urbanization, region of upbringing, immigrant generation, or home religious influence were not persuasive for explaining the long-range changes. The total number of American college students increased more than tenfold from 1920 to 1970, but this increase is relevant for explaining long-range value changes only if students' backgrounds shifted in the process.

The only important changes in students' lives prior to college which appear useful for explaining the long-range value changes are the rise in scholastic aptitude and the earlier physical maturity. We found marked rises in the Scholastic Aptitude Test scores of incoming students over the years. All the colleges except one (Los Angeles City College) experienced rises in median scores between 60 and 156 points from the middle 1950's to the late 1960's. Trends before the 1950's are not measurable, but they were probably increases over time, not decreases. The improvements in scholastic aptitude over the decades probably account for some of the long-term changes in religion and values, for higher scores have proven to be correlated with the changes we found. Especially higher *verbal* scores are associated with more liberal values. Research also shows earlier physiological maturity among youth today. Since 1920 the average age of puberty (menarche) for American girls has fallen about one and a half to two years (cf. Tanner, 1962; *The New York Times*, Jan. 24, 1971:1). The trend for boys is similar, but it is more difficult to measure. Although definite proof is lacking, it is likely that accelerated physiological maturation brings accelerated cognitive development. Indeed, one can interpret many of the long-range trends we have found as aspects of acceleration of the life cycle.

One long-range change in all American culture seems to underlie the five-decade changes found among students, and that is the gradual extension of tolerance and appreciation in American society for ethnic and religious diversity. The old-line Protestant domination of American cultural life has given way to greater pluralism during the past half century.

Durkheim predicted that long-range religious change in the modern world would be in the direction of greater individualism, increased tolerance, more free thought, and de-emphasis of local groupings and local loyalties. This prediction seems to coincide with the overall changes found in the present study. We may add that trends toward greater individualism and free thought will bring more liberal religious beliefs and lower levels of participation in traditional churches. American higher education today usually upholds the values of individualism and religious relativity, thereby accelerating the trends Durkheim predicted.

Most of our attention in this study has been directed not to the long-range changes but to the short-term fall-rise-fall pattern in religious commitments described in Chapter 2. The explanations for the short-range changes must be different. Also the long-range changes cannot serve alone as explanations for the short-range. Fifty-year trends cannot explain distinctive five-year developments on campuses, but they are important as a contextual background for more immediate explanations. An example is the Roman Catholic Church in the 1960's. For several decades prior to Vatican Council II social pressures in America had been building up for change in the church, but they had been successfully bottled up by its leadership. Only after the Council was there an "uncorking" which was followed by a surge of many diverse changes in short order. An understanding of them must include the broad context of social change as well as the immediate effects of the Council.

For purposes of projecting into the future the long-range trends are much more reliable than shorter five-year or ten-year trends. However, they will appear useless or even wrong for understanding some immediate events and fluctuations among young people. In the overall, a gradual weakening of traditional religious participation appears a more "normal" accompaniment of modernization of American society than the dramatic changes in the 1940's, 1950's, and 1960's. Especially the rising religious commitment, participation, and orthodoxy in the 1940's and early 1950's should be seen as a discrete occurrence and not a normal trend. Hence we pay more particular theoretical attention to it than to the falling indicators in the late 1950's and 1960's. They are in some sense a "return to the normal trend." In the 1960's, as in any other period, the long-range trends and their explanations make no pretense of explaining the richness and color of all the new events. They merely add an element of context to a series of more appropriate immediate explanations.

In Chapters 4 and 5 we also discussed possible explanations for the short-range pattern of commitment changes we found. Our analysis of religious attitude changes found economic indicators to be of no help. Research into student political activism has come to the same conclusion. Attempts to explain the baby boom in America in the late 1940's and early 1950's have also found economic indicators to be of little help (Blake, 1967; 1968). Theorizing from wants to religious behavior is a difficult approach, and when the wants are seen in purely economic terms it is too precarious to be recommended. The kind of historical events and experiences having impact on religious commitments must be more closely related to the integration of important social groups or the maintenance of prevailing social ideologies.

It may be helpful to sketch the Durkheimian model of interrelation of elements in social change. Arrows indicate causation, and stronger arrows are relatively stronger causation:

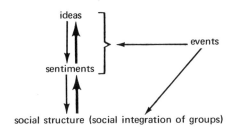

We have bracketed together "ideas" and "sentiments" for present purposes to indicate that both are included in the category "commitments." The two arrows from "events" may serve to depict two kinds of hypothesized linkages between historical events and personal commitments. First is the impact of events on the social integration of groups, a topic carefully studied by Durkheim:

> Great social disturbances and great popular wars rouse collective sentiments, stimulate partisan spirit and patriotism, political and national faith, alike, and concentrating activity toward a single end, at least temporarily cause a stronger integration of society. The salutary influence which we have just shown to exist is due not to the crisis but to the struggles it occasions. As they force men to close ranks and confront the common danger, the individual thinks less of himself and more of the common cause. (Durkheim, 1951:208)

For Durkheim the main type of social explanation of individual acts is in terms of changing social integration of groups important to the individual. Social integration is a factor closely related to investment of personal commitments. Indeed Durkheim sometimes tends to underplay individual variations in commitments beyond those determined by the integration of his social groups. Wars and similar national crises have the effect of strengthening social integration and social sentiments, thus depressing the suicide rate. The main factor is that the population feels a threat and becomes aroused. We have seen that the high point of traditional religious commitments was in the period 1952 to 1955, at the height of the cold war and the McCarthy era. Religious orthodoxy and commitment began rising about 1940 and continued rising to the high point in the early 1950's. It is plausible that a principal explanation for the trends has to do with World War II and the cold war. Insofar as American college students perceived a threat from European Fascism in the 1940's and Russian Communism in the early 1950's, social integration in those groups would increase. The particular social groups and organizations gaining most in integration should be those feeling most threatened. Stouffer, in his extensive 1954 study of anti-Communism, found that the aspect of Communism most distrusted by Americans was its opposition to traditional Judeo-Christian religion (Stouffer, 1955:166). Next most distrusted was its tendencies to political dictatorship, and third was its opposition to private enterprise and private property. This pattern of distrust suggests that anti-Communism during the early 1950's should be seen most of all in terms of a religious threat, second in terms of a political and economic threat. We would predict that traditional religious sentiments would strengthen most in this situation.

Durkheim also noted that in times of perceived threat or danger, social sentiments intensify and social symbols gain new sacredness. In times of perceived national crisis, nationalistic symbols and norms take on such sanctity that their violation is greeted with public outrage and repressiveness. "Men are always likely to be intolerant of opposition to their central ultimate values" (Robin Williams, quoted in Herberg, 1960:74). During the early 1950's we would also expect rising intolerance of deviance from "good" nationalistic and anti-Communistic behavior.

Data supporting the social integration explanation for rising traditional religious commitments during the 1940's and early 1950's have already been reviewed. We have seen that during the late 1940's fears of Communism strengthened and sentiments supporting civil liberties for deviant and suspect groups in society weakened. Historical accounts of the early 1950's all mention the heightened group-embeddedness of students, and from 1952 to 1969 we found a striking decline in other-direction and group-embeddedness. Social integration was intensified at the peak of the cold war fears and McCarthyism. Religious commitments, being associated with Americanism in many social groups, intensified as a result. The Durkheimian theory appears to be supported as one explanation of the impact of historical events.

From historical accounts we judged that another linkage between historical events and personal commitments was at least as important. We argued that dominant commitments shifted in the direction of *privatism*. The explanation for the shift is most commonly stated in terms of feelings of personal helplessness and meaninglessness amid the momentous international cold war forces and repressive domestic forces. Students were intimidated from speaking out on many controversial social, political, or religious issues and thus tended to shift commitments to the private spheres, which offered both more security and more personal meaning (cf. Herberg, 1960:61). The sociological explanation for the shift to privatism should probably include an analysis of differential social integration of various groups; it is not clear just how Durkheimian theory would handle the problem.

Secondly, we should look at the direct impact of events on personal commitments. A theory linking historical events with shifts in commitments was proposed by Max Weber in his discussion of "withdrawal of charisma" from institutions or leaders failing to deliver the expected satisfactions to their followers. The Weberian analysis emphasizes this problem under the rubric of "the problem of theodicy." Historical events may render the theodicy problem extremely acute and may cause major shifts in persons' commitments to particular creeds or institutions. The outcome of any crisis of theodicy depends partly on the actions of the social authorities and religious leaders. Weber's discussion of the theology of the Old Testament prophets amid a theodicy crisis demonstrates the importance of theological factors in a way not easily captured in Durkheimian thought. In short, historical events may impinge directly on strongly held sentiments and ideas, and their impact depends partially on the actions of institutional authorities and theologians. The outcome depends on a complex of factors including both intellectual orientations and mobilization of motivations of large numbers of people. The Weberian line of analysis requires a complex understanding of stresses in breakdowns in cultural, social, and personality systems, as was noted in Chapter 1. Its applicability for explaining the rising religious commitments in the 1940's and early 1950's is probably in terms of the challenge of the Depression, the failure of the

League of Nations, rising Fascism, and world war to certain religious and political ideologies stressing human social progress, internationalism, pacifism, and the goodness of human nature. The rise of neo-orthodox theology in the late 1930's and 1940's is possibly explainable in these terms.

CONCLUDING COMMENTS

Can one discern overall trends in college students' religious attitudes over five decades? We must be cautious. In the time span from 1914 to 1969 there is definite change away from religious orthodoxy, but in the time span 1914 to 1954 there is little change. What the change from 1914 to 1980 or 1990 will be seems rather unpredictable. None of the short-range trends we found are steady enough to serve as bases for projections into the future. Certainly the 1952 to 1969 trends should not be projected forward.

However, a more definite statement about long-range trends can probably be made, for two reasons. First, we have uncovered a long gradual decline in church attendance and have argued that it is a reflection of underlying modernization trends. Our guess is that this long-range gradual decline will continue, but it may be eclipsed by dramatic and more immediate changes of various sorts. Second, from the vantage point of theories of social change developed by Parsons and others, the early 1950's were more "abnormal" than the middle 1960's. Whereas the main axis of long-range development in social institutions is toward greater structural differentiation, the early 1950's were a time of de-differentiation. Whereas the main axis of development is toward more individual freedom and responsibility, the early 1950's were a time of reduced individualism. The McCarthyism phenomenon was the product of widespread withdrawal of commitments from the political system; lack of trust and "deflation" of commitments followed. These are regressive and abnormal tendencies. Therefore, to use the early 1950's as a measuring point for studying long-term trends is much more questionable than to use the middle 1960's. This is not to say that the conditions of the 1950's could not easily return; on the contrary, tendencies of backlash and malaise are always present, especially when there is widespread perception of threatening gaps between present institutions and deeply held value commitments. But from present social indications a return to the religious life of the 1950's seems somewhat unlikely. On this basis we can speak of overall liberalization of religious attitudes and reduction of traditional religious behavior over five decades.

In the near future we would predict lower church participation for two reasons. First, we have noted that young persons have tended recently to decline in church attendance and that research on attitude change suggests that they will "carry with them" this lower level of participation in the years ahead. Second, many campus ministers and observers describe a turning point in theological emphases since 1967–69, away from a theology of social involvement and toward immediate and personal concerns. The new emphasis is on the personal, the mystical, and the movement of the Spirit. Along with it there has appeared new religious interest in many places, which takes both Judeo-Christian and nontraditional forms. Survey data suggest that the Jesus movement, in spite of the attention given it, is not widespread, and in any event is not very much related to the organized church. The new religious interest is not likely to have much impact on overall church participation.

What sorts of events would be likely to cause a strengthening of traditional religious commitments such as occurred in the 1940's and early 1950's? That trend was a product of a general conservative movement in American life. More specifically it was probably a product of the perceived threat of atheistic Communism, the intimidation of liberal groups in society and on campus, calls for loyalty and solidarity of all Americans and all Christians, a widespread emotional reaction in many lower-middle-class groups to the threat of Communism and also to Eastern liberals, and the challenge to liberal ideologies resulting from the Depression, the rise of Fascism, and a world conflict. Which events and forces were most important is not known, but a recurrence of some of them would possibly produce another strengthening of traditional religious commitments among college students. It also depends on how theologians and church leaders respond to new configurations of religious interests and needs. In summary terms, any large-scale collapse of the political or cultural system or any other "breakdown of modernization" would probably produce new traditionalistic religious currents.

One main implication of this research is that social trends are to some extent interrelated, and certain social trends will predict others. The social changes usually desired by liberals today—greater individual freedom and autonomy, higher levels of education, greater participation in political and social movements, greater tolerance of political, cultural, and religious diversity, and reduced anti-Communism in American life, would tend to bring with them reduced religious orthodoxy and participation. We have shown the interrelation of these variables in Chapters 3 and 4. The present-day religious leader is faced with somewhat of a dilemma, in that some trends which he may welcome will, with certain levels of probability, bring with them other trends which he may not welcome. If he works toward greater individualism, greater political participation, and more tolerance of cultural and religious diversity in American life, he will probably also be working toward reduced participation in the traditional church. The intelligent discussion of religious change and church policy requires an understanding of the interrelation of these various social trends.

APPENDIXES

Appendix A

Description of the Studies
and Adjustment Procedures

Data in Chapters 2, 3, and 4 can be found in more detail in the original thesis, available in Harvard University Library: "College Students' Religion: A Study of Trends in Attitudes and Behavior," 1969. It is in three volumes, the first of which summarizes all the research and literature. The other two give details of the thirteen studies, including the questionnaires. Volume One can be obtained from University Microfilms in Ann Arbor, Michigan.

THE THIRTEEN STUDIES

Each of the replication studies was based on an older study selected from the literature on the basis of subject matter, quality, and reliability. The first three replicate 1946 and 1948 surveys of religious attitudes.

First is a twenty-year replication of Allport's 1946 study of Harvard and Radcliffe students (Allport *et al.,* 1948). The original study and the replication study were done in large social science courses. The original had five hundred respondents (hereafter: "N") and a response rate of 95 percent; the replication had an N of 449 and a response rate of 82 percent.

The second study used the Allport questionnaire at Williams College. In 1948, Philip K. Hastings made a study at Williams identical to that at Harvard, and in 1967 we repeated it. The survey group was a random sample of undergraduates; in 1948, N was 205 for a 96 percent return rate, and in 1967, N was 206 for a 93 percent return rate.

The third study used the Allport questionnaire at Los Angeles City College. In 1948 a study was made there identical to Allport's study, and in 1967 we replicated it. The N was 452 in 1948 and 477 in 1967. Los Angeles City College is unlike all others in our research. It is an "open door" college with no admission requirements besides a high school diploma or the age of eighteen and an ability to learn.

The fourth study was a 1968 replication of a 1948 study done at the University of Denver by Daniel G. Brown and Warner L. Lowe (1951). The 1948 sample was gathered in a series of classrooms; N was 887. In 1968 we worked with Thomas E. Drabek in a replication. We secured 488 completed questionnaires with a return rate close to 100 percent.

The fifth study was different in structure. At Haverford College all entering freshmen are required to take the Minnesota Multiphasic Personality Inventory (MMPI) and the Allport-Vernon Study of Values. With Dr. Douglas H. Heath we coded extensive data on samples of entering freshmen between 1944 and 1966. The total N was 855.

The sixth study replicated portions of five older studies of attitudes at Dartmouth College. In 1940 and 1956, Dr. Irving E. Bender studied samples of Dartmouth seniors using the Allport-Vernon Study of Values (Bender, 1958), and in 1968 we repeated the procedure. In addition, we replicated three earlier studies of random samples of Dartmouth undergraduates. The most important of these was the Cornell Values Study, a survey done in eleven universities in 1952 (Goldsen *et al.,* 1960). The second study was done in 1958, 1959, 1960, and 1961 (Sokol and Sykes, 1963). The third was a study of the Class of 1965 as freshmen and as seniors (MacNaughton, 1966). We received 368 questionnaires for a response rate of 89 percent.

The seventh study was done at Clark University. Between 1930 and 1935 Dr. Vernon Jones studied two undergraduate classes using three Thurstone scales on religious attitudes. Later he repeated the research six times between 1938 and 1960. We collaborated on a replication study of entering freshmen in 1967, receiving 369 questionnaires for a 91 percent return rate. At Clark University we have measures on freshmen at eight points in time.

The eighth study also used Thurstone scales. At Northwestern University, A. R. Gilliland administered Thurstone scales on religious attitudes to psychology classes in 1933, 1937, 1943, 1944, 1946, 1948, and 1949. In 1967 we worked with Dr. Carl P. Duncan in replicating the Gilliland studies, receiving 179 questionnaires with a return rate of nearly 100 percent.

The ninth study was done at Ripon College in Wisconsin. In 1929 and 1949 George J. Dudycha administered a short questionnaire on religious beliefs to entering freshmen (Dudycha, 1930; 1950). With Dr. Leonard Vaughan and Dean of Men David L. Harris we replicated the study in 1968, receiving 318 questionnaires for a response rate of 98 percent.

The tenth study was done at the University of Wisconsin, replicating a 1930 study by William H. Sheldon in which he administered a "Wisconsin Scale of Radicalism and Conservatism" to over three thousand students in psychology classes. In 1968 we arranged a replication and received 781 completed questionnaires, about 94 percent of all students surveyed.

The eleventh study replicated a 1926 study of all Syracuse undergraduates done by Daniel Katz and Floyd H. Allport (1933). It was one of the first high-quality surveys of college students' attitudes done in the nation. The total N was 4248 or about 99 percent of all students enrolled. In 1932 a partial replication was done by Dorothy Loeb. In 1967 and 1968 we worked with Dr. Maurice Troyer and George Dolch in setting up a replication study. We planned a survey in April, 1968, but due to mishaps data collection was delayed until October, 1968, when we gathered 359 completed questionnaires for a 91 percent return rate.

The twelfth study replicated several early studies by James H. Leuba (1916; 1934). In about 1906 he asked undergraduates in nine colleges to respond to questions about belief in God and immortality. We attempted a replication by including the same items in our Harvard-Radcliffe, Williams, Northwestern, Clark, and Bryn Mawr studies. The replication is not very reliable. Also in 1914 and 1933 Leuba surveyed all undergraduates at Bryn Mawr College. In spring, 1968, we replicated them at Bryn Mawr, gathering 230 responses for a 93 percent return rate.

The thirteenth study replicated three earlier surveys at the University of Michigan. First is a 1924 survey by John S. Diekhoff and Neil Staebler on religious attitudes and practices (Diekhoff and Staebler, 1925). Second is a series of surveys between 1938 and 1942 on religious attitudes and church attendance (Lane Hall:1938–1942). Third is the 1952 Cornell Values Study. In 1969 in the replication we received 400 questionnaires for an 89 percent return rate in a sample of undergraduate men. Also at Michigan we gathered the results of a series of religious censuses between 1896 and 1969.

ADJUSTMENTS

The purpose of calculating adjusted responses is to assess the generalizability of the findings in any one college. Attitude changes in any one college may be the product of shifting recruitment patterns peculiar to that college. If the shifts in recruitment may be statistically controlled, we can see the amount of change generalizable to broader groups of young people.

To calculate adjusted responses we weighted the replication data so that the distribution of background characteristics of the original sample would be reinstated. First we scrutinized all available background variables to see if they were related strongly enough to the target attitude items to be worth adjusting. Then we determined the background of the original sample group in terms of the important background variables. Whenever these data were not available for the original sample we made estimates based on data for the entire undergraduate student body or the entire freshman class. Several times we coded data from the college archives, and in one or two cases we had to rely on reports in old student newspapers or yearbooks and on interviews with persons knowledgeable about changes in the student body.

Thirdly, we calculated actual changes and "independent changes" in all

TABLE A.1

Calculation of Adjusted Score for Church Attendance,
University of Michigan, 1952 to 1969

Change*		DISTRIBUTION			CHANGE CAUSED		
		Weekly	Monthly	Less	Weekly	Monthly	Less
Religious Background							
Protestant	−12	.11	.32	.58	−1.3	−3.7	−7.0
Catholic	+10	.44	.19	.37	+4.4	+1.9	+3.7
Jewish	+1	.02	.02	.96	0	0	+1.0
Other, Mixed, No	+1	.13	.26	.60	+.1	+.3	+.6
Geographic Origin							
Detroit S.M.S.A.	+9	.22	.25	.53	+2.0	+2.3	+4.8
Other Michigan	−5	.17	.26	.57	−.9	−1.3	−2.9
N.E. states	−8	.03	.22	.75	−.2	−1.8	−6.0
Other	+4	.14	.20	.66	+.6	+.8	+2.6
Major Course							
Nat. science	+3	.17	.21	.62	+.5	+.6	+1.9
Soc. science	+12	.08	.23	.69	+1.0	+2.8	+8.2
Humanities	+1	.18	.23	.60	+.2	+.2	+.6
Engineering	−4	.27	.23	.50	−1.1	−.9	−2.0
Other	−12	.15	.35	.50	−1.8	−4.2	−6.0
S.A.T. Verbal Score							
Under 500	−42	.18	.21	.61	−7.5	−8.7	−25.8
500–600	0						
Over 600	+42	.12	.25	.63	+5.0	+10.5	+26.5
Total Change Caused					+1.0	−1.2	+.2

* Independent change. The change in S.A.T. verbal scores is approximate. Major course is considered a background variable here because it may reflect a change in the recruitment and enrollment practices of the University of Michigan.

background variables. The need for the "independent changes" arises because the background variables are not independent of each other. For example, at Syracuse University there was a shift in the student body, so that fewer came from upstate New York and more came from the New York City metropolitan area. In addition, there was a shift away from students of Protestant background to those of Jewish background. These two shifts are related, and after one variable is employed in the adjustment calculations only the "independent" portion of the second may be employed. In statistical terms, the covariance between the two variables must be eliminated. This was done with a procedure similar to that described below.

The adjustment calculation for an item on church attendance at the University of Michigan is shown in Table A.1. The responses to the item were divided into three parts—weekly or oftener, monthly or semimonthly, and less than monthly. The "total change caused" is subtracted from the actual change from 1952 to 1969 to get the adjusted change.

Appendix B

Responses to Twenty Attitude Items at the University of Wisconsin, 1930 and 1968

The Wisconsin study is one of our most revealing comparisons of student values over a long time period. During the academic years 1928–29, 1929–30, 1930–31 Professor William H. Sheldon administered a "Wisconsin Scale of Radicalism and Conservatism" to many of his psychology classes, and a friend in the sociology department administered it to some of his classes. Most questionnaires were completed in 1929–30. A total of 3,010 responses were received, about one sixth from sociology classes and five sixths from psychology classes, mostly introductory psychology. Of the respondents 50.5 percent were men and 49.5 percent were women.

In the fall of 1967 we pretested the Wisconsin questionnaire on Harvard and Radcliffe students and made several minor alterations in it to modify phrases and eliminate assumptions seen to be obsolete. In January and March, 1968, the questionnaires were administered to two sections of introductory psychology, one sociology class, and one social psychology class, with a total of 781 responses.

The 1930 questionnaire had twenty items, each with seven responses (Sheldon, 1942:491–498). The first five provided a range of attitude responses on the topic, and the sixth and seventh said "Insufficient familiarity with the problem" and "A different attitude, as follows." In 1930 an average of 3.05 percent of the stu ents chose responses 6 or 7 on any item, and in 1968 it was 4.67 percent.

Table B.1 shows the responses in percentages. The sexes are weighted so that the ratio remains exactly as that in 1930. Responses 6 and 7 were removed before percentaging.

Since the Sheldon questionnaire was constructed with maximally equal intervals between responses, mean scores may be calculated for each item. The responses were scored from 1 to 5. We also calculated adjusted scores on the means, eliminating the effect of changes in religious preference, family

TABLE B.1

Responses to Twenty Attitude Items,
University of Wisconsin, 1930 and 1968*
(*In percentages*)

	1930	1968
N =	2920	743

Item A: Limitation of Profit

Markets should be free, and profits should be unrestricted.	16	4
A few restrictions are necessary to prevent monopoly.	26	37
Some question about the whole principle.	39	25
Laissez-faire is probably unsound.	14	24
Uncontrolled profiting is one of the worst evils.	5	9

Item B: Wealth Distribution

Traditional capitalism provides for the best possible distribution of wealth.	11	8
The present distribution is probably a wise one.	28	32
Some question about the whole system.	31	25
The system is fundamentally unsound; wealth is not used well.	20	26
The system is altogether unsound and needs radical revision.	11	10

Item C: Inheritance of Wealth

Inheritance of great wealth is sound, natural, and needed for incentives.	22	34
Possibly inheritance should be restricted somewhat.	38	52
Transmission of large fortunes may be fundamentally unsound.	31	6
Inheritance is in need of revision and large inheritance stopped.	7	5
No individual should ever inherit great private wealth.	2	2

Item D: Economics of Fashion Change

Rapid style change is desirable since it increases volume of trade.	7	23
Certain extreme fashions are unduly wasteful.	19	44
Some question about exploiting fashion to stimulate trade.	35	17
Style changing is an abuse, it wastes resources and income.	31	15
The style-changing racket is vicious and insidious.	8	2

Item E: Advertising

Advertising is most beneficial; it raises living standards.	16	3
Advertising is beneficial but overdone today.	26	50
Some question about permitting uncurbed advertising.	29	30
Advertising does more harm than good; it is wasteful.	17	4
Advertising is a menace to humans; it creates false values and desires.	12	13

Item F: American Democracy

American democracy provides the wisest social control possible.	4	3
American democracy is satisfactory but has weaknesses.	31	61

* The response categories are abbreviated here.

TABLE B.1 (continued)

	1930	1968
N =	2920	743

Some question about the wisdom and efficacy of American government.	53	22
American democracy is unsound, failing to bring the best minds to power.	10	12
Democracy in America is a bad failure; too much mediocrity; uncivilized.	2	2

Item G: Patriotism

Every child should be taught strong patriotism; we cannot have too much.	2	8
Perhaps the present emphasis upon patriotism is enough.	25	57
Some question about the wisdom of patriotic emphasis in education.	30	16
Patriotism is a cause of war and should be de-emphasized.	30	13
All patriotism is vicious and criminal; no more worship of soldiers and flags.	13	7

Item H: Observance of Law

Breaking a law is never excusable and must be punished as criminal.	10	3
In some extreme cases breaking a law can be justified.	25	42
Some doubt about the wisdom of too strong respect for law.	24	15
It is good to break some laws deliberately to get rid of bad laws.	27	21
A man is duty-bound to break unfair and useless laws.	14	19

Item I: Free Speech

Public expressions hostile to government or morality must be prohibited.	4	2
On the whole, control subversive opinion but allow some debate.	16	10
Some doubt about the wisdom of trying to curb free speech.	32	6
Should be free expression except in wartime, in matters of decency, etc.	38	53
Should be absolute freedom to express publicly any opinion.	10	30

Item J: Socialism

Socialism is a wild impossible dream, not worthy of serious thought.	18	3
Socialism is interesting but probably out of the question.	20	28
Possibility that socialism may be worth serious consideration.	19	35
The most practicable form of government will prove to be socialism.	31	32
Socialism is the one practical answer; we should turn to it now.	13	2

Item K: Monogamy vs. Other Sexual Norms

Strict monogamy is the only natural and respectable form of human life.	34	25

TABLE B.1 (continued)

	1930	1968
N =	2920	743
Certain circumstances justify some temporary deviation from monogamy.	25	42
Some question about the psychological soundness of strict monogamy.	26	18
Serious doubt as to the wisdom of strict monogamy.	11	9
Monogamy is contrary to nature and has caused a great share of human misery.	4	5

Item L: Birth Control

	1930	1968
Man has no business meddling with birth control and should not interfere.	20	1
Maybe some population control will be justified, but let the matter alone.	28	2
Possibly a birth control program is worth considering.	18	4
Probably birth control is an important problem to be faced now.	16	23
We urgently need wide application of birth control and more research.	18	70

Item M: Special Value of the Family

	1930	1968
The family is the sacred and permanent unit of society; must be inviolate.	19	43
The family is subject to modification and perhaps should change.	24	48
Some question as to the soundness of the family idea.	31	4
Probably the family restrains human personality and should be changed.	23	4
The family inhibits and frustrates human happiness; must be replaced.	2	1

Item N: Premarital Sex for Women

	1930	1968
No young woman should ever experiment; absolute virginity.	27	7
Discourage experimentation, but some wisdom and experience is good.	26	20
Possibly limited experimentation may be wise for women.	18	21
Some wisdom and experience in sexual matters before marriage is good.	16	40
Rich sexual experience is very important for women entering marriage.	13	11

Item O: Elasticity of Sexual Morality

	1930	1968
Sexual morality is fixed and unchanging; applies to all men.	9	3
On the whole it is unchanging, but may vary somewhat.	20	13
Sexual morality is more elastic than in the above statements.	34	21
Sexual norms are changing rapidly; the moral code needs revision.	21	21
There is no fixed right and wrong; it depends on persons and situations.	16	43

TABLE B.1 (continued)

	1930	1968
N =	2920	743

Item P: The Church (Organized Religion)

The church is the one sure and infallible foundation of life.	4	3
Stands for the best in human life, but it has shortcomings.	25	55
Possibly it may do a good deal of harm; some doubt.	40	20
The total influence of the church may be on the whole harmful.	15	12
Stronghold of much that is unwholesome and dangerous; intolerant.	15	10

Item Q: Reality of Divine Inspiration

Divine inspiration is the one real and infallible source of truth.	6	17
Probably real, but not the most important source of truth.	33	23
The reality of divine inspiration is open to question.	34	25
Probably there is no such thing as divine inspiration.	20	23
It is a delusion, either wish fulfillment or a lie.	7	12

Item R: The Supernatural Idea

Religion should be primarily man's relation to the supernatural.	14	3
Religion should be concerned with supernatural and also human affairs.	35	29
Some question if religion is primarily supernatural or natural.	21	17
The supernatural should play only a minor part in religion.	21	36
Useful religion deals entirely with natural human functions.	10	14

Item S: Individual Immortality

We are individual immortal beings; otherwise life is meaningless.	16	20
We are probably immortal, but this is not vital to human purposiveness.	18	24
Possibly the idea is not necessary to purposiveness or happiness.	25	20
The idea is unnecessary to a good religious orientation.	29	25
The idea is unnecessary and preposterous, confusing young minds.	12	11

Item T: The Idea of God

God is personal and conscious of human affairs.	35	33
Maybe the idea of God is not necessary; maybe God is not conscious.	27	27
Perhaps the idea of God is not essential to human orientation.	13	13
We need not postulate God to build a positive human orientation.	12	24
The assumption of God is misleading, dangerous, and confusing.	13	3

TABLE B.2

Actual and Adjusted Means and Differences, Both Sexes

	1930	1968 Actual	Actual Difference	Adjusted Difference
A: Limitation of Profit	2.66	2.97	+.31	+.28
B: Wealth Distribution	2.93	2.97	+.04	−.02
C: Inheritance of Wealth	2.30	1.89	−.41	−.38
D: Econ. of Fashion Change	3.14	2.28	−.86	−.85
E: Advertising	2.82	2.74	−.08	−.09
F: American Democracy	2.73	2.49	−.24	−.29
G: Patriotism	3.25	2.53	−.72	−.83
H: Observance of Law	3.10	3.11	+.01	−.11
I: Free Speech	3.34	4.00	+.66	+.60
J: Socialism	3.01	3.03	+.02	−.03
K: Monogamy	2.25	2.26	+.01	−.07
L: Birth Control	2.85	4.59	+1.74	+1.74
M: Value of the Family	2.64	1.70	−.94	−.97
N: Premarital Sex for Women	2.63	3.28	+.65	+.54
O: Sexual Morality	3.16	3.88	+.72	+.60
P: The Church	3.11	2.71	−.40	−.49
Q: Divine Inspiration	2.91	2.92	+.01	−.13
R: The Supernatural Idea	2.79	3.29	+.50	+.43
S: Individual Immortality	3.01	2.85	−.16	−.28
T: The Idea of God	2.41	2.36	−.05	−.20

socioeconomic status, and major course distribution since 1930. The actual differences and adjusted differences are shown in Table B.2.

On five items (E, J, K, L, and M) the variance in 1968 is much smaller than in 1930. On these items the 1968 students tended to choose a moderate response, suggesting that the debate raging in 1930 on these topics is largely dead in 1968. In general, the alienation of Wisconsin students from the basic institutions of American society seems greater in 1930 than in 1968.

NOTES

1. See Stark and Glock (1968:199 ff.) for recent data strongly supporting this model of denominational dynamics in the United States. Also see Demerath (1968:358–359) for a review of church membership statistics from 1900 to 1954 showing that the conservative religious groups grew fastest and the liberal groups grew most slowly during that period.

2. Liston Pope (1942: Ch. 7) proposes a more elaborate model of sect-to-church development differing somewhat from the Niebuhr model. Also see Wilson (1959) for a discussion of types of sects and their development.

3. For more detailed outlines of these theoretical approaches to religious change, cf. Hoge (1969: Ch. 1).

4. For more theological and ecclesiastical aspects of religious change in the twentieth century, see H. Schneider (1963) and Gilkey (1967).

5. Questions are often raised about the "normalcy" of the college years compared to later life. Are college students still the same five or ten years later? Isn't college just a time for letting off steam before entering the "real world"? Feldman and Newcomb (1969: Ch. 10) reviewed the most important studies bearing on these questions. They assessed the impact of historical events on attitudes of all age groups, the impact of growing older quite apart from influences of historical events, and the impact of the peculiar college experiences of any single age cohort. Though the research evidence is not entirely consistent, the bulk of research shows that values are quite constant and stable from college years to later life. In a study of men and women students in Connecticut, E. Lowell Kelly (1955) found a moderately high degree of stability in values in the age-span between the twenties and the forties. Among Vassar alumnae Freedman found that in attitudes and values "the differences noted at the time of testing reflect differences which were present at the time of leaving college" (Freedman, 1962:858). And in a study

of graduates of eighteen colleges, Nelson found that "religious attitudes held in college tend to persist for at least 14 years" (Nelson, 1956:15). Feldman and Newcomb conclude that available data "provide rather consistent support for a general theory about the persistence of students' attitudes, more or less as they were on leaving college" (Feldman and Newcomb, 1969:323).

6. Besides studies which we replicated, the most important trend studies of college students' religion in the literature are five in number. First, John J. Cavanaugh reviewed a series of fifteen religious surveys carried out at the University of Notre Dame between 1921 and 1936 (Cavanaugh, 1939). Second and third, at Ohio State University two different studies provide very long-range data on value trends. One is a series of surveys of high school and college students' moral disapprovals, worries, and interests carried out in 1923, 1933, 1943, and 1953 (Pressey and Jones, 1955). The other is a 1958 replication of three earlier surveys of students done in 1929, 1939, and 1949 (but at two different universities). The questionnaire included fifty moral prohibitions to be ranked according to their seriousness (Rettig and Pasamanick, 1959). Fourth, each year since 1942 the Purdue University Opinion Panel has carried out several large surveys of high school students throughout the nation. By 1970 eighty reports were published, and several of them include replications of ten, twenty, or more years. Fifth, at the University of Texas, Robert K. Young and his co-workers completed three surveys of undergraduates' attitudes toward traditional religion depicting changes between 1955 and 1964 (Young, Dustin, and Holtzman, 1966).

7. Daniel Katz (1967) attempts to specify in detail the types and situations of behavior wherein the rational or the irrational views of man are most apt. A discriminating analysis of this problem is very much needed.

8. For the data supporting all summary statements in this chapter, cf. Hoge (1969: Ch. 4).

9. Stark and Glock draw a very similar conclusion from their survey of church members (1968: Ch. 11).

10. Adjusted scores remove the effect of changes in religious background, sex, socioeconomic status, veteran status, and major course. Since these changes were rather large, the actual and the adjusted responses at Ripon are quite far apart.

11. In the 1924 Michigan survey an item asked, "Do you sympathize with the 'modernists' or the 'fundamentalists'?" Of the students 30 percent called themselves modernists, 8 percent called themselves fundamentalists, 31 percent said they weren't concerned, and 31 percent said they didn't know or left the item blank. Interest in the modernist-fundamentalist controversy was low. Another item asked if the respondent believed in evolution. Sixty-five percent said they believed in evolution before coming to college, 22 percent more had accepted the theory since coming to college, and 13 percent still didn't believe in evolution. Among the Catholics 56 percent didn't believe in evolution; in contrast the figure was 4 percent among the Presbyterians and Congregationalists and 6 percent among the Jews.

12. The colleges are Amherst, Bucknell, University of Chicago, Cornell, Dartmouth, Grinnell, University of Illinois, University of Kansas, Massachusetts Agricultural College, University of Michigan, Middlebury, Mount Holyoke, Ohio Wesleyan, University of Pennsylvania, Princeton, Randolph-Macon, Rockford, Smith, Swarthmore, Wabash, Wellesley, University of Wisconsin, and Yale.

13. More accurately, the continuum is a U-shape in which the sense of conflict is the vertical dimension and the attitude toward science, ranging from extreme rejection to extreme acceptance, is the horizontal dimension. For a related U-shape in attitude theory, cf. Guttman and Suchman (1967). This interpretation of the science-religion conflict is strongly supported by the research of Espy on college teachers. He found that "in the conscious thought of the teacher, the issue of science and religion, or of other educational disciplines and religion, has, on the whole, been resolved, though there are exceptions in the cases of the more religiously conservative faculty members and of certain others at the opposite pole" (Espy, 1951:68). Also, like the students in our research, the college teachers with less orthodox views of God tended disproportionately to see conflict between science and religion (Espy, 1951:59; cf. Lehman and Shriver, 1968).

14. Several studies have asked students why they changed religious attitudes during college, and in each case the conflict between science and religion was the main reason given. However, questionnaire items asking a respondent *why* he made certain decisions or changed in certain ways are not reliable sources of scientific explanation. Psychoanalysis has taught us how little an individual understands his own motives, and Durkheim stresses that persons' own explanations of their behavior are not helpful sociological data (Durkheim, 1951:148). Nevertheless the responses show the conscious importance for college students of the conflict between science and religion. In 1927, Alma Pearle Stack asked Northwestern students what factors had influenced their religious thinking, and the main factors given were psychology, English, and natural science courses. A study at Beloit College in the early 1950's asking students to write on "Why I Hesitate to Be a Christian" found that the main reason given was the opposition of modern science to Christian religion (Walsh, 1953). A *Harvard Crimson* study in 1956 asked those students who did not affirm the existence of God why they did not; the most checked response was "the fact that contemporary science does not appear to require the concept of God to account satisfactorily for natural phenomena" (Levy *et al.*, 1959).

15. The replication study in 1969 also yielded data on participation in religious organizations on campus. In April, 1941, an item asked how many students ever had attended guilds or religious groups, and 22 percent of both sexes said they had. The 1969 questionnaire asked, "Have you participated in, or are you now participating in, the following groups or activities?" Among the groups listed was "Student religious groups." Eight percent of the

men reported participation. We may conclude that participation in student religious groups was lower in 1969 than in 1941. It should be noted that student religious groups have changed drastically in recent years, so that the term "participate in a student religious group" has a less clear denotation in 1969. Many campus ministers have no "group" as such but participate and cooperate in various social, action, and study programs on campus. This change in style may account for another finding. In December, 1938, an item asked, "This semester to what extent did you go to religious lectures and discussions?" Of the men 29 percent said they had gone at least "occasionally," and 71 percent said they had never gone. In 1969 an item asked, "In the last three months have you gone to any religious lectures or discussions?" Of the nonveteran men 25 percent said yes. Attendance at religious lectures and discussions seems about as frequent in 1969 as in 1938, suggesting that the level of interest is somewhat the same.

16. For further survey data on church attendance in the 1920's and 1930's, cf. Edwards, Artman, and Fisher (1929:242) and Hartshorne (1939:284).

17. In every study prior to 1966 asking both items we lacked the original data cards and thus could not calculate the index. However, in the Harvard-Radcliffe, Williams, and Los Angeles City College studies of 1946–48 we had the frequencies for both items, and this allowed calculation of an estimate. We used the ratio of index scores to "net preferences" from the 1966–67 studies to estimate the index scores in 1946–48. The net preferences are simply the ratios of those preferring any tradition to those reared in that tradition; such a ratio cannot discriminate between students switching *from* a tradition and those switching *to* the tradition.

18. Detailed data for this chapter may be found in Hoge (1969: Ch. 5; 1970; 1971).

19. Changes on this item since 1952 at Dartmouth do not totally coincide with changes in the Allport-Vernon scores since 1956. As a life satisfaction, political participation has risen markedly, but the Political score in the Allport-Vernon test has fallen. The most likely explanation is found in the particular focus of the Allport-Vernon Political score. It measures emphasis on developing *one's own* political power, influence, and prestige. In the case of a second inconsistency, that of the falling Allport-Vernon Religious score and the slightly rising choice of "religious beliefs and activities," the explanation is not clear.

20. A March, 1939, nationwide poll of students in fifty-six colleges asked, "If you had to make a choice, which would you prefer, Fascism or Communism?" Fifty-six percent responded, "Communism" (Belden, 1940).

21. The relation of traditional religion to dominant social values is clearly seen in an item stating, "If I found the person I was engaged to had had previous sex relations, I would break the engagement." In 1952, 7 percent at Dartmouth and 9 percent at Michigan agreed; in 1968–69 it was 3 percent at Dartmouth and 5 percent at Michigan. Of all the items on social, political, or

moral issues in the questionnaire this item had the strongest correlation with orthodoxy and traditional religious commitment.

22. In the Clark University studies in 1948–49, 1954–56, and 1967, freshman men and women were asked, "What do you think are the most important things which college can do for you?" The questionnaire listed eight responses to be ranked. Among Clark freshmen intellectual emphases increased from the late 1940's to 1967, and this is probably related to the improved scholastic standards of Clark students over that time. Emphasis on getting along with people and on good family and friendship life diminished. Clark students, like Michigan students, were more "academic" in the late 1960's than in the 1940's or 1950's. We could not adjust these data to assess the impact of rising scholastic standards among the freshmen recruited to Clark University.

23. This item was used in the 1962–1965 freshman-to-senior study at Dartmouth (MacNaughton, 1966). The major change from 1952 seemed to occur before 1962, not after. Also the major change was found among the freshmen upon arrival, for the seniors in 1952 and 1968 were much more alike than the freshmen. The main determinants of the drop in other-direction were brought to college from the wider society.

24. In the 1952 eleven-university data, Goldsen *et al.* (1960:190–195) demonstrated that traditional religious beliefs and commitment were mildly associated with intolerance of cognitive ambiguity. The indicator for intolerance of ambiguity was the item "How important is it for you to have your plans for the future known in advance?" At Dartmouth and Michigan from 1952 to 1968–69 the importance of knowing future plans declined. At Dartmouth in 1952, 78 percent said "very important" or "fairly important"; in 1968 the figure was 67 percent. At Michigan in 1952 the figure was 82 percent, and in 1969 it was 73 percent. It is plausible that the decline in traditional religious attitudes and the decline in intolerance of ambiguity are related, and the association between the two shown in 1952 supports the hypothesis. However, in 1968–69 at Dartmouth and Michigan strong associations between this item and the traditional religious indices failed to appear. They appeared in mild strength in only the Catholic and Jewish groups.

25. A second opportunity to test this hypothesis was provided by the Clark and Denver questionnaires. In both questionnaires we included three items on "concerns." One asked about concern about "the questions religion seeks to answer, such as questions of the meaning of life and death, evil, and destiny." The other two asked about concern about "questions of international relations and politics" and "questions of state and national politics." In neither Clark nor Denver did noteworthy correlations occur between religious concerns and either of the political concerns. Also at Clark the items on political concerns were unrelated to the three Thurstone scales on traditional religion. For the second time the hypothesis found no support.

26. All value changes are given in adjusted scores. For details, see Appendix B.

27. This item illustrates a general observation about the Wisconsin and Syracuse studies in 1930 and 1926. In both questionnaires was a theme emphasizing the elite status of college graduates in comparison with the rest of society. In this item on democracy the theme was manifest in the response proposing the objection that American democracy puts "a penalty on the more highly civilized personality." Such an attitude of college elitism is largely absent today. Likewise the importance of any person's social standing on campus in terms of fraternities, parties, and invitations is much diminished.

28. In 1930 a questionnaire answered by 75 seniors at Columbia University dealt with sex norms, marriage, and religion. Apparently these were hotly debated issues on campus at that time. The results show a strong tendency among the seniors to overthrow traditional moral codes regarding sex and marriage. A strong majority favored extramarital relations and said they would not require virtue in the woman they intended to marry. About half answered affirmatively to "Does religion have any appeal for you as part of a personal philosophy?" (*The New York Times*, Feb. 12, 1930:16.)

Also a 1934 survey of students in nine Eastern colleges showed a prevalence of liberal economic attitudes. Eighty-three percent favored a "much more equal distribution of wealth" than exists in America, while only 11 percent opposed it and 6 percent were neutral. Also 86 percent opposed dismissal of teachers who severely criticized the government. A majority believed that "workers must organize for the class struggle," that "violent strikes are sometimes justifiable," and that "hunger marches are justified." Only 13 percent favored Communism and revolution, while 50 percent believed that Communism would fail because of man's love for power. Thirty-seven percent agreed that "medicine and dentistry should be entirely state controlled." Twenty-two percent agreed that "unjust laws should be obeyed." (*The New York Times*, Dec. 10, 1934:23.)

29. A dramatic demonstration of the new claims of college students for their own individual autonomy and power is seen in changed attitudes toward lowering the voting age. In a nationwide survey in the spring of 1940, students in 56 colleges were asked, "Are you for or against lowering the voting age from 21 to 18?" Eleven percent were for, 89 percent were against (Belden, 1940). In a nationwide Gallup poll of students conducted in November, 1969, an item asked, "Do you think that persons 18, 19, and 20 years old should be permitted to vote, or not?" Seventy-six percent said yes, 23 percent said no, and one percent had no opinion (Gallup Opinion Index 55:25).

30. This conclusion is supported in our Clark University study. We asked about the importance of religious factors in ethical rules of conduct and about the relative importance of personal ethics and social ethics in those rules. There was a mild tendency for those stressing religious factors in their rules of

conduct to focus on the individual life rather than the society. Those without religious affiliation and those with liberal religious attitudes stressed social ethics a bit more than personal ethics.

31. For the data supporting summary statements in this chapter, cf. Hoge (1969: Ch. 6).

32. This coincides with the findings of Bernard Lazerwitz in a study of Jewish identification in the Chicago area. His study relied on differences in generation since immigration, not on measures of change over time, yet the similarity in findings is striking. He found that in the first generation (those who immigrated at the age of five or older) women were lower on an overall index of Jewish identity than men. Then from the first to the third generation the Jewish identity of the men weakened much more than of the women. By the third U.S. generation the index scores of the women were on average higher than the men (Lazerwitz, 1970). Age and socioeconomic status were not controlled in the Lazerwitz study, but probably they would not account for the sex differences. The pattern must probably be explained in terms of adaptation to American society.

33. At Wisconsin we used "religious preference" as a basis for establishing the groups. This is not properly a background variable, so the variance accounted for came out greater—38 percent for the men and 43 percent for the women on the Religion Index. Religious background groups, accurately identified, would account for much less of the variance than this. The statistic calculated to determine variance accounted for was Hays's estimated omega-squared (Hays, 1963:382).

34. Lazerwitz has done extensive work in testing the third-generation hypothesis (1969; 1970). He summarized his evaluation of it in personal correspondence: "Basically, I find that among Jews there is no dropping away and then a return. Instead, there is a downward decline in identity characteristics which is considerably more precipitous for men than for women. My opinion about the three-generation hypothesis is that it should be abandoned."

35. We compared public school and private school graduates in six colleges and found no differences in religious attitudes or behavior. The percentage of students who had attended parochial schools was very small.

36. Studies of student political activists tend to find a similar pattern. The bulk of activists are social science and humanities majors. Natural science majors are seldom activists. Also the activists tend to be religiously liberal or even antitraditional religion. These data categorize natural science majors as conservatives, not liberals or radicals, contrary to Feldman and Newcomb (cf. Lipset, 1971).

37. These conclusions have apparently been true since the 1920's. A 1927 poll assessed the orthodoxy of students in a large number of colleges, and each college was given an orthodoxy score based on percentages of students indicating certain beliefs. The average score for all the colleges was 87.

Dartmouth College had the lowest score for men's colleges with 52, and Wellesley had the lowest for women's colleges with 71. The highest orthodoxy scores were mostly in the South, where many colleges had nearly 100. The responses of college students were compared with responses on a newspaper reader poll, and the overall orthodoxy scores of the two groups were similar (*Literary Digest*, 1927).

38. This section is based largely on magazine articles and *The New York Times* for the period 1900–1955. In addition, it benefited from the analyses in Lipset (1966; 1971), Lipset and Altbach (1966), Altbach and Peterson (1971), Flacks (1967), F. Allen (1931), D. Allen (1967), Draper (1967), Rudolph (1962), and Lee (1970).

39. Our interviews with Catholic theologians and campus ministers supported the Durkheimian hypotheses that new technology facilitating communication across traditional group boundaries will tend to bring about religious change and that religious commitments in any ethnic group will weaken if the group assimilates into larger social groupings in the environment. In the interviews there was constant mention of the recent "opening up" of the urban Catholic subcommunities from their closed community life to a sense of participation in the total American culture. It was noted that many more Catholics recently have been attending secular colleges, that many more are in white-collar occupations, that Catholics tend increasingly to feel much in common with their urban Protestant neighbors, and that they now participate in main-line American culture via the new technology of mass media. Religious change in the Catholic community seems to be a good example of the effects of increased communications transcending traditional social barriers.

40. Future measurements of religious trends among students should distinguish several dimensions apparently fruitful for explanations of changes—individual versus social theological emphasis, optimism versus pessimism about the nation and the world, strength of motivation for social and political involvement, levels of commitment to dominant social institutions, intensity of interest in particular religious problems, and commitment to nontraditional religious forms. These dimensions should be added to the commonly studied measures of orthodoxy, church participation, and so on.

41. Data for the analysis of course enrollments were partly derived from Braden (1948), McLean and Kimber (1960), McLean (1967), Michaelsen (1965; 1967), and Welch (1971). Further data were gathered through correspondence, for which we would like to thank Paul Ramsey, David H. Smith, Robert Michaelsen, William A. Spurrier, D. B. Robertson, H. Ganse Little, and Fred Berthold, Jr.

42. Data on seminary applications and enrollments are mostly from H. R. Niebuhr *et al.* (1957), *The Official Catholic Directory*, reports from the American Association of Theological Schools, and articles in *The Christian Century*.

43. Table 6.5 has an interesting difference from our previous findings in that it shows less change among Catholics than among Protestants and Jews. This pattern was found in no other research. Also the table suggests that change among all Jewish adults from 1952 to 1965 exceeded that among Jewish college students. The pattern is difficult to understand.

44. The possible influence of World War II on religious interest in the American population is seen in a survey item asked by the Gallup organization in November, 1941, and in May, 1942: "Have you noticed an increase in interest in religion in this community since the war began?" In November, 1941, 31 percent said yes, 57 percent said no, and 12 percent didn't know. In May, 1942, the item asked, "Do you think interest in religion has increased in your community since the war began?" Forty-seven percent said yes, 31 percent said no, and 22 percent didn't know (Erskine, 1965:152). Probably the active entry of the United States into the war increased interest in religion.

45. It is possible that the religious trends among college students "anticipate" trends in the total population so that they represent a kind of "early turner" in a stock-market sense. This is not only true in the sense that young people inevitably grow older and their attitudes inevitably permeate the adult population after a while. It is plausible that college students are more sensitive to social and cultural changes and reflect them more quickly in their attitudes and behavior. It is plausible that because of the relative freedom of college students from social commitments and social structural constraints, they are freer to shift attitudes and commitments. The sole evidence for the "early turner" hypothesis is the earlier peak in religious orthodoxy and behavior among students than among adults (as measured by adults' church attendance). However, it has been put forth for many years. The Dean of the College at Princeton proposed it in 1932: "As undergraduates are almost invariably young, as they are still malleable, quicker and more generous in their responses to life than their elders, certain changes in the world about them, changes in what we used to call the Zeitgeist, are more pronounced on the campus and show themselves sooner than in communities of older men." (*The New York Times*, June 5, 1932.)

46. The association between anti-Communism and defense of American organized religion was quite strong in the general public in the 1950's. Probably it remains so today, but a lack of recent polls prevents our knowing. Stouffer found that in 1954 the aspect of Communism most feared by Americans was its anti-religious and ideological aspects opposing Christianity and American democracy (Stouffer, 1955:160–161). Stouffer asked, "If an American opposed churches and religion, would this alone make you think he was a Communist?" Sixteen percent said yes. The association between critics of American life and suspected Communists was even stronger. In 1953 a poll asked, "A teacher who tells his students that there are many things wrong in America—would you yourself be very suspicious that he was a Communist, or

just a little suspicious, or wouldn't you suspect him at all just because of that?" Thirty-four percent said "very suspicious." Among college-educated respondents the figure was 31 percent (N.O.R.C. poll on May 15, 1953).

47. The data are found in the *Public Opinion Quarterly*, Vol. 4, No. 1 (March 1940), p. 94; Vol. 11, No. 4 (Winter 1947–48), p. 657; Vol. 12, No. 3 (Fall 1948), pp. 557–578; Vol. 14, No. 1 (Spring 1950), p. 182; Vol. 14, No. 3 (Fall 1950), p. 603; American Institute of Public Opinion releases, April 9, 1954; Jan. 5, 1955; *Gallup Political Index*, No. 5 (October 1965), p. 4; *Gallup Political Index*, No. 7 (December 1965), p. 5.

48. An item asked, "As you hear and read about Russia these days, do you believe Russia is trying to build herself up to be the ruling power of the world or is Russia just building up protection against being attacked in another war?" Those saying "ruling power" increased from 58 percent in 1946 to 79 percent in 1953. The data are in the *Public Opinion Quarterly*, Vols. 10 to 15. See Vol. 15:1 (Spring 1951), p. 179. Also see American Institute of Public Opinion release, August 21, 1953.

49. The data are in American Institute of Public Opinion releases of May 16, 1958; July 27, 1960; Feb. 3, 1961; and Jan. 31, 1962.

50. The data are in *Public Opinion Quarterly*, Vol. 14, No. 4 (Winter 1950–51), p. 817; American Institute of Public Opinion releases, Sept. 23, 1951; July 5, 1953; Sept. 11, 1953; July 25, 1954; Aug. 8, 1954; June 4, 1955; Sept. 26, 1955; Feb. 23, 1958; Sept. 26, 1958; March 24, 1961; Oct. 6, 1961; Nov. 27, 1964; *Gallup Political Index*, No. 8 (January 1966), p. 15; No. 11 (April 1966), p. 11; No. 17 (October 1966), p. 16; No. 45 (March 1969), p. 18.

51. This summary section does not take into account the divergent findings at Los Angeles City College. Because of the great difference between Los Angeles City College and the other institutions in our research, not only geographically but in terms of admission policies, scholastic standards, and backgrounds of the students, it seemed wise for present purposes to simplify the analysis by ignoring Los Angeles City College.

52. For a graph showing the fertility rate in the United States from 1800 to 1960, see Heer (1968:51). The decline is quite constant from about 1830 to 1920, then it declines more rapidly until about 1937–39 and takes an upturn, peaking in the late 1950's.

53. As a further investigation into the relationship between traditional religious commitment and family we looked into trends in marriage rates, divorce rates, and age at marriage. These three indicators failed to relate to religious trends in any discernible way.

54. For data on the association between low traditional religious commitment and high political activism, see Lipset (1966), Flacks (1967:65), Marx (1967:98 ff.), Eckhardt (1970), and Glock and Stark (1965: Ch. 10).

55. An eighth commitment area is associated with these seven—anti-Semitism. One might interpret it as a specific instance of a more general ethnocentrism, suspicion of minorities, or lack of commitment to civil

liberties, but a close study of trends in nationwide polls studying anti-Semitism over the last four decades found a departure from our more general model. Charles H. Stember (1966) reviewed poll data on anti-Semitism from 1938 to the middle 1960's. He found that it rose from 1938 to 1946 and then fell constantly from then until the most recent polls. For example, a series of polls asked, "Do you think the Jews have too much power in the United States?" The percentage answering yes went up from 41 in 1938 to 58 in 1945, but by 1962 it had fallen to 17 and by 1964 to 11. In a scrutiny of breakdowns Stember found that the declines after 1946 were greatest among urban dwellers, upper-income groups, younger people, Catholics, and residents of the Eastern States. Considerable research has shown that anti-Semitism is associated with other forms of prejudice and with political conservatism. Yet it declined rather sharply after 1946 while other measures of ethnocentrism and anxiety about deviant social groups continued to rise until about 1953 or 1954. One possible explanation may lie in the perceived incompatibility of anti-Semitism with effective anti-Communism. For example, the John Birch Society and fundamentalist anti-Communist crusader Rev. Billy James Hargis have both been careful to avoid any anti-Semitism in their movements. Robert Welch, president of the John Birch Society, said that it is a "Communist tactic to stir up distrust and hatred between Jews and Gentiles, Catholics and Protestants, Negroes and Whites" (quoted in Stember, 1966). Perhaps anti-Semitism declined sharply right after World War II because of counterpressures in the early cold war years. Whatever the reason the analysis of anti-Semitism trends seems to advise us to be alert to the cumulative impact of specific historical events on overall patterns of personal commitments.

56. For a very suggestive analysis of social change probably accurate for the social forces of the early 1950's, see Shils (1958). He distinguishes "loose tradition" and "traditionalism." In normal times the adherence to tradition is rather loose, permitting certain deviations and modifications without arousing social hostility or personal guilt. However, reactions to social change or perceived threat may arise which have the character of "traditionalism." Such reactions affirm traditionalist norms with strong dogmatism and intolerance of deviation. Traditionalism demands exclusiveness of all former sacred claims in political, economic, and cultural realms as well as religious realms.

BIBLIOGRAPHY

Abrams, Ray H., 1937. "The Prospect for Youth and the Church," *The Annals of the American Academy of Political and Social Science*, November, 48–59.

Adorno, Theodor W., Frenkel-Brunswick, E., Levinson, D. J., and Sanford, R. N., 1950. *The Authoritarian Personality*. Harper & Brothers.

Allen, David, 1967. "Student Radicalism in Depression and Prosperity," unpublished B.A. honors thesis, Harvard University.

Allen, Frederick L., 1931. *Only Yesterday: An Informal History of the 1920's*. Harper & Brothers.

Allport, Gordon W., 1929. "The Composition of Political Attitudes," *American Journal of Sociology*, 35:2, 220–238.

———, Gillespie, James M., and Young, Jacqueline, 1948. "The Religion of the Post-War College Student," *Journal of Psychology*, 25, 3–33.

———, and Vernon, Philip E., 1931. *Study of Values: Manual*. Houghton Mifflin Company.

———, Vernon, Philip E., and Lindzey, Gardner, 1951. *Study of Values: Manual*. Rev. ed. Houghton Mifflin Company.

———, Vernon, Philip E., and Lindzey, Gardner, 1960. *Study of Values: Manual*. 3d ed. Houghton Mifflin Company.

Altbach, Philip G., and Peterson, Patti M., 1971. "Before Berkeley: Historical Perspectives on American Student Activism," *Annals of the American Academy of Political and Social Science*, 395, 1–14.

Argyle, Michael, 1958. *Religious Behaviour*. London: Routledge & Kegan Paul, Ltd.

Arsenian, Seth, 1943. "Change in Evaluative Attitudes During Four Years of College," *Journal of Applied Psychology*, 27:4, 338–349.

Astin, A. W., Panos, R. J., and Creater, J. A., 1967. "National Norms for Entering College Freshmen, Fall, 1966." *American Council of Education Research Reports*, 2:1. Washington: American Council on Education.

Bain, Read, 1927. "Religious Attitudes of College Students," *American Journal of Sociology*, 32:5, 762–770.

Barton, Allen H., 1959. *Studying the Effects of College Education: A Methodological Examination of Changing Values in College.* New Haven: Edward W. Hazen Foundation.

Belden, Joe, 1940. Collected reports of the Student Opinion Surveys of America, 1938 to 1940. Catalogued in library of Barker Texas History Center, Austin, Texas.

Bell, Daniel (ed.), 1963. *The Radical Right: The New American Right.* Doubleday & Company, Inc.

Bell, Howard M., 1938. *Youth Tell Their Story: A Study of the Conditions and Attitudes of Young People in Maryland Between the Ages of 16 and 24.* Washington: American Council on Education.

Bellah, Robert N., 1965. "Epilogue," in R. Bellah (ed.), *Religion and Progress in Modern Asia*, pp. 168–229. The Free Press.

———, 1967. "Civil Religion in America," *Daedalus*, 96:1, 1–22.

———, 1968. "The Sociology of Religion," in the *International Encyclopedia of the Social Sciences*, Vol. 13, pp. 406–414. The Macmillan Company and The Free Press.

———, 1970. *Beyond Belief: Essays on Religion in a Post-Traditional World.* Harper & Row, Publishers, Inc.

Bender, Irving, 1958. "Changes in Religious Interest: A Retest After 15 Years," *Journal of Abnormal and Social Psychology*, 57, 41–46.

———, et al., 1942. *Motivation and Visual Factors: Individual Studies of College Students.* Hanover: Dartmouth Publications.

Berelson, Bernard, and Steiner, Gary A., 1964. *Human Behavior: An Inventory of Scientific Findings.* Harcourt, Brace and World, Inc.

Betts, George H., 1928. "Religious Attitudes and Activities of University Students: A Report," *Religious Education*, 23:9, 917–919.

Blackmer, Alan, Jr., 1960. "Andover to Harvard: A Study of Role Transition," unpublished B.A. honors thesis, Harvard University.

Blake, Judith, 1967. "Income and Reproductive Motivation," *Population Index*, 33:3, 326.

———, 1968. "Are Babies Consumer Durables?" *Population Studies*, 22:1, 5–25.

Boldt, W. J., and Stroud, J. B., 1934. "Changes in the Attitudes of College Students," *Journal of Educational Psychology*, 25:8, 611–619.

Bond, Charles M., 1940. "College Student Attitudes Toward Some Basic Christian Values," *Religious Education*, 35:2, 109–116.

Braden, Charles S., 1948. "Enrollment Trends in Religion Courses," *Religious Education*, 43, 337–342.

Breemes, E. L., Remmers, H. H., and Morgan, C. L., 1941. "Changes in Liberalism-Conservatism of College Students Since the Depression," *Journal of Social Psychology*, 41, 99–107.

Brown, Daniel G., and Lowe, Warner L., 1951. "Religious Beliefs and Personality Characteristics of College Students," *Journal of Social Psychology*, 33, 103–129.

Brown, Donald, 1956. "Some Educational Patterns," *Journal of Social Issues*, 12:4, 44–60.

Bugelski, Richard, and Lester, Olive P., 1940. "Changes in Attitudes in a Group of College Students During Their College Course and After Graduation," *Journal of Social Psychology*, 12, 319–332.

Callahan, Daniel (ed.), 1966. *The Secular City Debate.* The Macmillan Company.

Campbell, Thomas C., and Fukuyama, Yoshio, 1970. *The Fragmented Layman.* Pilgrim Press.

Cantril, Hadley, 1946. "The Intensity of Attitude," *Journal of Abnormal and Social Psychology*, 41, 129–135.

———, and Allport, Gordon W., 1933. "Recent Applications of the Study of Values," *Journal of Abnormal and Social Psychology*, 28:3, 259–273.

Carlson, Hilding B., 1934. "Attitudes of Undergraduate Students," *Journal of Social Psychology*, 5, 202–213.

Cavanaugh, John J., 1939. "Survey of Fifteen Religious Surveys 1921–1936," *Bulletin of the University of Notre Dame*, 34:1, 1–128.

Chamberlain, Roy B., 1930. "Can Religion Recapture the Campus?" *The Christian Century*, 47:44 (Oct. 29), 1310–1313.

Clark, Burton R., and Trow, Martin, 1966. "The Organizational Context," in Theodore M. Newcomb and Everett K. Wilson (eds.), *College Peer Groups: Problems and Prospects for Research.* Aldine Publishing Company.

College Entrance Examination Board, 1965. *College Board Score Reports.* New York: College Entrance Examination Board.

Collins, Eleanor H., 1934. "Religion at Bryn Mawr," *Bryn Mawr Alumnae Bulletin*, 14:2, 7–8.

Corey, Stephen M., 1936. "Attitude Differences Between College Classes: A Summary and Criticism," *Journal of Educational Psychology*, 27:5, 321–330.

———, 1940. "Changes in the Opinions of Female Students After One Year at a University," *Journal of Social Psychology*, 11, 341–351.

Cox, Harvey, 1965. *The Secular City.* The Macmillan Company.

Demerath, N. J., III, 1965. *Social Class in American Protestantism.* Rand McNally & Company.

———, 1968. "Trends and Anti-Trends in Religious Change," in Eleanor B. Sheldon and Wilbert E. Moore (eds.), *Indicators of Social Change: Concepts and Measurements.* Russell Sage Foundation.

———, and Lutterman, Kenneth J., 1967. "Campus Religion and Student Values: Radical Rhetoric and Traditional Reality," paper presented to American Sociological Association Meeting.

Deutsch, Karl W., 1963. *The Nerves of Government: Models of Political Communication and Control.* The Free Press of Glencoe, Inc.

Diekhoff, John S., and Staebler, Neil, 1925. "Religion at Michigan," *Michigan Chimes*, 6:5, 20–21, 40–41.

Draper, Hal, 1967. "The Student Movement of the Thirties: A Political History," in Rita J. Simon (ed.), *As We Saw the Thirties*. University of Illinois Press.

Dreger, Ralph Mason, 1950. "Some Personality Correlates of Religious Attitudes as Determined by Projective Techniques," unpublished Ph.D. thesis, University of Southern California.

Dressel, Paul L., and Mayhew, Lewis B., 1954. *General Education: Explorations in Evaluation*. Washington: American Council on Education.

Dudycha, George J., 1930. "The Religious Beliefs of College Freshmen," *School and Society*, 31, 206–208.

———, 1933. "The Religious Beliefs of College Students," *Journal of Applied Psychology*, 17, 585–603.

———, 1950. "The Religious Beliefs of College Freshmen in 1930 and 1949," *Religious Education*, 45:3, 165–169.

Durkheim, Emile, 1933. *The Division of Labor in Society*. Free Press.

———, 1951. *Suicide: A Study in Sociology*. Free Press.

———, 1953. *Sociology and Philosophy*. Free Press.

———, 1961. *The Elementary Forms of the Religious Life*. The Free Press of Glencoe, Inc.

Eckert, Ruth E., and Marshall, Thomas O., 1938. *When Youth Leave School*. McGraw-Hill Book Co., Inc.

Eckhardt, Kenneth W., 1970. "Religiosity and Civil Rights Militancy," *Review of Religious Research*, 11:3, 197–203.

Edelstein, Alex A., 1962. "Since Bennington: Evidence of Change in Student Political Behavior," *Public Opinion Quarterly*, 26:4, 564–577.

Edwards, R. H., Artman, J. M., and Fisher, Galen M., 1929. *Undergraduates: A Study of Morale in Twenty-Three American Colleges and Universities*. Doubleday, Doran & Company, Inc.

Eells, Walter C., 1926. "Why Do College Students Go to Church?" *Religious Education*, 21:4, 342–347.

Emme, Earle E., 1932. "A Study of the Adjustment Problems of Freshmen in a Church College," unpublished Ph.D. dissertation, University of Chicago.

———, 1941. "Factors in the Religious Development of Thirty-Eight College Students," *Religious Education*, 36:2, 116–120.

Enroth, Ronald M., Ericson, Edward E., Jr., and Peters, C. Breckenridge, 1972. *The Jesus People: Old-Time Religion in the Age of Aquarius*. Wm. B. Eerdmans Publishing Company.

Erskine, Hazel G., 1965. "The Polls: Personal Religion," *Public Opinion Quarterly*, 29:1, 145–157.

———, 1971. "The Polls: Freedom of Speech," *Public Opinion Quarterly*, 34:3, 483–496.

Espy, R. H. Edwin, 1951. *The Religion of College Teachers*. Association Press.

Fallows, Alice K., 1903. "The Practical Religion of the College Girl," *The Outlook*, 74:14 (Aug. 1), 819–824.

Faulkner, Joseph E., and DeJong, Gordon F., 1966. "Religiosity in 5-D: An Empirical Analysis," *Social Forces*, 45:2, 246–254.

Feldman, Kenneth A., and Newcomb, Theodore M., 1969. *The Impact of College on Students.* 2 vols. San Francisco: Jossey-Bass, Inc., Publishers.

Ferguson, Leonard W., 1939. "Primary Social Attitudes," *Journal of Social Psychology*, 9, 217–223.

――――, 1944. "Socio-Psychological Correlates of the Primary Attitude Scales," *Journal of Social Psychology*, 19, 81–98.

――――, Humphreys, Lloyd G., and Strong, Frances W., 1941. "A Factorial Analysis of Interests and Values," *Journal of Educational Psychology*, 32:3, 197–204.

Ferman, Louis A., 1960. "Religious Change on a College Campus," *Journal of College Student Personnel*, 1, 2–12.

Fishbein, Martin (ed.), 1967. *Readings in Attitude Theory and Measurement.* John Wiley & Sons, Inc.

Flacks, Richard, 1967. "The Liberated Generation: An Exploration of the Roots of Student Protest," *Journal of Social Issues*, 23, 52–75.

――――, 1970. "Who Protests: The Social Bases of the Student Movement," in Julian Foster and Durward Long (eds.), *Protest! Student Activism in America.* William Morrow & Company, Inc.

Freedman, Mervin B., 1956. "The Passage Through College," *Journal of Social Issues*, 12:4, 13–28.

――――, 1962. "Studies of College Alumni," in N. Sanford (ed.), *The American College: A Psychological and Social Interpretation of the Higher Learning.* John Wiley & Sons, Inc.

Freedman, Ronald, Whelpton, Pascal K., and Campbell, Arthur A., 1959. *Family Planning, Sterility, and Population Control.* McGraw-Hill Book Co., Inc.

Gans, Herbert J., 1968. "Urbanism and Suburbanism as Ways of Life: A Re-evaluation of Definitions," in Sylvia Fava (ed.), *Urbanism in World Perspective.* The Thomas Y. Crowell Company.

Garrison, K. C., and Mann, Margaret, 1931. "A Study of the Opinions of College Students," *Journal of Social Psychology*, 2:2, 168–178.

Gates, Edward D., 1953. "The Religion of College Students with Special Reference to Bradley University Students," unpublished Ph.D. dissertation, Bradley University.

Gilkey, Langdon, 1967. "Social and Intellectual Sources of Contemporary Protestant Theology in America," *Daedalus*, Winter, 69–98.

Gillespie, James M., and Allport, Gordon W., 1955. *Youth's Outlook on the Future: A Cross-National Study.* Doubleday & Company, Inc.

Gilliland, A. R., 1940. "The Attitude of College Students Toward God and the Church," *Journal of Social Psychology*, 11, 11–18.

Gilliland, A. R., 1953. "Changes in Religious Beliefs of College Students," *Journal of Social Psychology*, 37, 113–116.

Glock, Charles Y., 1962. "On the Study of Religious Commitment," *Religious Education*, Research Supplement, 42, 98–110.

———, Ringer, Benjamin B., and Babbie, Earl R., 1967. *To Comfort and to Challenge.* University of California Press.

———, and Stark, Rodney, 1965. *Religion and Society in Tension.* Rand McNally & Company.

Goldsen, Rose K., Rosenberg, Morris, Williams, Robin M., Jr., and Suchman, Edward A., 1960. *What College Students Think.* D. Van Nostrand Company, Inc.

Greeley, Andrew M., 1963. *Religion and Career: A Study of College Graduates.* Sheed & Ward, Inc.

———, 1965. "The Religious Behavior of Graduate Students," *Journal for the Scientific Study of Religion,* 5:1, 34–41.

———, 1969. *Religion in the Year 2000.* Sheed & Ward, Inc.

Griffin, Helen C., 1929. "Changes in the Religious Attitudes of College Students," *Religious Education*, 24:2, 159–164.

Guttman, Louis, and Suchman, Edward A., 1967. "Intensity and a Zero Point for Attitude Analysis," in Martin Fishbein (ed.), *Readings in Attitude Theory and Measurement.* John Wiley & Sons, Inc.

Hadden, Jeffrey K., 1963. "An Analysis of Some Factors Associated with Religion and Political Affiliation in a College Population," *Journal of the Scientific Study of Religion*, 2:2, 209–216.

———, 1969. "The Private Generation," *Psychology Today*, 3, 32–35, 68–69.

Hall, Roy M., 1951. "Religious Beliefs and Social Values of Syracuse University Freshmen and Seniors, 1950," unpublished Ph.D. dissertation, Syracuse University.

Harrington, Michael, 1965. "Radicals, Old and New," *New Republic*, July 3.

Harris, A. J., Remmers, H. H., and Ellison, C. E., 1932. "The Relation Between Liberal and Conservative Attitudes in College Students, and Other Factors," *Journal of Social Psychology*, 3:1, 320–336.

Harris, D., 1933. "Group Differences in Values Within a University," *Psychology Bulletin*, 30:8, 355–356.

Harrison, Walter R., 1952. "A Study of Church Attitudes in the East Baton Rouge Area," *Religious Education*, 47:1, 39–51.

Hartshorne, Hugh (ed.), 1939. *From School to College: A Study of the Transition Experience.* Yale University Press.

Hastings, Philip K., and Hoge, Dean R., 1970. "Religious Change Among College Students Over Two Decades," *Social Forces*, 49:1, 16–28.

Havemann, Ernest, and West, Patricia Salter, 1952. *They Went to College: The College Graduate in America Today.* Harcourt, Brace and Company, Inc.

Havens, Joseph, 1963. "The Changing Climate of Research on the College

Student and His Religion," *Journal for the Scientific Study of Religion*, 3:1, 52–69.

Hays, William L., 1963. *Statistics for Psychologists*. Holt, Rinehart, and Winston, Inc.

Heath, Douglas H., 1965. *Explorations of Maturity: Studies of Mature and Immature College Men*. Appleton-Century-Crofts.

———, 1969a. *Growing Into Maturity: The Process of Becoming Educated*. Jossey-Bass, Inc., Publishers.

———, 1969b. "Secularization and Maturity of Religious Beliefs," *Religion and Health*, 8:4, 335–358.

Heer, David M., 1968. *Society and Population*. Prentice-Hall, Inc.

Herberg, Will, 1960. *Protestant—Catholic—Jew*. New ed. Doubleday & Company, Inc.

Hirschberg, Grace, and Gilliland, A. R., 1942. "Parent-Child Relationships in Attitude," *Journal of Abnormal and Social Psychology*, 37:1, 125–130.

Hodges, George, 1906. "Religious Life in American Colleges," *The Outlook*, 83 (July 28), 693–701.

Hoge, Dean R., 1969. "College Students' Religion: A Study of Trends in Attitudes and Behavior," unpublished Ph.D. dissertation, Harvard University.

———, 1970. "Value Trends and Religious Trends at the University of Michigan." Xeroxed report, University of Michigan Library.

———, 1971. "College Students' Value Patterns in the 1950's and 1960's," *Sociology of Education*, 44:1, 170–197.

Horne, E. P., and Stender, William J., 1945. "Student Attitudes Toward Religious Practices," *Journal of Social Psychology*, 22, 215–217.

Horton, Paul B., 1940. "Student Interest in the Church," *Religious Education*, 35:4, 215–219.

Howells, Thomas H., 1928. "A Comparative Study of Those Who Accept as Against Those Who Reject Religious Authority," *University of Iowa Studies in Character*, 2:2.

Hunt, Richard A., 1968. "The Interpretation of the Religious Scale of the Allport-Vernon-Lindzey Study of Values," *Journal of the Scientific Study of Religion*, 7:1, 65–77.

Hunter, E. C., 1951. "Attitudes of College Freshmen, 1934–1949," *Journal of Psychology*, 31, 281–296.

Huntley, C. William, 1965. "Changes in Study of Values Scores During the Four Years of College," *Genetic Psychology Monographs* 71, 349–383.

Hyman, Herbert H., 1963. "England and America: Climates of Tolerance and Intolerance," in Daniel Bell (ed.), *The Radical Right*. Doubleday & Company, Inc.

———, and Sheatsley, Paul B., 1953. "Trends in Public Opinion ᴄ ɔ Civil Liberties," *Journal of Social Issues*, 9:3, 6–16.

Jacob, Philip E., 1957. *Changing Values in College*. Harper & Brothers.

Jones, Edward S., 1926. "The Opinions of College Students," *Journal of Applied Psychology*, 10:4, 427–436.

Jones, Vernon, 1938. "Attitudes of College Students and the Changes in Such Attitudes During Four Years in College," *Journal of Educational Psychology*, 29:1, 14–25, 114–134.

———, 1942. "The Nature of Changes in Attitudes of College Students Toward War Over an Eleven-Year Period," *Journal of Educational Psychology*, 33:7, 481–494.

———, 1970. "Attitudes of College Students and Their Changes, A 37-Year Study," *Genetic Psychology Monographs*, 81, 3–80.

Katz, Daniel, 1967. "The Functional Approach to the Study of Attitudes," in Martin Fishbein (ed.), *Readings in Attitude Theory and Measurement*. John Wiley & Sons.

———, and Allport, Floyd H., 1933. *Students' Attitudes: A Report of the Syracuse University Reaction Study*. Syracuse: Craftsman Press.

Kelly, E. Lowell, 1955. "Consistency of the Adult Personality," *American Psychologist*, 10, 659–681.

Keniston, Kenneth, 1965. *The Uncommitted: Alienated Youth in American Society*. Dell Publishing Co.

———, 1967. "The Sources of Student Dissent," *Journal of Social Issues*, 23:3, 108–137.

King, Morton B., and Hunt, Richard A., 1969. "Measuring the Religious Variable: Amended Findings," *Journal for the Scientific Study of Religion*, 8:2, 321–323.

King, Stanley H., 1967. "The Harvard Influence," *Harvard Today* (Autumn), 27–32.

Kirkpatrick, Clifford, 1949. "Religion and Humanitarianism: A Study of Institutional Implications," *Psychological Monographs*, 63:9, 304.

———, and Stone, Sarah, 1935. "Attitude Measurement and the Comparison of Generations," *Journal of Applied Psychology*, 19:5, 564–583.

Kiser, Clyde V., Grabill, Wilson H., and Campbell, Arthur A., 1968. *Trends and Variations in Fertility in the United States*. Harvard University Press.

Kitay, Philip M., 1947. *Radicalism and Conservatism Toward Conventional Religion*. Teachers College, Columbia University, Publication No. 919. Columbia University Press.

Knight, Walker L. (ed.), 1971. *Jesus People Come Alive*. Tyndale House, Publishers.

Kosa, John, and Schommer, Cyril O., S.J., 1961. "Religious Participation, Religious Knowledge, and Scholastic Aptitude: An Empirical Study," *Journal for the Scientific Study of Religion*, 1:1, 88–97.

Krech, David, Crutchfield, Richard S., and Ballachey, Egerton L., 1962. *Individual in Society*. McGraw-Hill Book Co., Inc.

Kuhlen, Raymond G., 1941. "Changes in the Attitudes of Students and Relations of Test Responses to Judgments of Associates," *School and Society*, 53:1373, 514–519.

Lane Hall Surveys, 1938–1942. Collected mimeographed reports of surveys at the University of Michigan. Ann Arbor: Office of Religious Affairs, University of Michigan.

Lazarsfeld, Paul F., and Thielens, Wagner, Jr., 1958. *The Academic Mind: Social Scientists in a Time of Crisis.* The Free Press of Glencoe, Inc.

Lazerwitz, Bernard, 1968. "The Components of Jewish Identification," paper delivered to the American Sociological Association.

———, 1969. "The Consequences of Religio-Ethnic Identification," dittoed.

———, 1970. "Contrasting the Effects of Generation, Class, Sex, and Age on Group Identification in the Jewish and Protestant Communities," *Social Forces*, 49:1, 50–59.

———, and Rowitz, Louis, 1964. "The Three Generations Hypothesis," *American Journal of Sociology*, 69, 529–538.

Lebergott, Stanley, 1968. "Labor Force and Employment Trends," in Eleanor B. Sheldon and Wilbert E. Moore (eds.), *Indicators of Social Change: Concepts and Measurements.* Russell Sage Foundation.

Lee, Calvin B. T., 1970. *The Campus Scene: 1900–1970.* David McKay Company, Inc.

Lehman, Edward C., Jr., and Shriver, Donald W., Jr., 1968. "Academic Discipline as Predictive of Faculty Religiosity," *Social Forces*, 47:2, 171–182.

Lehmann, U. J., and Ikenberry, S. O., 1959. "Critical Thinking, Attitudes, and Values in Higher Education: A Preliminary Report." U.S. Department of H.E.W. Cooperative Research Report No. 590. East Lansing, Michigan: Michigan State University.

Lenski, Gerhard, 1963. *The Religious Factor.* Doubleday & Company, Inc.

Leuba, James H., 1907. "Religion as a Factor in the Struggle for Life," *American Journal of Religious Psychology and Education*, 2:2–3, 307–343.

———, 1916. *The Belief in God and Immortality.* Boston: Sherman, French & Co.

———, 1934. "Religious Beliefs of American Scientists," *Harper's Monthly Magazine*, 169, 292–300.

Levy, Richard N., McNees, John E., and Maier, Charles S., 1959. "Religious and Political Attitudes," commencement supplement to the *Harvard Crimson*, June 11, 1959.

Lipset, S. M., 1963a. *The First New Nation.* Basic Books, Inc., Publishers.

———, 1963b. "The Sources of the 'Radical Right,' (1955)" and "Three Decades of the Radical Right: Coughlinites, McCarthyites, and Birchers (1962)," in Daniel Bell (ed.), *The Radical Right.* Doubleday & Company, Inc.

———, 1966. "Student Opposition in the United States," *Government and Opposition*, 1:3, 351–374.

———, 1968. "The Activists: A Profile," *The Public Interest*, 13, 39–51.

———, 1971. *Rebellion in the University.* Little, Brown & Company.

Lipset, S. M., and Altbach, Philip G., 1966. "Student Politics and Higher Education in the United States," *Comparative Education Review*, 10:2, 320–349.

Literary Digest, 1927. "Youth Gives the Lie to Gossip," 93:5 (April 30), 28–29.

Lundberg, George A., 1926. "Sex Differences on Social Questions," *School and Society*, 23:593, 595–600.

Lynd, Staughton, 1969. "The New Left," *Annals of the American Academy of Political and Social Science*, 382, 64–72.

McLean, Milton D. (ed.), 1967. *Religious Studies in Public Universities.* Southern Illinois University Press.

———, and Kimber, Harry H., 1960. *The Teaching of Religion in State Universities.* Ann Arbor: Office of Religious Affairs, University of Michigan.

MacNaughton, William S., 1966. "Comparative Profiles of Emergent Value Patterns in Undergraduate Life at Dartmouth," Dartmouth College, multilithed.

Malan, C. T., 1935. "Effects of College Education on Religion," *Religious Education*, 30:2, 132–134.

Mallory, Edith B., 1933. "Father's Occupation and Boarding School Education as Related to the Individual's Judgment of Values," *Psychological Bulletin*, 30:9, 717.

Marty, Martin E., Rosenberg, Stuart E., and Greeley, Andrew M., 1968. *What Do We Believe? The Stance of Religion in America.* Meredith Press.

Marx, Gary T., 1967. *Protest and Prejudice.* Harper & Row, Publishers, Inc.

Maslow, Abraham, 1943. "A Theory of Human Motivation," *Psychological Review*, 50, 370–396.

Michaelsen, Robert, 1965. *The Study of Religion in American Universities.* New Haven: The Society for Religion in Higher Education.

———, 1967. "Religion and Academia," paper read to the Consultation, Department of Higher Education, National Council of Churches.

Miller, Norman, 1958. "Social Class and Value Differences Among American College Students," unpublished Ph.D. thesis, Columbia University.

Moore, Gwyn, and Garrison, K. C., 1932. "A Comparative Study of Social and Political Attitudes of College Students," *Journal of Abnormal and Social Psychology*, 27:2, 195–208.

Morse, Josiah, and Allan, James, Jr., 1913. "The Religion of One Hundred and Twenty-Six College Students," *Journal of Religious Psychology*, 6:2, 175–194.

Moss, Milton, 1968. "Consumption: A Report on Contemporary Issues," in Eleanor B. Sheldon and Wilbert E. Moore (eds.), *Indicators of Social Change: Concepts and Measurements.* Russell Sage Foundation.

Murphy, Gardner, and Likert, Rensis, 1938. *Public Opinion and the Individual.* Harper & Brothers.

———, Murphy, Lois Barclay, and Newcomb, Theodore M., 1937. *Experimental Social Psychology.* Rev. ed. Harper & Brothers.

Nathan, Marvin, 1932. *The Attitude of the Jewish Student Toward His Religion.* Bloch Publishing Company, Inc.

Nelson, Erland, 1938. "Radicalism-Conservatism in Student Attitudes," *Psychological Monographs,* 50:4, 1–32.

———, 1940. "Student Attitudes Toward Religion," *Genetic Psychology Monographs,* 22, 323–423.

———, 1956. "Patterns of Religious Attitude Shifts from College to Fourteen Years Later," *Psychological Monographs,* 70:17, 1–15.

Newcomb, Theodore M., 1943. *Personality and Social Change: Attitude Formation in a Student Community.* Henry Holt & Company, Inc.

———, Koenig, Kathryn E., Flacks, Richard, and Warwick, Donald P., 1967. *Persistence and Change: Bennington College and Its Students After Twenty-Five Years.* John Wiley & Sons, Inc.

———, and Svehla, George, 1937. "Intra-Family Relationships in Attitude," *Sociometry,* 1:1, 180–205.

Niebuhr, H. Richard, 1957. *The Social Sources of Denominationalism.* Meridian Books, Inc.

———, Williams, Daniel Day, and Gustafson, James M., 1957. *The Advancement of Theological Education.* Harper & Brothers.

Parsons, Talcott, 1949. "The Role of Ideas in Social Action," in *Essays in Sociological Theory.* Rev. ed. Free Press.

———, 1960. "Some Comments on the Pattern of Religious Organization in the United States," in *Structure and Process in Modern Societies.* The Free Press of Glencoe, Inc.

———, 1963a. "Social Strains in America (1955)" and "Social Strains in America: A Postscript (1962)," in Daniel Bell (ed.), *The Radical Right.* Doubleday & Company, Inc.

———, 1963b. "Christianity and Modern Industrial Society," in E. Tiryakian (ed.), *Sociological Theory, Values, and Socio-cultural Change.* The Free Press of Glencoe, Inc.

———, 1964. "Evolutionary Universals in Society," *American Sociological Review,* 29:3, 339–357.

———, 1966a. "Religion in a Modern Pluralistic Society," *Review of Religious Research,* 7:3, 125–146.

———, 1966b. *Societies: Evolutionary and Comparative Perspectives.* Prentice-Hall, Inc.

———, 1968. "On the Concept of Value-Commitments," *Sociological Inquiry,* 38:2, 135–160.

Peabody, Francis G., 1901. "The Religion of a College Student," *The Forum,* 31, 442–452.

Peterson, Richard E., 1965. *Technical Manual, College Student Questionnaires.* Princeton, N.J.: Educational Testing Service.

Pintner, Rudolf, 1933. "A Comparison of Interests, Abilities, and Attitudes," *Journal of Abnormal and Social Psychology,* 27:4, 351–357.

Pixley, Erma, and Beekman, Emma, 1949. "The Faith of Youth: As Shown by a Survey in Public Schools of Los Angeles," *Religious Education*, 44:6, 336–342.

Poit, Carl H., 1962. "A Study Concerning Religious Belief and Denominational Affiliation," *Religious Education*, 57:3, 214–216.

Pope, Liston, 1942. *Millhands and Preachers*. Yale University Press.

———, 1948. "Religion and the Class Structure," in Reinhard Bendix and S. M. Lipset (eds.), *Class, Status and Power*. The Free Press.

Potter, Allen, 1953. "A Study of the Religious Views of Students at the Massachusetts Institute of Technology," unpublished B.S. thesis.

Pressey, S. L., and Jones, A. W., 1955. "1923–53 and 20–60 Age Changes in Moral Codes, Anxieties, and Interests, as Shown by the X-O Tests," *Journal of Psychology*, 39, 485–502.

Purdue Opinion Panel, Nos. 1 to 84. Bound mimeographed reports on surveys conducted by the Purdue Opinion Panel under the direction of H. H. Remmers. Authors of the reports vary.

Rankin, Fay S., 1938. *The Religious Attitudes of College Students: A Comparative Study*. Contributions to Education, George Peabody College for Teachers, No. 206. Nashville: George Peabody College for Teachers.

Remmers, H. H., and Radler, D. H., 1957. *The American Teenager*. The Bobbs-Merrill Company, Inc.

Rettig, Salomon, and Pasamanick, Benjamin, 1959. "Changes in Moral Values Over Three Decades, 1929–1958," *Social Problems*, 6:4, 320–328.

———, 1960. "Differences in the Structure of Moral Values of Students and Alumni," *American Sociological Review*, 25:4, 550–555.

Riesman, David, with Glazer, Nathan, and Denney, Reuel, 1950. *The Lonely Crowd*. Yale University Press.

Ross, Murray G., 1950. *The Religious Beliefs of Youth*. Association Press.

Rosten, Leo (ed.), 1963. *Religions in America*. Simon & Schuster, Inc.

Rudolph, Frederick, 1962. *The American College and University, A History*. Random House, Inc.

Salisbury, W. Seward, 1958. "Religion and Secularization," *Social Forces*, 36:3, 197–205.

———, 1962. "Religiosity, Regional Sub-culture, and Social Behavior," *Journal of the Scientific Study of Religion*, 2:1, 94–101.

Salner, E., and Remmers, H. H., 1933. "Affective Selectivity and Liberalizing Influence of College Courses," *Journal of Applied Psychology*, 17:4, 349–355.

Sametz, A. W., 1968. "Production of Goods and Services: The Measurement of Economic Growth," in Eleanor B. Sheldon and Wilbert E. Moore (eds.), *Indicators of Social Change: Concepts and Measurements*. Russell Sage Foundation.

Sampson, Edward E., 1967. "Student Activism and the Decade of Protest," *Journal of Social Issues*, 23:3, 1–33.

Sanford, Nevitt (ed.), 1962. *The American College: A Psychological and Social Interpretation of the Higher Learning*. John Wiley & Sons.

Schneider, Herbert W., 1963. *Religion in 20th Century America.* Rev. ed. Atheneum Publishers.

Schneider, Louis, and Dornbusch, Sanford M., 1958. *Popular Religion: Inspirational Books in America.* The University of Chicago Press.

Searles, Herbert L., 1926. "An Empirical Inquiry Into the God Experience of One Hundred and Forty College Students," *Religious Education,* 21:4, 334–342.

Sheldon, Eleanor B., and Moore, Wilbert E. (eds.), 1968. *Indicators of Social Change: Concepts and Measurements.* Russell Sage Foundation.

Sheldon, William H., 1942. *The Varieties of Temperament.* Harper & Brothers.

Shils, Edward, 1958. "Tradition and Liberty: Antinomy and Interdependence," *Ethics,* 68:3, 153–165.

Shuttleworth, Frank K., 1927. "The Influence of Early Religious Home Training on College Sophomore Men," *Religious Education,* 22:1, 57–60.

Simmel, Georg, 1950. "The Metropolis and Mental Life," in Kurt H. Wolff (ed.), *The Sociology of Georg Simmel.* Free Press.

Smith, John E., 1958. *Value Convictions and Higher Education.* New Haven: Edward W. Hazen Foundation.

Smith, M. Brewster, Bruner, Jerome S., and White, Robert W., 1956. *Opinions and Personality.* John Wiley & Sons.

Smith, Robert O., 1947. *Factors Affecting the Religion of College Students.* Ann Arbor, Michigan: R. O. Smith.

Smith, Timothy L., 1960. "Historical Waves of Religious Interest in America," *The Annals of the American Academy of Political and Social Science,* 332 (November), 9–19.

Sokol, Robert, and Sykes, Carla A., 1963. "The Dartmouth Student: A Summary Report of Studies Carried Out from 1958 to 1963." Mimeographed, Dartmouth College.

Spengler, Joseph J., 1966. "Values and Fertility Analysis," *Demography,* 3:1, 109–130.

Srole, Leo, 1956. "Social Integration and Certain Corollaries: An Exploratory Study," *American Sociological Review,* 21, 709–716.

Stack, Alma Pearle, 1928. "A Survey of the Religious Agencies and Activities of Northwestern University," unpublished M.A. thesis, Northwestern University.

Stark, Rodney, 1963. "On the Incompatibility of Religion and Science: A Survey of American Graduate Students," *Journal of the Scientific Study of Religion,* 3:1, 3–20.

———, and Glock, Charles Y., 1968. *American Piety.* University of California Press.

Stember, Charles H. (ed.), 1966. *Jews in the Mind of America.* Basic Books, Inc., Publishers.

Stern, George G., 1965. "Student Ecology and the College Environment," in

College Entrance Examination Board, *Research in Higher Education: Guide to Institutional Decisions.* Princeton: College Entrance Examination Board.

Stouffer, Samuel A., 1955. *Communism, Conformity, and Civil Liberties.* Doubleday & Company, Inc.

Streiker, Lowell D., 1971. *The Jesus Trip: Advent of the Jesus Freaks.* Abingdon Press.

Symington, Thomas A., 1935. *Religious Liberals and Conservatives.* Teachers College Contributions to Education, No. 640. Teachers College, Columbia University.

Symonds, Percival M., 1925. "A Social Attitudes Questionnaire," *Journal of Educational Psychology,* 16:5, 316–323.

Tanner, J. M., 1962. *Growth at Adolescence.* 2d ed. Oxford: Blackwell Scientific Publications.

Telford, C. W., 1934. "An Experimental Study of Some Factors Influencing the Social Attitudes of College Students," *Journal of Social Psychology,* 5:3, 421–428.

Tillich, Paul, 1958. *Dynamics of Faith.* Harper & Brothers.

Toch, Hans H., and Anderson, Robert, 1964. " 'Secularization' in College: An Exploratory Study," *Religious Education,* 59, 490–502.

Todd, J. Edward, 1941. *Social Norms and the Behavior of College Students.* Teachers College Contributions to Education, No. 833. Teachers College, Columbia University.

Underwood, Kenneth, 1969. *The Church, the University, and Social Policy.* 2 vols. Wesleyan University Press.

U.S. Bureau of the Census, 1960. *Historical Statistics of the United States, Colonial Times to 1957.* Washington, D.C.: Government Printing Office.

U.S. Bureau of the Census, 1968, 1969, 1972. *Statistical Abstracts of the United States.* Published annually. Washington, D.C.: Government Printing Office.

U.S. Department of Health, Education, and Welfare, 1969. *Toward a Social Report.* Washington: Department of H.E.W.

Van Tuyl, Mary C. T., 1937. "A Study in Student Thinking," *Religious Education,* 32:4, 255–262.

———, 1938. "Where Do Students 'Lose' Religion?" *Religious Education,* 33:1, 19–29.

Vetter, George B., 1930. "The Measurement of Social and Political Attitudes and the Related Personality Factors," *Journal of Abnormal and Social Psychology,* 25:2, 149–189.

Vincent, Lena Duell, 1956. "The Religious Concepts and Attitudes of One Hundred College Students," unpublished Ph.D. dissertation, University of Michigan.

Vreeland, Rebecca S., 1971. "The Changing Functions of Dating: Dating Patterns of Harvard Men 1960–1970," paper delivered to the American Sociological Association.

Walsh, Chad, 1953. *Campus Gods on Trial.* The Macmillan Company.

Walter, Erich A. (ed.), 1964. *Religion and the State University.* University of Michigan Press.

Weber, Max, 1946. *From Max Weber: Essays in Sociology,* ed. by Hans Gerth and C. Wright Mills. Oxford University Press.

————, 1947. *The Theory of Social and Economic Organization,* ed. and with an Introduction by Talcott Parsons. Free Press.

————, 1958. *The Protestant Ethic and the Spirit of Capitalism.* Charles Scribner's Sons.

————, 1963. *The Sociology of Religion,* with an Introduction by Talcott Parsons. Beacon Press.

Webster, Harold, 1956. "Some Quantitative Results," *Journal of Social Issues,* 12:4, 29–43.

————, 1958. "Changes in Attitudes During College," *Journal of Educational Psychology,* 49:3, 109–117.

Welch, Claude, 1971. *Graduate Education in Religion: A Critical Appraisal.* University of Montana Press.

Westoff, Charles F., Potter, Robert G., Jr., Sagi, Philip C., and Mishler, Elliot G., 1961. *Family Growth in Metropolitan America.* Princeton University Press.

Whitely, Paul, 1933. "A Study of the Allport-Vernon Test for Personal Values," *Journal of Abnormal and Social Psychology,* 28:1, 6–13.

————, 1938. "The Constancy of Personal Values," *Journal of Abnormal and Social Psychology,* 33, 405–408.

Wickenden, Arthur C., 1932. "The Effect of the College Experience Upon Students' Concepts of God," *Journal of Religion,* 12:2, 242–267.

Wilson, Bryan R., 1959. "An Analysis of Sect Development," *American Sociological Review,* 24, 3–15.

Wirth, Louis, 1938. "Urbanism as a Way of Life," *American Journal of Sociology,* 44, 1–24.

Woodward, Luther Ellis, 1932. *Relations of Religious Teaching and Life to the Adult Religious Life.* Teachers College, Columbia University, Publication No. 527. Columbia University Press.

Yankelovich, Daniel, 1972. *The Changing Values on Campus.* Washington Square Press.

Young, Robert K., Clore, Gerald, and Holtzman, Wayne H., 1966. "Further Change in Attitude Toward the Negro in a Southern University," in Donn Byrne and Marshall L. Hamilton (eds.), *Personality Research: A Book of Readings.* Prentice-Hall, Inc.

————, Dustin, David, S., and Holtzman, Wayne H., 1966. "Change in Attitude Toward Religion in a Southern University," *Psychological Reports,* 18, 39–46.

Zimmerman, Franklin K., 1934. "Religion a Conservative Force," *Journal of Abnormal and Social Psychology,* 28:4, 473–474.

INDEX

related to other attitudes, 100
and scholastic aptitude, 121, 127
and socioeconomic status, 116, 128
Religious behavior, 110, 124, 127
predicted by religious upbringing, 113
Religious beliefs, 34, 35, 36, 38, 39, 41, 44, 102, 103, 106, 169
challenged by college experience, 122
changes from 1914 to 1968, 49
and liberalism, 125
liberalized between 1927 and 1930, 52
in life after death, 164
parental influence, 114, 115
predicted by home background, 112, 118
Religious change, 153, 192
caused by changes in dynamic density, 19
explained by social factors, 17, 18, 27, 107, 156
and greater intellectualism, 20
models for explanation, 180
not explained by third-generation hypothesis, 120
sources of, 165
and structural differentiation, 23
in the twentieth century, 26
Religious commitments, 85, 128, 132–135, 145–146, 152, 154
and cold war, 103
correlation with other-direction, 88
and the Depression, 189
dimensions of, 34
in Durkheim, 18
and family commitments, 127
and family size, 178
impact of historical events, 187
and individualism, 19
long-range changes, 186
in the 1940's, 188
and other commitments, 183
and population curves, 175
a product of conservatism, 191
relation to political commitments, 87, 106
and social mobility, 20

trends in, 28, 50, 169, 182
varies over life cycle, 114
varies with national commitments, 72
Religious Emphasis Weeks, 138
Religious identification
in third generation, 21
no relation to political interest, 156
Religious interest
and college religion courses, 159
distinguished from orthodoxy, 156
no impact on church participation, 191
product of personality and social system, 157
Religious participation, 46, 134, 145, 152, 185, 186, 191, 192
decline in the 1930's, 137
increases in the 1950's, 140
increases with urban residence, 119
varies over life cycle, 114
See also Church attendance
Religious preference, 51, 52, 67, 68, 71, 111, 131, 144
and home religion tradition, 66–67
Religious upbringing, 113
Reserve Officer Training Corps (ROTC), 133, 136
Revival
and the baby boom, 26
of conservative Christianity, 143
in the 1950's, 174
Riesman, David, 22, 105. *See also* Other-direction
Roosevelt, Franklin D., 137
Roper poll, 167
Rural-urban differences, 120
and educational level, 119
and orthodoxy, 117, 128
and socioeconomic status, 118
See also Urbanization
Russia, 172

Salvation religion, and political withdrawal, 20
Schneider, Louis, 26
Scholastic aptitude, 29, 109, 121, 127, 185

Scholastic Aptitude Test, 109, 185
Science, and religious belief, 49, 55, 56, 57, 58, 59, 70, 124, 127
Second Vatican Council, 149, 151, 173, 186, 191
Sectarian movements, 20
Secular City, 24
Secular theology, 148
Secularization, 14, 21, 23, 27, 118, 119, 127, 151, 174
Seminary, applications and enrollment, 160, 161, 162, 163
Sex differences
  and economic and political attitudes, 41
  generalized trends, 110
  and orthodoxy, 110
Sex norms, 90, 106, 107, 146
Silent generation, 138
Simmel, Georg, 23
Social change, 22, 182, 186, 190, 191
Social class
  related to religious commitment, 88
  and religious attitudes, 116
Social constraint, 77, 87, 111, 116, 121
Social gospel, 147
Social integration, 187
Social mobility, 128, 151
  and church membership, 27
  and religious change, 20, 120
Social service, rather than doctrine, 130
Socioeconomic status, 184
  and college admissions, 109
  and major course of study, 123
  and religious attitudes, 116, 128
  and rural-urban differences, 118
Spengler, Joseph J., 178
Stalin, Joseph, 141
Stark, Rodney, 34, 57
Stouffer, Samuel A., 104, 119, 170, 188
Strike for Peace, 136
Structural differentiation, 190
  defined, 22
  related to religious participation, 22, 23

See also Parsons
Student autonomy, 53, 54, 55, 106
Student Christian Association, 140, 147
Student Christian Volunteer Movement, 131, 138, 147
Student League for Industrial Democracy, 133
Students for a Democratic Society, 142, 145
Suburbanization, 117
  after World War II, 22
Subversion, 172
Suffrage movement, 172
Supernaturalism, 45, 90
Symbols, 18, 118

Thematic Apperception Test, 183
Theodicy, 189
Theological change, 147, 151
  little relevance to students, 144
  product of historical events, 151
Third-generation hypothesis, 21, 120, 128, 174
  explains upswing in organized religion, 21
  See also Herberg, Will
Tillich, Paul, 148, 182
  definition of religion, 30
Totalitarianism, 73, 102

Ultimate concern, 31
United Nations, 171
Urbanization, 148, 174, 184
  produces secularization, 118, 119, 127
  and religious change, 24
  weakens religious ties, 23

Value changes, 125, 145
  among high school students, 97–98
  survey of literature, 94
Value cluster, 181
Values
  interrelations summarized, 100, 101
  of students, 73
Vatican II. *See* Second Vatican Council
Vietnam war, 102, 103, 142, 148, 151